Creating Resilient Economies

Creating Resilient Economies

Entrepreneurship, Growth and Development in Uncertain Times

Edited by

Nick Williams

Centre for Enterprise and Entrepreneurship Studies, University of Leeds, UK

Tim Vorley

Centre for Regional Economic and Enterprise Development, University of Sheffield, UK

 Edward Elgar
PUBLISHING

Cheltenham, UK • Northampton, MA, USA

Published by
Edward Elgar Publishing Limited
The Lypiatts
15 Lansdown Road
Cheltenham
Glos GL50 2JA
UK

Edward Elgar Publishing, Inc.
William Pratt House
9 Dewey Court
Northampton
Massachusetts 01060
USA

A catalogue record for this book
is available from the British Library

Library of Congress Control Number: 2017931764

This book is available electronically in the **Elgar**online
Business subject collection
DOI 10.4337/9781785367649

ISBN 978 1 78536 763 2 (cased)
ISBN 978 1 78536 764 9 (eBook)

Typeset by Servis Filmsetting Ltd, Stockport, Cheshire
Printed and bound in Great Britain by TJ International Ltd, Padstow

Contents

Contributors

David Bailey is Professor of Industrial Strategy at Aston Business School, has written extensively on industrial and regional policy – especially in relation to manufacturing and the auto industry – and is a regular newspaper columnist and media commentator.

Dr Gill Bentley lectures on Urban and Regional Economic Development at Birmingham Business School, specialising in industrial and regional development, policy and governance at different spatial scales. She has published widely on local and regional economic development, including writing about the restructuring of the European auto industry and the closure of MG Rover.

Daniel Braithwaite studied Business Management at the University of Birmingham. As part of his degree programme he completed a placement year for Vauxhall Motors at their headquarters. The year inspired him to undertake further research on the automotive industry and trends in the UK economy.

Dr Chay Brooks is a Lecturer in International Entrepreneurship at the University of Sheffield. His research focuses on entrepreneurship and philanthropy as well as local and regional development in the UK and internationally.

Dr Cédric Brunelle is Assistant Professor in Urban Studies at Centre Urbanisation Culture Société (UCS) at the Institut National de la Recherche Scientifique (INRS) in Montreal. His research focuses on urban and regional development, including the industrial dynamics of peripheral and metropolitan regions, as well as economic resilience.

Dr Jennifer Clark is Associate Professor in the School of Public Policy and Director of the Center for Urban Innovation at the Georgia Institute of Technology. Her research focuses on urban and regional economic development, urban innovation, and technology and policy diffusion in the context of smart cities.

Dr Stuart Dawley is Senior Lecturer in Economic Geography in the Centre for Urban and Regional Development Studies (CURDS) at Newcastle

University. His research interests are around evolutionary approaches within economic geography, particularly in developing a broader geographical political economy approach to path creation.

Dr Paolo Di Caro is an economist at the Department of Finance, Italian Ministry of Economy and Finance, and a Research Associate at the Centre for Applied Macro-Finance, University of York (UK). He earned a PhD in Economics from the University of Catania (Italy) and is main research interests focus on regional economics, spatial econometrics and the theory and applied analysis of regional and local issues in public economics.

Dr Rachel Doern is a Senior Lecturer in Entrepreneurship at Goldsmiths University of London. Drawing on micro-sociological and psychological approaches, her research examines the cognitions, emotions and behaviours of different groups of entrepreneurs and in relation to adverse conditions.

Dr Emil Evenhuis is a Research Associate at the Department of Geography, University of Cambridge. His research focuses on long-term economic transformation in cities, drawing on evolutionary, institutional and political economy approaches within economic geography and the social sciences more widely.

Huiwen Gong is a PhD Student at the Department of Geography, Kiel University, Germany. Her research focuses on creative industries (particularly the video games industry), co-evolution of institutions and industries, as well as theories and paradigms of economic geography.

Nick Gray is a Doctoral Researcher and Research Associate at Newcastle Business School, Northumbria University. His research interests include local and regional development, subnational governance, labour markets and welfare reform.

Robert Hassink is Professor of Economic Geography at Kiel University, Germany, and Visiting Professor of at the Institute of Socio-Economic Geography and Spatial Management at the Adam Mickiewicz University, Poznań, Poland. His research focuses on the restructuring of old industrial areas, regional innovation policy, as well as theories and paradigms of economic geography.

Robert Huggins is Professor of Economic Geography and Director for Economic Geography at the School of Geography and Planning, Cardiff University, UK.

Christian Kjær Monsson works with innovation policy as a Special Consultant at the Danish Ministry for Higher Education and Research.

He has a PhD in Social Science and his research focuses on regional and small business development.

Lee Pugalis is Professor of Urban Studies at the University of Technology Sydney. His research traverses local and regional economic development, urban regeneration and strategic planning, and he has a particular interest in urban entrepreneurship.

James Simmie is Emeritus Professor of Innovation Studies in the Faculty of Technology, Design and the Environment at Oxford Brookes University. His research is focused on the economic geography of innovation, evolutionary theory, and the competitiveness of urban and regional economies.

Ben Spigel is Chancellor's Fellow and Lecturer in Entrepreneurship at the University of Edinburgh Business School. His research focuses on entrepreneurial ecosystems, digital entrepreneurship and the geography of high-growth entrepreneurship.

Dr Piers Thompson is a Reader in Small Business and Local Economics at Nottingham Trent University, UK.

Alan Townsend is Emeritus Professor of Regional Regeneration and Development Studies at Durham University. His research interests include local and regional planning and economic development.

Tim Vorley is Professor of Entrepreneurship at the University of Sheffield. His research focuses on the role of place in economic resilience, as well as local and regional economic development.

Nick Williams is Associate Professor in Enterprise at the University of Leeds. His research primarily focuses on entrepreneurship and institutions, including institutional change in crisis and post-conflict economies, as well as economic resilience.

Foreword

Certain terms periodically capture the imagination of the social sciences. *Our Common Future*, the final report of the Brundtland Commission, launched *sustainability* as a central metaphor. From sustainable growth to sustainable environments, social scientists have sought to understand the implications for individuals, organizations and economies. Working toward sustainability implied then, and still does today, the sense that a suitable equilibrium could be found that balanced good outcomes for the environment, the economy and social equity.

Starting around 2000, however, resilience emerged as another prominent catchword in academic and policy agendas, owing mainly to shocks and stresses that have disrupted social systems throughout the world. Urban development has placed increasing numbers of people in harm's way, especially with escalating threats from climate change. The September 11, 2001 terrorist attacks reinforced a climate of fear in the US, with subsequent attacks in Madrid (2004), London (2005), Mumbai (2008), Paris (2015) and other global cities reinforcing the climate of uncertainty. And the 2007–8 economic crisis manifested structural weaknesses in the global financial system. That crisis—occurring less than a decade after the dot-com crash of 1999–2001—reinforced the understanding that capitalism is prone to speculative bubbles.

If disequilibrium is the norm, rather than the exception, then sustainability needs resilience as a counterpart metaphor to fully encompass our understandings of the economy. Perpetual disequilibrium requires strategies for surviving today and being prepared for future shocks and stresses. Resilience isn't just a useful metaphor for understanding non-equilibrium systems, however. Indeed, many researchers use it as a way to describe whether and how fast a system returns to its previous (equilibrium) state once exposed to a shock. Others look for understanding of how a shock can cause a system to move to a new equilibrium. While some critics of the construct reject it precisely because of this fuzziness, others embrace it for exactly the same reason: it can help illuminate how systems respond to surprises and stresses, regardless of whether these are normal or unusual.

In any case, social scientists deploy the resilience metaphor in part because it has normative appeal, just as sustainability does. Who doesn't want to recover from a shock? Who doesn't want to grow after experiencing adversity? When they embrace the metaphor enough, however, they can sometimes create a need for yet another round of metaphor deployment. Resilience, as originally posited by ecologists and psychologists, really does mean "returning to normal." But if it also means "getting better because of a strain or shock," then maybe it would be useful to call the process something different: transformation, perhaps. Maybe that's a metaphor for another decade.

It has been a privilege to provide a short foreword to this volume, which brings together key research on this important topic, demonstrating the breadth and potential of economic resilience as an approach. The book highlights the application of resilience to be wide-ranging, from individual level, businesses, sectors, as well as national and subnational economies. As the editors state, resilience offers an opportunity to reframe economic development policy and practice. Given the emergent nature of resilience research, the book sets the foundations to advance these debates. In doing this, *Creating Resilient Economies* provides a probing and thoughtful collection that analyses how external shocks can positively shape the economic future of individuals, organizations and places.

Rolf Pendall
Director, Metropolitan Housing & Communities Policy Center
Urban Institute
Washington, DC

1. Introduction

Nick Williams and Tim Vorley

We live in uncertain economic times. The 2007/8 global financial crisis and ongoing economic fallout, as well as the UK Brexit vote, have brought issues of economic volatility to the fore. These events are, however, just the most recent to affect the global economy. The world has been punctuated with a series of economic rises and falls over the past 100 years, from the oil crisis of the 1970s, to interest rates and unemployment of the 1980s, the prosperous digital decade of the 1990s, the rise of the Asian Tiger economies, the dot-com bubble of the early 2000s and fluctuations in the economic fortunes of the USA and China. Economic volatility has become a norm.

Academics and policymakers have long since been interested in the booming and busting of economies, with research focused on understanding the underlying dynamics. Much of this work has understandably centred on economic growth, recession and recovery. However, over the past few years the concept of economic resilience has been applied to a range of contexts. As opposed to focusing on the phases of economic and business cycles, economic resilience has become a fashionable lens for understanding the factors that shape and determine the nature of economic change and performance over time.

Despite the growing interest in economic resilience as an analytical theory, it is still regarded as comparatively underdeveloped and characterised as fuzzy. The concept of resilience stems from the disciplines of ecology and social psychology, and there remains no universally agreed definition of resilience. In developing the common foundations of resilience as an analytical concept, there has been a growing body of work led by different fields of the social sciences. Notably economic geography and management studies have led the quest to refine and develop the concept and its application. It is important to note that the concept of resilience is not without its critics. For example, Walker and Cooper (2011: 2) argue that resilience has succeeded in 'colonising multiple arenas of governance' and reflects its ideological fit with neoliberalism. MacKinnon and Derickson (2013) note that the importation of naturalistic concepts and metaphors to the social sciences should be treated with caution, while Davoudi and Porter (2012) opine that care needs to be taken with regard to the adoption of resilience into public policy discourse.

As an analytical concept, the notion of resilience has undoubtedly been hindered by a lack of definitional clarity. That said, the appropriation of economic resilience has occurred within commercial strategy and policy rhetoric at pace, being widely regarded as critical to the performance of organisations, regions and nations. In understanding the nature of performance there have been a growing number of aggregated indices of resilience that have sought to systematically measure and define resilience. In parallel to this race to capture the essence of resilience there have been a number of leading scholars working to establish and consolidate the conceptual and theoretical underpinnings of resilience as a field of research.

This in itself is not unusual of fields of enquiry in their formative stages of development. Arguably the challenge of developing economic resilience as an analytical lens has been exacerbated by its application across different spaces and scales. Increasingly we see the same approach applied to researching the microeconomic (i.e., individual businesses and organisations), the mesoeconomic (i.e., industry sectors or markets) and the macroeconomic (i.e., all economic activity). The fact that the concept is researched across these different spaces and scales is testament to its relevance and strength, but heightens the need for conceptual clarity and development.

This edited collection offers different perspectives on resilience. The intention is not to unify the many arguments made by the contributors; indeed given the varied foci of the chapters this would be futile. Instead the aim of the collection is to illuminate how in this diversity there is an emerging consensus about how and why resilience is important as a conceptual lens. The remainder of this introductory chapter reflects on the emergence of resilience debate before introducing the collection of essays that explore resilience in different contexts.

INTRODUCING RESILIENCE

Rather than constraining the contributors by imposing our interpretation of economic resilience, instead the book assumes a bottom-up approach. The contributors to this volume have all grounded their own thinking in the literature, which serves to highlight similarities as well as differences concerning how the economic resilience lens is employed.

The notion of resilience is not new, having been widely studied in different disciplinary contexts. However, as a conceptual lens and analytical approach it has only recently become part of the vocabulary of social scientists. Previously the nature of resilience research has been implicit to discussions of economic cycles and business cycles. However, the growing interest in resilience as a first-order concept in its own right has seen it developed empirically and conceptually, as well as exploring the implications for policy and practice.

The original interpretation of resilience focused primarily on responding to external changes and shocks. However, in recent years the notion of resilience has become more nuanced, from a concept associated with 'bouncing back' to one of 'bouncing forward'. More than semantics, the nature of bouncing forward acknowledges that resilience does not simply mean returning to business as usual. It is this view that distinguishes equilibrium-based approaches towards resilience from evolutionary interpretations, and sees change as inherent to resilience. Consequently, following any type of crisis (economic or otherwise), change is a likely if not inevitable outcome.

More than disaffecting growth, the nature of any change occurring as a result of a crisis will shape the ways that organisations, regions and nations develop and evolve in the future. Such changes, often framed in terms of adaption, have led scholars to think more about responses, both in terms of anticipating shocks as well as how to respond to them. In particular, recent work on 'adaptive cycles' has found that higher levels of resilience are commonly associated more creative and flexible approaches (Pendall et al., 2010; Simmie and Martin, 2010). Continual adaption has come to represent an innate strength, as this can aid the ability to anticipate, prepare, respond to and recover from exogenous shocks.

Whether conceived in terms of frameworks or systems, adaption is critical to resilience, and distinguishes it from the related but distinct concepts of vulnerability and sustainability. Where it is not the norm to embrace change and adapt, and there is no attempt to respond to the external shock(s), the prospect of bouncing back – let alone bouncing forward – is seriously undermined and survival threatened. This means that resilience is not typically considered in terms of an individual organisation, region or nation, but rather in relation to the wider socio-economic system of which they are a part. Consequently, resilience is best understood as the ability of an organisation, region or nation to accommodate change, withstand systematic discontinuities and to do so without disrupting the wider system.

The following chapters offer insights about the nature of resilience across different spaces and scales. In this way the collection avoids the danger of 'concept stretching' described by Shaw (2012). Instead, as noted above, each chapter frames and elaborate the concept of resilience, the outcome of which serves to contribute to our collective understanding.

The interpretations of the contributing authors highlight the value and merit of resilience as an analytical lens through a series of case studies focused on the economic resilience of entrepreneurs, industrial sectors and cities in Part I, and local and regional economies in Part II.

PART I: THE RESILIENCE OF ENTREPRENEURS, INDUSTRIAL SECTORS AND CITIES

In Chapter 2, Rachel Doern explores the resilience of entrepreneurs in the context of the London 2011 riots, a human-induced crisis. While the rioting made international news headlines, this chapter considers the impact of the crisis on small businesses and their recovery in the aftermath of the looting, vandalism and/or arson during four days of rioting. In exploring the strategies and approaches of entrepreneurs, in particular the chapter highlights the importance of the personal dimension in understanding how entrepreneurs manage and respond to crises.

In the context of what is another human-induced crisis, Chapter 3 examines the experiences of entrepreneurs and small business in the context of the recessionary crisis in Greece. In exploring the link between entrepreneurship and the institutional environment, Nick Williams and Tim Vorley demonstrate how individual entrepreneurs have responded to the crisis. Despite the importance attributed to entrepreneurship as a driver of economic growth and renewal, the chapter details how entrepreneurship is being undermined as a driver of resilience and change.

The focus of much resilience research has tended to emphasise how shock and crises disaffect firms. However, in Chapter 4 Christian Kjær Monsson focuses on the resilience of small and medium-sized enterprises (SMEs), and in particular their ability to resist and recover from shocks. Considering resilience as a firm-level concept, and drawing out the distinction between vulnerability and adaptability, Monsson finds that many SMEs experiencing decline in the wake of a recession tend to turn performance around. Moreover, he contends that short-term decline can be an indicator of future growth potential.

Chapter 5 sees Gill Bentley, David Bailey and Daniel Braithwaite find the resilience of the automotive industry is premised on firms reinventing themselves. As opposed to bouncing back, the emphasis here is much more about bouncing forward. The resilience of the automotive industry is argued to be based on its ability to reorganise production across national and global supply chains both in response to and in anticipation of shocks to individual firms and the sector as a whole.

Picking up again on the theme of reinvention in Chapter 6, James

Simmie's focus is on the economic resilience of cities. Assuming a longitudinal approach examining data from English and Welsh cities from 1911, the chapter focuses on employment change and the development of knowledge-based private-sector service industries and digital firms. The chapter find that those cities with the highest levels of knowledge-based employment in 1911 have emerged as the most resilient economies, while those with the highest levels of low-knowledge-intensity jobs exhibit lower levels of resilience. A striking finding explored concerns the tendency of places to replicate and reproduce themselves, which has implications for resilience and long-run economic growth paths.

Chapter 7 is a study of the resilience of St Johns, the capital city of Newfoundland, as an example of a resource-dependent economy. Cédric Brunelle and Ben Spigel explore the evolutionary lock-in and lock-out processes in St John's oil and gas industry, focusing on the role of entrepreneurship to promote path creation as the basis of resilience and renewal. However, given the lock-in and lock-out associated with resource-dependent economies, such as St Johns, while entrepreneur-led diversification is arguably important it remains rare.

The cross-scalar nature of resilience is explored by Jennifer Clark in Chapter 8, and how resilient regions are premised on underlying innovation capacities of the cities and sectors of which they are comprised. Drawing on a case study of Atlanta, the chapter explores intersections between resilience and innovation in a civic context as a city that has had to adapt to economic transformation and social change. The chapter highlights economic resilience to be contingent on how the public and private sectors both interact and relate.

PART II: THE RESILIENCE OF LOCAL AND REGIONAL ECONOMIES

Also focusing on the public–private dynamic, Chay Brooks uses the lens of civic leadership in Chapter 9 to examine the resilience of city-regions. The chapter explores how local communities of public–private stakeholders work together to design and deliver strategic priorities to promote economic resilience and foster competitiveness. The chapter discusses the importance of governance as a dimension of resilience, and how new capabilities and capacities can be developed through partnerships.

Building on the theme of local economic resilience, Robert Huggins and Piers Thompson examine the role of entrepreneurship and culture in fostering economic resilience and the impact on local economic performance in Chapter 10. While finding that entrepreneurial activity increases the resilience of local economies, it is found to be highly contingent on the mix of other factors including culture. So while entrepreneurship is certainly a factor, the chapter argues that it alone cannot ensure the resilience of local economies.

In Chapter 11, Lee Pugalis, Nick Gray and Alan Townsend focus on Local Enterprise Partnerships (LEPs) as public–private partnerships constructed across functional economic areas. In analysing the plans for growth and recovery articulated in the Strategic Economic Plans of these localities, they find the largely conservative approach to persist. Consequently, there is little evidence of local economies making economies more resilient, a challenge exacerbated by the continued preoccupation of the partnerships with growth.

Paolo Di Caro focuses on the nature of local economic resilience in Chapter 12, drawing on case study evidence from three Italian local areas – the city of Turin (north-west), the province of Ragusa (south) and the eyewear district in the province of Belluno (north-east). The chapter argues that the economic resilience of these places differs according to the balance of five driving forces: innovation, entrepreneurship, human capital, civic capital and local policies/strategies. The chapter concludes by reflecting on how policy proposals serve to shape the long-term resilience of places and regions.

Emil Evenhuis and Stuart Dawley assume an evolutionary perspective towards economic resilience in regional development in Chapter 13. With a focus on governance and policy models, their findings highlight the key intersections between innovation and resilience. It is argued that innovation performs a key role in maintaining resilient regional economies, serving as a driver of competitiveness and growth. The challenge for regional economies is sustaining innovation as a driver of resilience and, with it, growth.

To explain the differences in regional resilience, Huiwen Gong and Robert Hassink ask why it is that some regional economies manage to renew themselves, whereas others remain locked in decline. As well as there being an evolutionary answer, Chapter 14 draws a wider interpretation of resilience, obtained from different disciplines, to develop new and useful insights. The conceptual contribution of this chapter further advances our understanding of regional economic adaptability and how evolutionary economic geographies shape resilience.

RESILIENCE INSIGHTS

This volume presents 13 accounts that all explore the nature of economic resilience, and in so doing seek to advance and refine our understanding of this fuzzy concept. In concluding the book, Chapter 15 offers some editorial reflections by the editors regarding the nature and development of economic resilience as a conceptual lens. As noted earlier, all of the contributors have identified and framed their work in their own under-standing of economic resilience without a framework being imposed on their approach. While it would therefore be remiss to presume a particular interpretation, the final chapter draws out the commonalities and identifies avenues for further conceptual and empirical development.

This collection advances our understanding of economic resilience in the social science by bringing together contributions exploring resilience across organisational and spatial scales, from the entrepreneur to regional economies. As the chapters demonstrate, the concept has been employed in relation to a variety of themes. However, in developing the concept, the chapters also show that while an aspect of resilience is often about responding to exogenous shocks, the concept is increasingly as much about adaptability and transformation.

PART I

The Resilience of Entrepreneurs, Industrial
Sectors and Cities

2. Strategies for resilience in entrepreneurship: building resources for small business survival after a crisis

Rachel Doern

INTRODUCTION

> We're not making a million pounds. We're just day-to-day activities. Since 2003, seven years, we didn't even go on holiday. My little girl says, 'Daddy, we have a shop, we have money, we have a passport, and why don't we get on an airplane?'... I say, 'OK darling, from next year, every single year, we go on holiday'. I told her, 'Baby I promise'... It's just, you know, it [the riots] changes a lot of things in your life. This is going to be huge.
>
> (OM5)

This quotation, taken from an interview with the owner-manager of a small shop in London (UK) damaged in the summer riots of 2011, captures an emergent emotional distance towards the business. This chapter examines this strategy and others adopted by owner-managers of small businesses impacted by the riots that followed the killing of Mark Duggan (a 29-year-old black male) by police on 4 August 2011. More than 2,000 commercial premises across London and other English cities were looted, vandalised and/or burned down (Reading the Riots, 2012).

Riots are social, human-induced, conflict-orientated crises (Barton, 1970), which, like other crises, negatively impact businesses by creating ambiguity and decision-making time pressures (Pearson and Clair, 1998). While much has been written about crisis planning and post-crisis management (e.g., Fink, 1986; Offer, 1998; Pedone, 1997), little is known about the kinds of strategies small businesses employ to minimise losses incurred, the role of resources in recovery, and how these strategies can, if at all, make businesses more resilient. Instead, studies on small business recovery after a crisis tend to concentrate on identifying the characteristics of firm survival (e.g., Alesch et al., 2001; Tierney et al., 1996; Dahlhamer and Tierney, 1998) and barriers to recovery (Irvine and Anderson, 2004; Runyan, 2006; Herbane, 2010).

Resilience has been defined as the ability – after a trauma, disruption or adversity generally – to bounce back or adapt in a positive fashion, to maintain healthy functioning in the process (Bonanno, 2004; Luthans, 2002; Luthar et al., 2000) or show good recovery (Masten, 1994, 2001). While this chapter draws on the broader resilience literature to highlight the importance of resources for recovery in the aftermath of a crisis, it pays particular attention to the Conservation of Resources (COR) theory (Hobfoll, 1988, 1989, 2001) to explain *why* these resources are important for resilience. The study featured here is based on qualitative interviews with 15 owner-managers of small businesses across London that were victimised during the riots. It makes several contributions to entrepreneurship research. First, it reveals the kinds of strategies small businesses adopt following a crisis and the resources they protect or build. Second, it shows how these strategies may enhance resilience (or vulnerability). Third, it introduces COR theory to the field of entrepreneurship, which provides an alternative to other theories that emphasise the value of resources for firms, such as the resource-based view. Fourth, it highlights the importance of personal recovery strategies and resources alongside the social and economic following a crisis, and suggests how small businesses and policymakers might better prepare for a crisis.

LITERATURE REVIEW

Resilience is a relatively new topic to entrepreneurship and has been discussed in relation to entrepreneurial teams, business start-ups, family and rural businesses, and in the contexts of disruptive business model innovations, economic recessions and other external shocks (e.g., Williams and Vorley, 2015a; Saridakis, 2012; Smallbone et al., 2012a; Glover, 2012; Blatt, 2009; Dewald and Bowen, 2010). Resilience, in the context of entrepreneurship, is conceived as business survival or growth following a crisis and is often measured by an increase in sales or profits or in terms of adopting positive/creative strategies (e.g., expanding the customer base, hiring more staff, investing in the business). Small businesses are generally regarded as being less resilient than large businesses because they have fewer resources, less bargaining power and are less able to spread risk over a larger customer base or product line (Smallbone et al., 2012a). Equally, they can be more flexible or adaptive in the face of adversity, in terms of adjusting inputs, products or prices (Reid, 2007).

While we know that an abundance of certain resources may make businesses more resilient, and that resources are important for business continuity generally following a crisis (Herbane et al., 2004), it is unclear just *why* or *how* this is the case. Thus, although in psychology there is a rich understanding of the relationship between resources and resilience (e.g., Hjemdal et al., 2006; Masten et al., 2004), in the field of entrepreneurship such understanding is largely absent. Additionally, studies on resilience in the field of entrepreneurship tend to neglect the critical human element, which is somewhat problematic when looking at small businesses wherein the motivations and energies of owner-managers are entwined with the business. This individual element is something that Conservation of Resources (COR) theory can bring to the entrepreneurship literature. Further, COR theory can explain why resources are important and bolster resilience.

According to COR theory, people are motivated to create resources and the act of doing so makes them more resilient (Hobfoll, 2002). The theory has been used to explain the link between threats to – or losses of – resources and resulting stress. It suggests that resources – including but not limited to physical objects (such as a business), conditions (such as seniority), personality characteristics that buffer against stress (such as self-esteem) and energies that help with the acquisition of resources (such as money, time or knowledge) – are valuable and should be protected. People can protect their resources and minimise the effects of potential losses to such during times of adversity by ensuring they have previously built up an abundance of such resources. This offsets future losses, strengthens resilience and leads to 'gain spirals' – i.e., the likelihood of acquiring more resources in the future (Hobfoll, 2001). When resources are limited or suddenly lost, however, the individual is more vulnerable and may experience stress; recovery may be more difficult and loss spirals may result – i.e., they are more likely to incur losses in the future (e.g., Hobfoll, 2001; Hobfoll and Lilly, 1993).

COR theory has been applied mostly to studies of stress management, burnout/well-being at work and work–family conflict (e.g., Hobfoll and Shirom, 2001; Grandey and Cropanzano, 1999; Westman and Eden, 1997), where resource losses and psychological distress are mostly gradual. Nevertheless, its basic tenets are supported by other studies where resource losses and psychological distress are sudden or acute, as in the case of a natural disaster or act of terrorism (e.g., Ironson et al., 1997; Hobfoll et al., 2006). In this study, COR theory helps explain the relationships between an adverse event (the riots), the strategies that owner-managers adopt for minimising losses, and resilience. The application of COR theory is extended here to highlight the importance of resources not only for small business owner-managers, but also for their businesses.

Thus, entrepreneurship provides a unique context in which to study both individual *and* organisational resilience simultaneously.

METHODOLOGY

The research approach adopted was phenomenological, part of the interpretivist tradition (Holstein and Gubrium, 1994). For phenomenologists, 'the world and the objects we perceive exist to us through the meanings we give to them, through an act of interpretation' (Berglund, 2007, p. 77). It has been used in other studies on entrepreneurship to understand entrepreneurial risk, learning and failure (Berglund and Hellström, 2002; Cope, 2011) and more recently crises (Doern, 2016). These studies share a focus on the perspective of the entrepreneur and his/her experiences.

The research sample consisted of owner-managers from 15 small businesses in London directly affected by the riots through looting, vandalism and arson. As with other phenomenological (and indeed crisis-focused) studies, the research sample was small (Buchanan and Denyer, 2013), allowing for a deep level of analysis (Hycner, 1985; King, 2004), theory-building and theoretical generalisation (e.g., Buchanan, 2012; Eisenhardt and Graebner, 2007), and the sampling strategy included only those with direct experience of the research phenomenon (the riots) (Hycner, 1985). Small businesses were identified by referral, media stories or via visible damage, and were drawn from the main riot-affected areas (Tottenham, Wood Green, Croydon, Hackney, Clapham Junction, Peckham, Ealing, Blackheath and Islington). The businesses included sold clothing, food and beverages, recreational goods and/or items for the home. Two were less than two years old, while about half were more than 15 years old. All had fewer than 50 employees while the majority were micro-businesses with fewer than ten employees. Most owner-managers were male (a fifth were women), and over the age of 40. More than half were white British (see Table 2.1).

In-depth semi-structured interviews began two months after the riots, between October and December 2011, taking advantage of the opportunity to collect data close to the events (e.g., Runyan, 2006). Participants were asked about their background and goals prior to the riots, how events unfolded in terms of where they were, when and how they were made aware of the riots, what happened to their businesses, how they responded, what motivated them to carry on, and what factors facilitated/inhibited their recovery. They were also asked what they believed were the causes of the riots, whether they might happen again, and what they had learned. All interviews were recorded and transcribed, and lasted between 45 minutes and two hours.

Table 2.1 Profile of participants

Participant code	Business type	Bus age (yrs)	Bus Size (employee numbers)	Bus damage Looting (L), vandalism (V) and/ or arson (A)	OM ethnicity	OM age (approx. yrs)	OM gender	OM Previously owned business
OM1	Clothing	15	4/5	LVA	Indian	45	M	Y
OM2	Furniture	50+	15–20	LVA	W British	55	M	N
OM3	Clothing	6	7	LV	B British	40	M	N
OM4	Services	40+	1	LV	W British	60+	M	Y
OM5	Convenience	11	3	LV	Other	40	M	N
OM6	Supplies	15	30	LVA	W British	55+	M	Y
OM7	Electronics	50+	>10	LV	W British	60+	M	N
OM8	Bar	1	>10 (temp)	LV	African	45	M	Y
OM9	Supplies	50+	2	LV	W British	60+	M	N
OM10ab	Clothing	20	2	LV	B British	30/55	FF	N
OM11	Electronics	40+	1	LV	W British	60+	M	N
OM12	Clothing	9	6	LV	W British	40+	F	N
OM13ab	Bar	30	4	LV	W Euro/W British	45/55	FM	N
OM14	Clothing	12	5/6	LV	W British	45	M	Y
OM15	Recreational	1.5	5	LV	W British	45	M	Y

15

The purpose of the study was to understand more about the strategies employed by small businesses following a crisis to minimise losses, the role of resources in these strategies and how, if at all, these strategies make businesses more resilient. A resource has been defined as anything of value to an individual that contributes to their well-being (Hobfoll, 2001; Dewe et al., 2012). This definition is extended here to include anything of value to the owner-manager that contributes not only to their well-being but also the well-being of their business. Data analysis was informed partly by the wider resilience literature and by COR theory. Transcripts were examined by addressing these analytical questions:

1.   What do owner-managers do in order to minimise losses?
2.   In each case, do owner-managers utilise existing resources or invest in additional resources?
3.   Do businesses lack resources or do owner-managers neglect to utilise the resources available to them?
4.   How, if at all, do these strategies lead to resource losses or gains?

The analysis began by repeatedly going through each transcript to identify themes (King, 2004), before reducing the data and drawing comparisons both within and across cases using data matrices (Nadin and Cassell, 2004). Some time was spent establishing the meaningfulness of individual accounts, examining each in detail by drawing from Interpretive Phenomenological Analysis (Smith, 1996). This technique develops interpretations of experiences from participant accounts, rather than 'simple descriptions of true experience' (King et al., 2002, p. 332).

FINDINGS

Three types of recovery strategies were identified from the data: *social*, *economic* and *personal* (see Table 2.2 for those that enhance resource gains and resilience). This section describes each strategy and gives examples from the data. It also discusses whether or not these strategies drew on existing resources or if resources were lacking and why, if owner-managers were actively investing in additional resources, and how, if at all, recovery strategies led to resources gains or losses.

Social Recovery Strategies

Following the riots, most participants relied on their existing social resources, networks of friends and family for support. Some drew further

Table 2.2   Recovery strategies for enhancing resource gains and resilience after a crisis

Strategies for resilience	Strategies reliant on existing resources	Strategies reliant on building resources	Resource gains
Social	Drawing resources from networks of friends, family, local community members (people/businesses), professional associations, local councils, government representatives	Generating publicity in order to draw additional attention and resources to the business	Boosting energy, self-esteem and/or status, providing financial assistance, building materials, information/advice, and practical or hands-on support
Economic	Drawing resources from personal savings, credit cards, bank overdrafts or other businesses	Applying for funding or business relief, devising in-store promotions or engaging in expansion	Rebuilding businesses by replacing damaged or stolen fittings, fixtures or stock, paying the rent and other bills, covering loss of turnover, keeping staff employed; also boosting energy and esteem
Personal	Drawing from own resources such as inner strength, self-determination and/or self-belief	Counting blessings, adopting a problem-solving mentality, engaging in emotion regulation, emotional distancing or withdrawal	Boosting energy, focusing on what is important and the tasks ahead, conserving energy

support from professional associations, local councils or government representatives, and many took comfort from the words and actions of both people and businesses in their local communities. The owner-manager of one small shop in North London (OM9), spoke about working in his community for over 40 years; after his business was looted, members of his local church came to assist: 'He [one community member] comes straight through the door and said, "What are we going to do? Alright let's get cracking!" On the Sunday afternoon they all came out of church in their Sunday best to do some work around here.' Not everyone was so lucky. In a few cases, the social resources of participants were limited either because these individuals were not so deeply embedded in the local community or because they were afraid to ask for help. In the latter instance, one owner-manager said: 'So you're off in this vacuum of "I really need support, but I can't really ask people for the support that I need because it's too much". So you want to just say, "somebody just fix all of this", but there's no fixing this thing' (OM10a).

Only a handful of participants were actively building their social resources following the riots. A few spoke about how this was being achieved by generating publicity. One owner-manager of a high-end clothing shop said it was his strategy to let members of his local community know what had happened and that he needed their support: 'We have three weeks of bad trading and it's game over so luckily we were resourceful and we made sure that a lot of people were aware we had been affected and they needed to support us . . . The people who live here. Because I am a great believer that if you don't support your local retailer, then they don't survive' (OM14). Similarly, another said: '[W]e took a business decision to make sure we didn't turn anything away . . . because the publicity, not only for us, but for the riots, if we do it well and people want to hear what we say . . . then it keeps the riots and things in the public eye' (OM2). Prior research suggests that such proactive attempts to draw resources to businesses strengthens organisational resilience (Mallak, 1998), while the act of engaging in new relationships enhances individual resilience (Bonanno, 2005).

The social strategies outlined above led, in turn, to a number of resource gains for both small businesses impacted by the riots and the owner-managers responsible for them. They produced economic and knowledge resources for the businesses, including financial assistance, building materials, information/advice and practical support, and sped up business recovery. A few benefited significantly from fundraising activities initiated by their communities. One business owner without adequate insurance said: 'The local people . . . they really want to help me, so they . . . created the webpage [to raise money] . . . So it makes you feel very very comfortable and you want to like, "I want to come back to this shop"' (OM5). Social resources boosted the morale of owner-managers, giving them the energy to carry on. One said: 'Although the riots might have been the catalyst to stopping me altogether . . . A lot of encouragement from local people [helped me carry on]' (OM11). It also protected their self-esteem, buffering them against stress (Rosenberg, 1979), and elevated their status in the community: 'I got an award, "Best Community Retailer of the Year"... It was a big award' (OM5). Only a couple mentioned that social interactions were time-consuming and drained their energy, leading to resource losses. 'Everybody is like, "Shit, [name of participant], what happened?" It's like I'm tired of telling people. I just scream . . . So I close the door' (OM1).

Economic Recovery Strategies

Many participants drew on existing economic resources such as personal savings or bank overdrafts to keep businesses operational and compensate for losses caused by paying for repairs and the sudden reduction in turnover. A few had other businesses from which they could draw resources. Unlike with social resources, owner-managers spoke with more desperation and frustration about using their economic resources: 'I had an overdraft with HSBC only £3,000, now it increases up to £20,000. I'm using £20,000. Because you're stuck! I have to use it. There's no choice. Because business is day to day trading and [if at] one point you stop, you will come up to the neck' (OM5).

For a number of reasons, most felt their economic resources were in short supply. First, some businesses were already suffering prior to the riots due to the recent recession and increased competition. This heightened concerns about the viability of businesses following the riots, as financial reserves were small. Second, not all businesses were fully insured (three in total), making them particularly vulnerable. Third, even those who were insured had to deal with insurance companies that were bureaucratic, slow to pay or unwilling to cover all of their losses, adding to their vulnerability. Fourth, some of those who tried to acquire funding or financial relief from local government (i.e., business rate reductions) were unsuccessful. Fifth, not everyone applied for funding quickly or confidently (e.g., 'I felt reluctant to [apply for financial support]', OM12; '[T]hey made it so complicated. . . and in the end it became so problematic you thought, "Sod it"', OM14).

Following the riots, most owner-managers were actively trying to build up their economic resources. Several spoke enthusiastically about the High Street Fund, a charity set up by the private sector to help small businesses affected by the riots: 'The High Street Fund has been brilliant. The first time ever, I thought, "I'm going to tap in to that. I'm not just going to stand on my own if there's an opportunity. I'm going to investigate it"' (OM14). They sang the praises of the fund for being a 'proactive', 'efficient', 'no-quibble' source. Additionally, a few owner-managers successfully obtained business rate reductions: 'We applied for business rate reduction. We got a quarter's worth of relief. So to coincide with us opening now, now we have that, which for us is good. Initially they [the council] just wanted to give us two weeks' (OM10a). Such persistence is critical to survival following a hardship (Flach, 2003). Other strategies reported by owner-managers included in-store promotions or business expansion. One participant described how he used his new fame to expand into a department store chain: 'By this time I was a media star. I said, "The publicity I could bring you". I said, "We could actually bring you thousands of new customers"' (OM6). Like building new relationships, this kind of creativity shows the owner-managers' capacity for generative experiences (Bonanno et al., 2001; Luthans, 2002), a feature of individual resilience.

Economic recovery strategies led to a number of resource gains. That is, in utilising existing economic resources or investing in new resources, owner-managers were able to begin rebuilding their businesses and work towards bringing them back to normal by replacing fittings, fixtures or stock, paying bills, covering loss of turnover and keeping staff employed. One said: 'Without the High Street Fund I wouldn't have been able to pay the rent' (OM15). Also, as with social recovery strategies, where economic strategies were successful, they had the effect of increasing owner-managers' energy and self-esteem. Nevertheless, a few implied these strategies also led to personal losses of time and energy: 'It's like you've got two businesses, the business that's running and the business you've got to sort out with insurance' (OM2). Another explained, 'I nearly cracked up over it all, chasing people and trying to get things done' (OM11). It has been argued that psychological stress may be produced when resource losses are threatened or incurred, and when investments in resources do not lead to resource gains (Hobfoll, 1989). Findings here further suggest that, following a crisis, the act of investing in resources may also be stress-inducing for owner-managers.

Personal Recovery Strategies

Many participants drew on existing personal resources such as an inner strength, self-determination and/or self-belief following the riots. Several attributed business continuity to a strong desire to prove to themselves and the rioters that they would not be defeated: 'I suppose the biggest motivator is . . . wanting to, to show whoever perpetrated the crime that I can bounce back' (OM12). For others, their determination to carry on came from life experience: 'I haven't told you half the *shit*, I've gone through in life . . . what the hell, it's a shop' (OM6). Another made reference to both factors: 'Well, I'm not going to be driven out by the riots . . . I had, six years ago, there was a big fire, the whole of the building around me was all burned down and the shop was flooded and we lived in temporary accommodation for 18 months and we worked through it all' (OM9).

There were few accounts of failing to use existing personal resources or reports relating to a lack of such personal resources. Nevertheless, as noted earlier, a few owner-managers complained of low energy levels, which was partly the product of investing in other social and economic strategies, particularly continuous dealings with members of the public or media, and a rise in workload. The literature on resilience (e.g., Bonanno, 2005) does not consider these potentially negative effects.

There was evidence that owner-managers were actively trying to increase personal resources through strategies such as counting blessings, adopting a problem-solving mentality, emotion regulation and emotional distancing or withdrawal. Many appreciated that the riots could have been worse: 'I'm a lot better off than some people in the way their businesses have been burned out and that sort of thing. It would not be possible then, to start again. You know, I kind of look at it from that angle as well, that I should be grateful that I am able actually to carry on, and pick myself up, and go on' (OM11). By counting blessings, positive emotions (e.g., gratitude) are generated, which in turn build psychological resources and resilience that buffer against depression (Fredrickson et al., 2003). Resilience may also be enhanced when individuals demonstrate problem-solving skills (Bonanno, 2004). This quality was present in some accounts: 'I have a habit like, if anything happen to me, I worry, one hour, two hours, and then, I'm always like, "How can I overcome that?"' (OM5). Some owner-managers were also building reserves by focusing on the positive and/or minimising the negative. 'The people that did [this], that stole from me, I'm not going to waste any time, any emotion on them' (OM11). Finally, a couple spoke about how the riots had created a wedge between themselves and their businesses: '[W]e're less precious about [our location]. . . If there comes a time where we can't be sustainable anymore, then we've done 20 years here and I think we've proven. . . that yes, something interesting and positive can thrive within a disadvantaged area . . . We've taken a hit and we're trying to pull things together as best as we can' (OM10a).

Personal recovery strategies that entailed using existing resources or building new resources led to a number of resource gains. As with both social and economic strategies, they provided entrepreneurs with the energy to continue; they also helped owner-managers identify what was important. For instance, several reported they had to be strong for family and staff. Emotion regulation and withdrawal helped in the short-term to conserve energy: 'I had to think what to do as quick as possible because if I don't do it, I get more down. I get more depression' (OM1). However, in the longer-term, distancing oneself from the business might also reduce the willingness to invest energy, time and passion in it. Not dealing with or learning from negative emotions can also lead to problems. One participant resorted to hiding her stock daily as she feared more riots would occur and wondered whether if she and her business partner should have received counselling.

DISCUSSION

The purpose of this study was to understand the kinds of strategies small businesses adopt following a crisis, the role of resources in these strategies and how they may create resilience. Three categories of recovery strategies, *social*, *economic* and *personal*, were identified. Conservation of Resources (COR) theory posits that strategies for conserving resources are successful when people use existing resources or seek to create new resources (Hobfoll, 1989, 2001). In turn, these strategies help to minimise or offset the losses incurred by a crisis. There was evidence in the current study that, after the riots, owner-managers drew on existing resources where possible – for example, social networks, personal savings and inner strength. These resources provided short-term relief and the motivation to focus on recovery. Nevertheless, in all cases, owner-managers did not rely solely on existing resources. Rather, they invested in additional resources – for example, creating new social resources by generating publicity, new economic resources through expansion or new personal resources by focusing on the positive and counting blessings. This investment in resources occurred where they lacked resources, were left vulnerable by the suddenness of the riots, and were unprepared or constrained for reasons relating to the size of the business. Prior research also shows small businesses tend not to be prepared for a crisis and are more focused on the post-crisis phase (Runyan, 2006; Irvine and Anderson, 2004). This can make them more vulnerable.

COR theory suggests that when resources are abundant, resistance to stress and resilience are enhanced, and more resources may be acquired leading to 'gain spirals' (Hobfoll, 2001). One example from the current study concerns an owner-manager (OM9) who spoke about the strong social network he had built up within his local community and through such, how he had acquired emotional and physical support, as well as access to building materials. Moreover, his business had previously recovered from a crisis (a fire and flooding), that gave him the experience, the inner strength and determination, to succeed after the riots. This case shows that resources accumulated prior to the riots led to resource gains for both the individual and the business following the riots. By developing resources, individuals/organisations can, when needed, increase their knowledge, speed of learning, response repertoires and even their ability to improvise (Weick and Sutcliffe, 2007, p. 68). Thus, the owner-manager in question was able to draw from a broad response repertoire, reducing his losses and stress, and ultimately enhancing resilience. It can also be said that an abundance of resources in one area can substitute for limitations in another. This was observed in those instances where businesses did not have adequate economic resources such as insurance but were able to carry on because they had built up social resources that led to community fundraising.

Not all participants, however, had an abundance of resources or were proactive in acquiring them. For example, one owner-manager (OM10a) said she could not rely on existing social networks for support due to the skilled nature of her work. She was unable to quickly access money from her insurance company, and was reluctant to apply for a loan or funding. In contrast to the previous case, this individual had a more narrow range of responses in her repertoire from which to draw. She adopted a strategy of emotional distancing as a means of conserving her personal resources. Her business took a long time to reopen and she experienced significant economic and personal losses. She was less resistant to stress; she continued to feel angry and fearful and questioned her future in the business. Thus, existing resource limitations, in conjunction with the nature of the business and a limited resource building approach made this participant more vulnerable to the effects of the riots. As with other studies (e.g., Hobfoll, 2001), these findings show that when losses are experienced without resource gains, the experience of psychological distress is more likely.

COR theory argues that recovery strategies are unsuccessful when resources are lacking, people do not use the resources available or create new resources (Hobfoll, 1989, 2001). This can lead to additional losses, stress, vulnerability and fewer resources in the future – 'loss spirals' (Hobfoll, 1989, 2001). When businesses are vulnerable, it is more likely they will experience future losses (Anderson, 1995). Where resources were limited in this study, as observed in the case above, it took longer to repair damages and reopen the business. As a result, businesses may have lost contact with customers and goodwill (see Herbane et al., 2004). Limited resources also increased the workload and psychological vulnerability of owner-managers. In the words of one individual, 'If I don't do it [recover quickly], I get more down' (OM1). A quick recovery can minimise the negative psychological effects of a crisis, which may be particularly salient following riots (Aguilera, 1998) (see Figure 2.1).

COR theory does not explain all of the findings, however. Specifically,

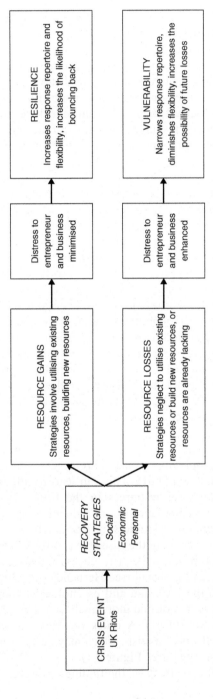

Figure 2.1 A model of the processes by which recovery strategies elicited by small businesses in the immediate aftermath of a crisis may lead to their resilience or vulnerability

it does not account for situations in which participants were actively trying to create new resources but were constrained or unsuccessful in their attempts, nor does it account for the implications. For example, while several participants in the current study actively pursued financial relief, some found the processes overly bureaucratic, which delayed their recovery and created frustration. Second, it does not take into consideration situations in which resource limitations in one area further deplete resources in another. For example, limited financial or social resources had a knock-on effect for some, depleting time and energy, leading to negative emotions that can make it more difficult for entrepreneurs to attract resources in turn (Baron, 2008). Third, post-crisis recovery strategies may be unsuccessful and lead to further losses when they deliberately deplete resources (e.g., by withdrawing effort via emotional distancing) or resource losses occur as an unintended consequence (of chasing up insurers or doing repairs). Future losses or 'loss spirals' may result. Finally, while COR theory places an emphasis on being proactive and assumes people are motivated to create and protect resources (Hobfoll, 2002), this tendency was not always apparent here. Instead, there were instances of being more reactive than proactive (e.g., where social and economic resources were received rather than actively sought). Therefore, further research is needed in order to explore these issues in full.

CONCLUSIONS

This study makes several contributions to our understanding of resilience in entrepreneurship. First, it identifies different kinds of strategies small businesses adopt following a crisis, the resources these strategies serve to protect or build, and the role they play in making businesses and entrepreneurs more resilient (or vulnerable). These strategies were found to be *social*, *economic* and *personal* in nature. Second, it introduces a new theory, Conservation of Resources (Hobfoll, 1989, 2001), to the field of entrepreneurship to develop our understanding of crises in this context. The theory sheds light on why resources are valuable to small businesses during the recovery phase and how they may facilitate resilience. It shows that when small businesses possess an abundance of resources they can offset the losses incurred from a crisis and provide a buffer against stress. On the other hand, resource limitations may lead to more losses and stress unless an outside intervention fills this resource gap, at least in the short term (e.g., community fundraising or government/private sector funding). Third, the study highlights the importance of personal recovery strategies and resources alongside the social and economic. While previous literature places an emphasis on the role networks and financial reserves play in business survival following a crisis (Smallbone et al., 2012a), personal resources such as self-determination, and the recovery strategies used to protect and build them (e.g., counting blessings, emotion regulation), have been overlooked.

One key limitation of the study is that it took place a couple of months after the London riots. While this captured the data close to the event (Runyan, 2006), it is a short time frame for assessing business recovery, especially as many participants were still waiting for funding or insurance payments. However, a second round of data collection was carried out two years later that should, once analysed, provide a fuller picture of recovery. It will also reveal whether and how strategies adopted by owner-managers evolved, and if they were successful in terms of leading to longer-term resource gains and resilience. Future research should seek to further develop and test the model (Figure 2.1) on different small business populations under similar or different crisis situations. There is also more scope for investigating the interdependencies between the different groups of strategies or kinds of resources identified, and the knock-on effects of such, where resource limitations in one area further deplete resources in another. Future research should also compare the effects of proactive and reactive strategies used by entrepreneurs and the implications for business survival.

The findings have a number of implications for practitioners and policymakers. First, they suggest entrepreneurs need to invest continually in resources, not just in the aftermath of a crisis, to prepare for the unexpected. These resources can buffer against the loss and stress that may follow crises and help them acquire additional resources. The findings should encourage entrepreneurs to ask for help, draw on the support provided and, importantly, to move on quickly in order to minimise stress and other losses to the business. Policymakers also need to act quickly in order to support small businesses affected by a crisis, particularly those affected by large-scale crises with significant social and economic repercussions – providing financial assistance, advice and emotional support. These efforts will likely help fill resource gaps common to small businesses, show businesses they are valued and enhance the self-belief of owner-managers, giving them the energy to carry on. Practically speaking, policymakers should also ensure that processes for attaining support following a crisis are simple and clear. Finally, they should recognise other kinds of difficulties faced by small businesses in terms of workload and psychological strain and provide appropriate support. Outside interventions might make the difference between business survival and failure for resource-limited or depleted individuals and businesses, while offering those with more abundant resources the respite they need in order to accumulate further resources (Westman and Eden, 1997).

ADDITIONAL READING

Bonanno, G., Papa, A. and O'Neill, K. (2001), 'Loss and human resilience'. *Applied and Preventative Psychology* **10**(3): 193–206.

Herbane, B. (2010), 'Small business research: time for a crisis-based view'. *International Small Business Journal* **28**(1): 43–64.

Mallak, L. (1998), 'Putting organizational resilience to work'. *Industrial Management* **40**(6): 8–13.

Weick, K.E. and Sutcliffe, K.M. (2007), *Managing the Unexpected*, 2nd edn. San Francisco: Jossey-Bass.

3. The resilience of entrepreneurs and small businesses in the depths of a recessionary crisis

Nick Williams and Tim Vorley

INTRODUCTION

The chapter focuses on a study of Greece, a country that has been adversely and severely affected by the global economic crisis that began in 2008, and has been slow to recover (Matsaganis and Leventi, 2013; Williams and Vorley, 2015a). Greece has been severely affected by the crisis, leading to both endogenous and exogenous institutional change. Endogenous change has resulted from the Greek government's attempts to restructure the economy in response to the crisis while exogenous change has been experienced due to the international bailouts Greece has received, which are conditional on tax increases and austerity measures (Matsaganis and Leventi, 2013). These changes have led to formal and informal institutional change, which will influence the competitiveness of the Greek economy in the longer term. This chapter examines how changes to the institutional environment brought about by the recent crisis have impacted on entrepreneurs. The chapter shows that Greece's institutional environment was weak prior to, and has worsened as a result of, the crisis. Further, we posit that negative changes to formal institutions brought about by the impact of the crisis will have a consequent and congruent negative impact on informal institutions, as the entrepreneurial culture weakens in response to changes in rules and regulations. It is only by reversing the trend of weak institutions that Greece can properly emerge as a competitive country in the longer term.

Whereas previous research has shown that policymakers have improved the institutional environment in response to a crisis (see, for example, Smallbone et al., 2012a), this chapter shows how policy decisions can have a cumulatively negative impact on entrepreneurship. Some of the institutional changes (such as a lack of credit) have been imposed upon policymakers and they are unable to alleviate these issues – for example, by changing formal institutions – due to the direct fiscal impacts of the crisis on government. However, other decisions made by policymakers that aim to improve the national economy have inadvertently undermined entrepreneurial activity, the support of which is crucial for recovering from crisis and achieving growth. The chapter develops a more nuanced understanding of how institutional reforms can negatively affect entrepreneurial activity in a crisis-hit economy, and thereby undermine the contribution that entrepreneurship can make to recovery.

LITERATURE REVIEW

Although entrepreneurship is often portrayed as an individual endeavour, it is important to recognise that it both affects and is affected by the institutional environment that governs and directs economic activity (Acs et al., 2008; Bruton et al., 2008). The 'rules of the game' (North, 1990, 1994) incorporate formal institutions such as the ease of starting up, licensing and registration laws and access to finance, and informal institutions such as perceptions of opportunity and prevailing culture, impose direct and indirect effects on both the supply of and demand of entrepreneurs' behaviours (Acs et al., 2008). As such, the extent to which entrepreneurship is socially productive and contributes to economic growth depends on the institutional context in which it occurs (Baumol, 1990; Acs et al., 2008).

FORMAL INSTITUTIONS

Formal institutions can be defined as the rules and regulations that are written down or formally accepted and give guidance to the economic and legal framework of a society (Tonoyan et al., 2010; Smallbone et al., 2012a). Informal institutions can be defined as the traditions, customs, societal norms, culture, unwritten codes of conduct (Baumol, 1990; North, 1990; Smallbone et al., 2012a). These norms and values are passed from one generation to the next and can therefore be resistant to change (Bruton et al., 2010). We posit that it is the interaction between formal and informal institutions that will have a long-term impact on entrepreneurship and its ability to contribute to emergence from this crisis.

Formal institutions are created to provide rules, regulations and property rights that enable decision-makers to engage in transactions with greater certainty (Smallbone et al., 2012a). Where formal institutions are strong and well-enforced, over time entrepreneurial activity will be fostered that contributes to economic growth (Acs et al., 2008). However, where formal institutions are weak, they impose costly bureaucratic burdens on entrepreneurs and increase uncertainty as well as the operational and transaction costs of firms (Djankov et al., 2002; Puffer et al., 2010). Entrepreneurs in such settings can often be faced with incoherent and constantly changing regulations (Manolova and Yan, 2002; Aidis et al., 2008), meaning that, for example, they are unable to calculate their tax bills due to changing tax rates (Tonoyan et al., 2010). Furthermore, gaining credit can be difficult, as banks can favour larger businesses and lack willingness to finance small enterprises (Smallbone and Welter, 2001). As such, getting credit can act as a strong constraint on entrepreneurial activity (Guseva, 2007). Moreover, in a crisis situation, credit constraints become much more acute. Smallbone et al. (2012a) demonstrate how a credit crunch caused by the recent economic crisis impacted on both the supply of and demand for small firm financing in the UK and New Zealand, and Cowling et al. (2012) show that the crisis in the UK led to finance being more readily available to larger and older firms throughout the recession. In common with these economies, finance has become more difficult to obtain in Greece as a result of the crisis (European Commission, 2012).

In light of recent economic crises, academic and policy interest has focused on how economies can rebound and cultivate greater resilience and competitiveness following an external shock (Hayward et al., 2010; Pike et al., 2010; Davidsson and Gordon, 2016; Martin et al., 2015; Lai et al., 2016). In order to respond effectively to a crisis, a country or region's ability to adapt institutional and organisational structures is of paramount importance (Dawley et al., 2010). The organisations and institutions that make up an economy are continually adapting to the wider economic environment, and indeed policy can be proactive in being 'prepared' for external shocks (Simmie and Martin, 2010). Similarly, policymakers must also seek to positively respond to external factors such as crisis if an economy is to emerge positively (Pike et al., 2010), and where policy is proactive or responds positively to external shocks, disturbances and stresses can be minimised (Pendall et al., 2010). Smallbone et al. (2012a) show that policymakers in New Zealand sought to minimise the impacts of the crisis by introducing an export credit scheme, expansion of business advice services, a prompt payment requirement for government agencies, and a relief package of 11 tax changes. Similarly, in the UK, the government introduced a relief package for small firms, financial help involving a system of loan guarantees and financial advice, a temporary cut in the value-added tax (VAT) rate, an acceleration of capital investment projects and accelerated roll-out of broadband, and measures to combat unemployment (Smallbone et al., 2012a). However, such policy options are only available to governments with budget flexibility. In Greece, which has been reliant on international bailouts to prevent fiscal collapse, the ability to fund such changes is severely restricted due to the shrinking of the state purse brought about by the crisis (Kaplanoglou and Rapanos, 2013), meaning that positive institutional change is stymied. For example, Greece has introduced VAT increases that served to dampen demand for products and services as prices rose (Matsaganis and Leventi, 2013). As a consequence, it is clear that changes to the formal institutions prior to or in the midst of a crisis is important for determining how an economy can support entrepreneurs and ultimately how effectively it will emerge from the external shock.

INFORMAL INSTITUTIONS

Bruton et al. (2010) describe how the informal institutions of norms and behaviours present within a society define and determine models of individual behaviour based on subjectivity and meanings that affect beliefs and actions. These norms are the often taken-for-granted culturally specific behaviours that are learned living or growing up in a given community or society (Scott, 2007) and engender a predictability of behaviour in social interactions that is reinforced by a system of rewards and sanctions to ensure compliance and over time become an informal institution (DiMaggio and Powell, 1983, 1991).

Understanding informal institutions is important to entrepreneurship in terms of how societies accept entrepreneurs, inculcate values and create a cultural milieu whereby entrepreneurship is accepted and encouraged (Bruton et al., 2010). Indeed informal institutions are widely acknowledged as critical to explaining different levels of entrepreneurial activity across countries (Davidsson, 1995; Puffer et al., 2010). Since entrepreneurship is always embedded in a cultural context, understanding informal institutions is critical to fostering entrepreneurship (Bruton et al., 2010). Yet despite the importance attributed to culture in relation to entrepreneurship and economic development, it remains an elusive concept (Huggins and Williams, 2011). This elusiveness represents a substantive challenge for academics and policymakers alike, as affecting cultural change demands a clear understanding as to the intended objectives of such interventions and the mechanisms by which they are achieved.

Reforming informal institutions is difficult but not impossible. It is often a slow process, since the norms and values passed from one generation to the next can be resistant to change (Estrin and Mickiewicz, 2011). As entrepreneurship becomes more visible and valued in a society it gains legitimisation, and the growth of entrepreneurial aspirations and ambitions can in turn serve to reinforce the emergence of a pro-entrepreneurship culture

(Krueger and Carsrud 1993; Minniti, 2005). In this sense, although government is clearly important in influencing entrepreneurial activity (Smallbone
and Welter, 2001; Acs et al., 2008), institutional change is not simply the
responsibility and domain of policymakers. Entrepreneurs themselves can
act as change agents and influence the institutional landscape (McMullen,
2011). At the cultural level, entrepreneurship is also self-reinforcing, as
individuals follow societal clues and are influenced by what others have
chosen to do, thereby slowly moving society to a more entrepreneurial
culture as people see others succeeding (Minniti, 2005). However, unchang-
ing cultures can contribute to a lack of economic resilience, meaning that
responses to crises may be slow (Simmie and Martin, 2010). In this sense,
a culture that is supportive of entrepreneurship and allows flexibility and
diversity will foster greater resilience and emerge from crisis more quickly
(Hill et al., 2008), whereas informal institutions that foster a weak culture
of entrepreneurship will undermine entrepreneurial activity. While they are
more difficult to affect as they are slow to change (Estrin and Mickiewicz,
2011), consideration of informal institutions is important as they will have
a long-term impact on entrepreneurship and its ability to contribute to
emergence from crisis.

Perceptions of entrepreneurship can change as a result of crisis, with
some individuals less willing to take risks while others see opportunities
to exploit, and societal views of entrepreneurs can shift if they are seen
to have contributed to the crisis (European Commission, 2012; Amoros
and Bosma, 2013). As such, informal institutions are as important to the
development of entrepreneurship as formal institutions (Williams and
Vorley, 2015b) and should be properly considered by policymakers seeking
to facilitate emergence from a crisis.

EMPIRICAL FOCUS AND METHODOLOGY

The recent economic crisis has highlighted the weaknesses of the Greek
economy and its institutional environment, and understanding the nature
of these challenges is critical to managing its fragile recovery. While the
enduring Eurozone crisis and speculation concerning the membership of
Greece within the Eurozone provides the backdrop to our research, the focus
of this chapter is on the nature of institutional change and entrepreneurial
activity in the context of the crisis. In doing so, the chapter demonstrates that
in responding to external shock, the ability of governments to affect positive
institutional change is limited by the extent of the crisis. We show that
institutional changes can be negative in terms of promoting entrepreneurship
and that this can be caused by a lack of policy flexibility available in a crisis.

Structural problems in the Greek economy see the country ranked as 81st out of 140 world economies (World Economic Forum, 2015) and 54th out of 189 world economies in the 'ease of doing business' index, with the primary reasons cited as government bureaucracy, poor access to finance, corruption, tax regulations and rates and political instability (World Bank, 2016). Prior to the recent crisis, Greek economic competitiveness had been declining (Koufopoulos and Morgan, 1994; Featherstone and Papadimitriou, 2008; Featherstone, 2010) and the crisis and ensuing recession has brought many of the systemic problems to the fore. As a result, Greek competitiveness has further declined due to the crisis, and it is now ranked as the least competitive economy in the European Union (World Economic Forum, 2015).

Today, Greece is a developed economy with above-average rates of early-stage entrepreneurial activity and a high level of established business ownership (Xavier et al., 2012). Greece also has a high rate of small, family-owned enterprises, but a cultural resistance to the iconic 'entrepreneur' (Drakopoulou Dodd and Hynes, 2012). Greek cultural perceptions of entrepreneurship are often negative, with entrepreneurs seen as having selfish motives (European Commission, 2012), and common metaphors used to describe them including 'thieves', 'fraudsters', 'pimps' and 'vampires' (Drakopoulou Dodd et al., 2013). The percentage of total early-stage entrepreneurship in 2012 was 6.5 per cent, but has declined as a result of the crisis as the recession has negatively affected the survival potential of businesses (Global Entrepreneurship Monitor, 2013). Perceived opportunities to start a business are low, although perceived capabilities are quite high, and the nature of entrepreneurial activities tends to be of low ambition and often driven by necessity (Amoros and Bosma, 2013). At the same time, there is a large and often ineffective public sector, and with it has emerged a significant informal economy (Piperopoulos, 2009).

This chapter critically analyses how changes to the institutional environment have affected entrepreneurial activity in Greece in light of the financial crisis. This study employs a qualitative case study of entrepreneurs based in Thessaloniki, the second most populous city in Greece and a major economic, industrial, commercial and political centre (Moussiopoulos et al., 2010). In-depth interviews with 26 entrepreneurs were conducted between April and June 2012 and lasted 50 minutes on average. Table 3.1 provides a profile of the participants in terms of the sector their business operates in, the size of the business and its age.

The interviews were recorded with the respondents' consent and transcribed, before assuming an inductive approach towards thematically analysing and coding the data to explore emergent themes (Bryman, 2012). In the analysis and discussion we use quotes from the interviews to add

Table 3.1   Profile of participants

Respondent	Sector	Size of business (number of employees)	Age of business
1	Financial services	11–50	1–5 years
2	IT	1–10	6–10 years
3	Food and drink	11–50	1–5 years
4	Tourism	1–10	6–10 years
5	Electronics	11–50	1–5 years
6	IT	1–10	Less than a year
7	Tourism	11–50	1–5 years
8	Construction	51–250	10+ years
9	Construction	51–250	10+ years
10	IT	1–10	Less than a year
11	Real estate	1–10	1–5 years
12	Media	11–50	1–5 years
13	Telecommunications	51–250	10+ years
14	Pharmaceutical	11–50	1–5 years
15	IT	11–50	10+ years
16	IT	1–10	1–5 years
17	Tourism	1–10	10+ years
18	Media	1–10	Less than a year
19	Electronics	1–10	1–5 years
20	Construction	51–250	6–10 years
21	Food and drink	1–10	6–10 years
22	Financial services	11–50	1–5 years
23	IT	1–10	1–5 years
24	Food and drink	11–50	1–5 years
25	Financial services	1–10	6–10 years
26	Textiles	11–50	10+ years
27	IT	11–50	1–5 years

voice to the study. In many cases, consensus was found regarding the key areas of exploration and these responses can therefore be considered to be representative of the views of the majority of the respondents.

FINDINGS

This section furthers the existing debates outlined in the literature review by presenting a more nuanced analysis of how reforms to the institutional environment in the midst of a crisis can have a negative impact on entrepreneurship. The institutional environment prior to the crisis provides the context for understanding the prevailing rules and culture, and to analyse how they have changed as a result of the crisis. Prior to the crisis, Greece showed evidence of institutional asymmetry with stable but bureaucratic formal rules and weak informal norms that stymied entrepreneurship, as individuals circumvented or avoided rules. Negative changes to formal institutions caused by the crisis have a consequent and congruent negative impact on informal institutions, as the entrepreneurial culture weakens in response to changes in the rules and regulations. The findings are presented in two sections: the first examines how the practices of entrepreneurs have changed as a result of institutional reforms in Greece; while the second considers how the institutional environment has shaped the culture of entrepreneurship in Greece and thus what role culture may play in any economic recovery.

Institutional Responses to the Crisis

Prior to the crisis, the consensus among respondents was that Greece was 'overly bureaucratic', an 'overly managed economy' that did little to support entrepreneurs. Yet it is not simply the prevailing institutional environment that has affected entrepreneurial activity, but that institutional reforms have created further obstructions which serve to disincentivise or undermine entrepreneurial activity. One recurring theme in the interviews related to how the institutional environment was becoming more challenging in the wake of the crisis as the government sought to restructure the economy. Some of the impacts of the crisis, such as the availability of credit, have been outside of the direct remit of Greek policymakers. Given the shrinking of the Greek state purse, the government has had no public money available to extend and/or support credit as a response to a fall in bank lending, as has occurred in other countries (Smallbone et al., 2012a). This has meant that 'government is no longer a customer' (INT9) due to the formal institutional change in access to finance. In addition, several entrepreneurs stated that bank lending to small businesses had 'completely stopped' (INT6), and that the government was not able to stimulate, underwrite or provide funding itself to plug this gap. In many cases, this has meant that many entrepreneurs had adjusted their growth plans to reflect more limited and constrained opportunities. One respondent stated that 'we can't expand now as we can't get access to finance . . . we are just aiming to survive not grow' (INT19), while another said 'we have had to cut back our workforce because some of our business has stopped . . . we used to provide IT services to a company that worked for the government but that work isn't there anymore' (INT27).

While the lack of private-sector finance may have been outside the ability of government to solve given their financial constraints, other decisions made by policymakers have had a direct impact on entrepreneurial activity. Despite attempts to reform the taxation system in the early to mid-2000s, the Greek government has since been forced to increase taxation rates on enterprises and income tax on employees (Katsimi and Moutos, 2010). In an attempt to generate higher public revenues as a result of the economic crisis, some sectors of the economy have had tax rates increased, which has curtailed growth and consequently seen tax revenues from these sectors fall. In addition, Greece has introduced VAT increases that have served to dampen demand for goods and services further as prices have risen (Matsaganis and Leventi, 2013).

The entrepreneurs interviewed expressed how the austerity programme in Greece, which has included variable VAT increases on different sectors, had created a sense of increased uncertainty with regards to the taxation system. One entrepreneur explained: 'Business taxes have gone up and they could easily go up again . . . businesses are being strangled with increased taxes and uncertainty' (INT16). Such uncertainty means that entrepreneurs have difficulties in planning over the medium to long term (Puffer et al., 2010; Williams and Vorley, 2015a). As one entrepreneur stated: 'Taxes on my business have changed five times in two years . . . it is impossible to plan ahead properly if the goalposts keep being moved' (INT4). In situations where institutions are stable, planning and coordination is promoted and the ad hoc expropriation of the fruits of entrepreneurship is prevented (Henrekson, 2007).

A further unintended consequence of reforms identified by the interviewees was a rise in informal activities. A number of the entrepreneurs reported that increased taxation and uncertainty had encouraged them to shift some entrepreneurial activities 'off-the-books' where possible. In the case of Greece, this poses an interesting challenge, as while Tonoyan et al. (2010) emphasise the importance of a strong institutional environment to tackle informal activity, our findings suggest that while Greece is implementing institutional reform it is at the same time regressing as an entrepreneurial environment. Consequently, as opposed to promoting the formalisation of entrepreneurial activity, Sepulveda and Syrett (2007) describe a coming out of the shadows whereby weak and changing institutional environments can be seen to inadvertently promote informal entrepreneurial activity while disincentivising legitimate entrepreneurship. All of the entrepreneurs interviewed stated that they had either engaged in informal economic activity themselves or knew of other entrepreneurs who had in order to avoid the time and/or costs of complying with the rules of the game. This was exemplified by one entrepreneur who commented that it was commonplace for business owners to under-report their revenues to avoid paying taxes. One respondent stated that in order to reduce their costs they had begun under-declaring employee's wages: 'We pay what we paid before but some of it goes to the employees in cash to avoid tax' (INT7). Another respondent stated that he did not declare his total number of employees as some were paid cash-in-hand to keep them 'off-the-books', so that perceived regulatory burdens such as tax and social security payments could be avoided. Such behaviours were regarded by the entrepreneurs as becoming more commonplace and were considered to be normal rather than deviant, although entrepreneurs (including those partaking in informal entrepreneurship) recognised the detrimental effect on the Greek economy.

These findings support the view that the institutional reforms in Greece intended to aid the recovery are in fact compounding the impact of the crisis, as the rules of the game are becoming increasingly burdensome and expensive. The consequence has been to curtail 'formal' and productive forms of entrepreneurial activity and lead to a rise in unproductive forms of informal entrepreneurship.

Post-crisis Institutional Development in Greece

The cumulative impact of the institutional arrangements in Greece prior to and post-crisis will inevitably have an impact on the long-term entrepreneurial culture and thus the country's entrepreneurial capacity. The consensus among the interviewees was that fostering entrepreneurial activity in Greece had not been a political priority prior to the crisis, and was not regarded as a priority in terms of the economic recovery; and as such this has led to a weak culture of entrepreneurship. As one entrepreneur commented: 'The government has never supported the private sector. It has just got in the way' (INT2). The interviewees stated that this lack of policy priority has meant that entrepreneurship is not seen as a viable or desirable option for many people in Greece. The interviewees repeatedly stated the culture in Greece is not supportive of entrepreneurship and therefore people do not have the ambition to be entrepreneurs. As one respondent stated: 'Many people want to work for the state. That is the culture. They don't see setting up a business as a worthwhile option when they can get a safe job in the public sector' (INT20).

Many of the respondents stated that the culture of entrepreneurship had deteriorated during the crisis. Several interviewees explained that the crisis had made people even more risk-averse as people do not see the potential of starting a business due to a lack of demand caused by the recession. At the same time, despite austerity measures, the interviewees stated that public sector employment levels had remained comparatively consistent, meaning that many people still saw working for the state as a 'safe' option. However, despite the crisis causing a general deterioration in the entrepreneurial culture (European Commission, 2012), some of the respondents stated that the economic crisis should provide an impetus for cultural change in Greece. Creating an institutional environment that is more conducive to starting businesses is no easy task, and requires positive institutional reforms. While entrepreneurial environments have common characteristics, Henrekson and Stenkula (2010) assert that the difference between the institutional environments means that developing an entrepreneurial culture is necessarily country-specific. In the case of Greece, there is a need to promote a more positive societal attitude towards entrepreneurship and entrepreneurial opportunities, else the country will remain devoid of entrepreneurial-led growth, which will further stifle its economic recovery.

While informal institutions are difficult to influence, Estrin and Mickiewicz (2011) contend that positive change is possible although this may take a generation to occur. Within Greece, unless the deterioration of informal institutions is addressed the institutional environment is in danger of regressing and the level of entrepreneurship will decline further. In this respect, the challenge for Greece is to ensure that the formal institutional environment does not hinder entrepreneurship while also promoting the reform of informal institutions to ensure that more people see entrepreneurship as a positive option.

CONCLUSIONS

This chapter has examined how changes to the institutional environment in a crisis-hit economy have impacted on entrepreneurial activity. Although the recent economic crisis was global, its impact in different countries has been varied, as has their recoveries. This can in part be explained by their exposure to the crisis, but also the resistance of institutions and their ability to adapt. Given it is the interaction of formal and informal institutions that determine the level and productivity of entrepreneurship, institutional change as a result of the recent crisis merits research.

Through the case of Greece, which has been severely affected by the crisis, this chapter finds that the interventions of policymakers to improve the national economy has had an overall negative impact on entrepreneurial activity, which has further hindered the ability of Greece to emerge from the crisis. While the economic challenges faced by Greece are large and numerous, in contributing to a better understanding of the institutions and entrepreneurship, this chapter provides lessons for how such economies may positively harness entrepreneurship in emerging from a crisis. Our findings suggest that ineffective institutional arrangements have undermined the country's entrepreneurial environment and meant that entrepreneurial activity has not contributed to economic growth as much as it could. As the country contemplates many years of government austerity and falling living standards, the need to restructure the economy and improve the institutional environment brings with it opportunity for positive reforms. Any institutional reforms need to be mindful about inadvertently undermining and/or disincentivising entrepreneurial activity, as harnessing entrepreneurial-led growth is imperative.

Previous research on crisis-hit economies has provided some indications of how support for entrepreneurs may be extended through government spending (Cowling et al., 2012; Parker et al., 2012; Smallbone et al., 2012a). However, given the fiscal constraints facing Greece and the conditions of the bailout, policy flexibility has been severely limited. The Greek state purse has shrunk as a result of the crisis (Kaplanoglou and Rapanos, 2013) meaning that direct government support for entrepreneurs has been severely curtailed. The institutional changes that have taken place have had an overall negative impact on entrepreneurship, by making entrepreneurial activity harder through worsening and frequently changing rules that have created uncertainty and a consequential worsening of the enterprise culture. At its most simple level, policymakers should adhere to a principle of 'do no harm' in terms of entrepreneurship. That is to say that they should avoid any policy actions that limit entrepreneurial activity and its potential contribution to economic growth. This means avoiding adding further unnecessary bureaucratic burdens on business as well as avoiding punitive tax increases. While this is not easy given the need for the Greek government to repay debt, if entrepreneurship is stymied then emerging from the crisis will take longer as a valuable contributor to growth and future resilience is being held back.

The chapter demonstrates that formal institutions can change in both positive and negative ways in response to a crisis. Previous research has shown that although reforms to formal institutions may be a positive step in fostering entrepreneurship, if they are not congruent with informal institutions then economic development within a country will not be positively affected (Williams and Vorley, 2015b). Our chapter builds on this avenue of research by demonstrating that although some countries may be able to respond positively to crisis to limit its impact (Cowling et al., 2012; Smallbone et al., 2012a), in countries that are severely restricted in terms of the public purse, both formal and informal institutions can deteriorate in a consequential manner, leading to a weakening of overall resilience. Changes that serve to further weaken formal institutions lead to a weakening of informal institutions as the entrepreneurial culture adjusts to the new environment, meaning that the long-term path to competitiveness is damaged.

ADDITIONAL READING

Acs, Z.J., Desai, S. and Hessels, J. (2008), 'Entrepreneurship, economic development and institutions'. *Small Business Economics* **31**(2–3): 219–234.

Drakopolou Dodd, S., Jack, S. and Anderson, A. (2013), 'From admiration to abhorrence: the contentious appeal of entrepreneurship across Europe'. *Entrepreneurship & Regional Development* **25**(1–2): 69–89.

Martin, R., Sunley, P. and Tyler, P. (2015), 'Local growth evolutions: recession, resilience and recovery'. *Cambridge Journal of Regions, Economy and Society* **8**(2): 141–148.

4. Vulnerability and adaptability: post-crisis resilience of SMEs in Denmark

Christian Kjær Monsson

INTRODUCTION

Small and medium-sized enterprises (SMEs) account for a considerable part of the production value and the employment in most regions. In the European Union (EU), SMEs account for around 67 per cent of the total employment in the private sector and generate 58 per cent of the production value (Hope, 2015). Thus it seems obvious that the organisational resilience of SMEs, understood as the ability to resist and recover from shocks, will affect the larger territorial resilience of regions in the case of major external shocks.

SMEs are, however, often argued to be more sensitive to shocks, implying a low level of resilience. This is owing to a variety of reasons that relate primarily to SMEs having fewer resources available and being vulnerable to inter-organisational dependence (Bhamra and Dani, 2011; Guglielmetti, 2012; Lee et al., 2015). Because of this, much academic research in relation to economic resilience focuses on other aspects than established SMEs. Still, it has also been suggested that SMEs can be a source of economic resilience owing to their flexibility and their ability to change after a shock (Smallbone et al., 2012a, 2012b; Cowling et al., 2015; Bartz and Winkler 2016). Thus there remains a somewhat inconclusive picture of resilience in SMEs in the literature.

In this chapter, I examine the different perspectives on resilience in SMEs. This first includes a brief conceptual discussion of what constitutes SME resilience. I argue that one must distinguish between the ability of SMEs to resist and the ability of SMEs to recover from external shocks to their economies. The vulnerability of SMEs determines their ability to resist shocks, while the adaptability of SMEs determines their ability to recover from such shocks. SME managers can make strategic and operational decisions in order to manage their vulnerability and adaptability, but they face several short-term and long-term trade-offs, as SME managers must balance concerns regarding short-term profits with the need for robustness and flexibility as well as innovation and learning.

In the second part of the chapter, I examine a large sample of Danish SMEs in order to study how the resilience of those firms unfolded empirically in the period following the recession of 2009. The analysis demonstrates that while SMEs may be vulnerable, many SMEs are also able to recover from a major shock to their economy. There are, of course, differences among the firms in both their ability to resist and their ability to recover. Finally, I draw some implications for industrial policy based on the findings.

ORGANISATIONAL RESILIENCE: VULNERABILITY AND ADAPTABILITY

Applying the concept of resilience to the organisational level is not a new idea. Even before the financial crisis, Sheffi (2005) argued that 'the resilient enterprise' could achieve a competitive advantage by applying the right design principles and promoting a culture of flexibility, which would make the firm more resilient, while balancing concerns for short-term profits. To Sheffi, resilience was related not only to the ability to avoid shocks such as disruptions and disasters in the first place, but also to the ability to 'bounce back' after these events. Not surprisingly, Sheffi's work received considerable attention after the 2008 financial crisis and the recession of 2009.

While Sheffi focused mainly on larger companies, the organisational resilience of SMEs has also received attention. In some parts of the literature on SME resilience, shocks and disruptions have been argued to be many types of event, including weather events (Ingirige et al., 2010), natural disasters, pandemic diseases and terrorist attacks, but also firm-specific disruptions such as machine failure and human error have been addressed (Bhamra et al., 2011). Other parts of the literature have focused primarily on system-wide external economic shocks that affect a larger number of firms (Pal et al., 2014), which are also the main focus of this chapter.

In spite of the wider discussions on the organisational resilience of firms, there does not seem to be a general definition of the concept. And as Bhamra et al. (2011) argued, it is sometimes unclear what the concept of organisational resilience really refers to. On the one hand, organisational resilience can refer to a capability, and Banahene et al. (2014), for instance, define it as 'a capability which enables organisations to adjust to perturbation, moderate the effects of risk and uncertainty and take advantage of emergent opportunities'. But resilience can also be seen as a feature or a set of characteristics that influences the capabilities of the firm. Resilience at the organisational level can thus also be thought of as a property embedded in the individuals, systems, structures, infrastructure, procedures and parameters of the organisation (Burnard and Bhamra, 2011) that enables the ability to respond to decline or shocks.

Independently of whether resilience refers to a capability or to a set of characteristics, what seems to be clear is that the concept of organisational resilience relates both to the ability of firms to resist and to the ability of firms to recover after an external shock. The main argument of this chapter is, thus, that it also makes sense to differentiate between these two abilities. In order to be resilient, firms can have two kinds of ability: one related to resisting the external shock and another related to enabling recovery. For Bhamra et al. (2011), SME resilience is related to vulnerability and adaptive capacity. For my purposes, vulnerability and adaptive capacity (or short adaptability) can be interpreted as the two specific abilities of being able to resist and to recover from shocks. Vulnerability can thus be interpreted as the ability of firms to resist external shocks, while adaptability on the other hand can be interpreted as the ability of firms to recover from such shocks.

Vulnerability

In the popular use of the word, vulnerability typically refers to something negative for organisations and firms such as being susceptible to exogenous shocks. But vulnerability is also the inverse of 'resistibility'. In this way, vulnerability and 'resistibility' can be seen as different labels for the same concept that describes a continuum where the ability to avoid the negative impacts of shocks varies from firm to firm. Since vulnerability, however, is the most commonly used label, it makes sense to apply it here in order to describe the varying abilities of firms to resist external shocks.

As mentioned in the introduction, SMEs are often argued to be more vulnerable to shocks owing to having fewer resources available and being vulnerable to inter-organisational dependence (Bhamra and Dani, 2011; Guglielmetti, 2012; Lee et al. 2015). But many aspects of SME vulnerability have further been addressed by the literature on risk management, where vulnerability is seen as leading to risk (Cardona, 2004). Based on the literature reviews on risk management in SMEs of Verbano and Venturini (2013) as well as Falkner and Hiebl (2015), it is possible to classify at least six types of risk that are particularly relevant when addressing the vulnerability of SMEs to external shocks. Those risk types are:

1. hazard risks, including property damage and natural disasters;
2. financial risks, including exchange rate and interest rate risks;
3. product price risks;
4. liquidity risk;
5. supply chain risks; and
6. strategic risks, including competition and market changes.

As much of the literature on risk management shows, SMEs can mitigate several of these types of risk through strategic and operational actions.

Insurance can be used to mitigate hazard risks to the firm such as fire, flooding, property damage and personal injury (Sparrow, 1999) as well as natural disasters (Cioccio and Michael, 2007). Financial instruments such as swaps can be used to reduce the exchange rate and interest rate exposure of SMEs (Bodnar et al., 2013), while futures and options can be used to manage product price risks (Pennings and Garcia, 2004). In fact, banks often serve SMEs with a wide range of financial products and services (De la Torre et al., 2010) that can help SMEs to mitigate these risks.

Liquidity risk posed a major problem for SMEs during the financial crisis of 2008 and the subsequent recession, since a harsh reduction in the availability of credit for SMEs followed (Guglielmetti, 2012). Here the dependency of SMEs on bank credit as the main source of external finance proved to be a serious problem for many of them (Guglielmetti, 2012). Hence the availability of liquid financial assets became paramount for SMEs in this period as one of the few elements that could reduce their vulnerability to liquidity risk. While SMEs can address liquidity risk through working capital management (García-Teruel and Martinez-Solano, 2007), the primary mitigating tactic for liquidity risk is simply to have excess cash available. Still, when using this mitigating tactic, SMEs must face a trade-off between having the extra cash at hand and the opportunity cost of these holdings (Orens and Reheul, 2013).

Supply chain risks typically are risks associated with flows of information, materials and products across organisation borders from suppliers to users (Jüttner et al., 2003). The supply chain risks of SMEs have received particular attention because SMEs are often dependent on single suppliers (Falkner and Hiebl, 2015). SMEs can take several actions to reduce their supply chain risks, as described by Jüttner et al. (2003). For instance, they can increase their flexibility by applying multiple sourcing, or they can increase their control through vertical integration of production. They can also simply make strategic decisions to avoid certain risky markets and suppliers. Further, SMEs can mitigate supply chain risks in their daily operations by increasing stockpiling and making use of buffer inventory. Similarly, SMEs can increase their flexibility to deal with unstable supplies, by maintaining excess capacity in production and having contractual postponement options (Jüttner et al., 2003). By applying these mitigating actions, SMEs can thus change their characteristics and competitive dynamics, which Pal et al. (2014) classify as the flexibility, robustness and redundancy that can help to absorb external shocks.

The strategic risks of SMEs are complex, but relate to general market developments, competition and customer demands. It is in this regard clear that some firms are more vulnerable to cyclical changes in the market than others. For instance, after the financial crisis of 2008 and the recession of 2009, European SMEs from the construction and manufacturing sectors were particularly prone to economic decline (Hope, 2015). Dealing with strategic risks obviously requires strategic actions, and while it is not the aim here to address all of the strategic possibilities for SMEs, many actions to mitigate strategic risks also relate to the ability of firms to create new growth paths, which shall be addressed in the next section.

For now, however, the lesson from the literature on risk management and vulnerability is that SMEs can apply a series of mitigating strategies, financial instruments and operational tools in order to reduce their vulnerability to external shocks. However, these mitigating actions carry costs (Sheffi, 2002; Jüttner et al., 2003). The vulnerability of SMEs is thus also a managerial trade-off between the ability to resist external shocks and the costs that follow the mitigating actions. Because of the limited resources in SMEs, these costs not only reduce the short-term profitability of the SMEs, but, as addressed in the next section, they may also limit other abilities of the firms such as the ability to create new growth paths.

Adaptability

Even if SMEs may be vulnerable to shocks, arguments have been made that many SMEs are capable of showing adaptive behaviour that enables recovery from external shocks. I label this as the adaptability of SMEs. In relation to the financial crisis of 2008 and the depression of 2009, scholars have argued that many SME managers appeared to desire renewed growth quickly after the shock (Cowling et al., 2015) and SMEs were able to respond in various contexts by developing new growth paths through innovation and increased sales initiatives (Smallbone et al., 2012a, 2012b) or market and product diversification (Kitching et al., 2011). The ability of established SMEs to grow following a shock has also been interpreted as a flexibility advantage of small size (Bartz and Winkler, 2016).

A key argument from the literature is that adaptability in relation to resilience is not merely the ability to reproduce old responses in order to recover; it is also the ability to find new growth paths (Gilly et al., 2014).

In the regional literature, proponents of an evolutionary perspective have argued that it is possible to distinguish between adaptation and adaptability. Here adaptation deals with changes within a preconceived growth path, while adaptability is about developing new growth paths (Pike et al., 2010; Boschma, 2015). There is, however, typically a trade-off between the two processes, since resources have to be focused on either adaptation or adaptability (Grabher, 1993; Boschma, 2015). This is mirrored in organisational level theories in what is labelled the trade-off between exploration of new possibilities versus exploitation of old certainties (March, 1991).

Adaptation and adaptability can thus also be interpreted as different processes within firms, as firms during a shock period can decide to exploit a preconceived growth path or to explore and develop a new growth path. At least two arguments can be made for why the trade-off between adaptation and adaptability becomes more important for SMEs during and following an external shock. First, during and following a shock there can be an extra limit to financial resources, which are often used to absorb the shock in the first place. In particular, innovative SMEs appear to face more severe problems with access to finance (Lee et al., 2015). At the same time, however, there is an eminent need to respond in order to ensure the profitability and long-term value creation of the firm (Kitching et al., 2011). The lack of financial resources can thus make the trade-off between adaptation and adaptability more apparent. Second, shocks are often closely linked with the unfolding of broader, slow and longer-run processes of change (Pike et al., 2010). External shocks can thus also highlight the trade-off between the two responses, as the ability to create new growth paths becomes more important for many SMEs.

A series of arguments have been made as to how SMEs can create new growth paths. While it is beyond the scope of this chapter to touch upon all of these, a few arguments can be emphasised. The literature on entrepreneurial orientation, for instance, highlights that small firms may need to be proactive, innovative, risk-willing and competitively aggressive as well as to have management autonomy in order to create growth (Lumpkin and Dess, 1996). The innovativeness of SMEs has been particularly addressed in much research, where the resource limits of SMEs are once again argued to be a main obstacle, as SMEs lack the financial resources to finance innovation projects and hire specialised workers (Van de Vrande et al., 2009). It has also been argued that of major importance is the possession of knowledge (Scott and Bruce, 1987; Macpherson and Holt, 2007) as well as the ability of SME managers to learn (Deakins and Freel, 1998). From the market-based perspectives, the ability of SMEs to reposition (Mayr et al., 2017) or develop new markets and find new customer bases (Smallbone et al., 1995) has further been emphasised as a way of developing new growth paths. Likewise, business group affiliations have been argued to positively affect the growth of SMEs during adverse conditions (Bamiatzi et al., 2014).

The adaptability of SMEs can thus be seen as being constituted by a combination of strategic characteristics and resources that enables the firms to create new growth paths that result in recovery. The strategic characteristics of SMEs that influence their adaptability include their entrepreneurial orientation as well as their focus on the exploration of new possibilities and new markets. The resources of SMEs that influence their adaptability include financial possessions, skilled labour and knowledge as well as learning abilities. While the adaptability of SMEs can be of major importance in the case of an external shock, the external shock can at the same time reduce their adaptability, if resources are depleted in order to absorb the shock.

The Relationship Between Resilience, Vulnerability and Adaptability

The vulnerability and adaptability of SMEs are fundamentally different abilities. Both can be managed through strategic and operational actions. But while managing vulnerability is about managing risk, managing adaptability is about creating new growth paths. Still, the vulnerability and adaptability of firms can be very well related. Some resources and characteristics of firms that influence their vulnerability may also influence their adaptability. The financial resourcefulness and flexibility of firms as well as their possession of knowledge and skilled labour can positively affect both their vulnerability and their adaptability. In times of an external shock, the ability to respond successfully to a crisis may further influence the ability of SMEs to create new growth paths (Kitching et al., 2011) if the response, for example, ensures that the financial resources of the firm are not depleted.

On the other hand, creating new growth paths often requires risk-taking, while managing vulnerability is primarily about reducing risk. Thus, there are fundamentally conflicting elements of managing vulnerability and adaptability. Further, since financial resources are limited within most SMEs, we must also expect a trade-off between vulnerability and adaptability, since the management of both vulnerability and adaptability carries cost. In pre-shock periods, managers of SMEs must, for instance, decide whether to invest in robustness or innovation. Finding the right fit between vulnerability and adaptability is thus an important strategic managerial decision.

In sum, the key for attaining resilience within SMEs can be conceptualised as the strategic, operational and organisational management of vulnerability and adaptability. Vulnerability can, among other elements, be reduced through financial risk management, resourcefulness, redundancy and flexibility. Adaptability can be achieved through risk-taking, innovation, learning and the exploration of new possibilities. Both abilities carry cost and may negatively influence short-run profitability. Hence, the ability to prioritise the right ability at the right time is a key determinant of whether SMEs are able to resist or recover from severe external shocks.

A Model of Development Paths Through Shock Periods

Based on the conceptualisation of SME resilience already provided, we can make a simple model that highlights the different development paths of SMEs in the event of an external shock and the roles of vulnerability and adaptability. The model is displayed in Figure 4.1 and differentiates between three periods, that is, (a) the pre-shock period, (b) the shock period and (c) the post-shock period. In the pre-shock period, the development of most SMEs is relatively stable, although firms can potentially follow both declining development paths and growth paths before the shock. The shock period is a shorter or longer period of a system-wide unstable and hostile environment for the majority of firms. In the shock period, the production value of most firms thus declines, although not for all firms. In the post-shock period, the environment for the majority of firms turns stable and firms once again follow various development paths.

We can classify five ideal development paths of SMEs during and after

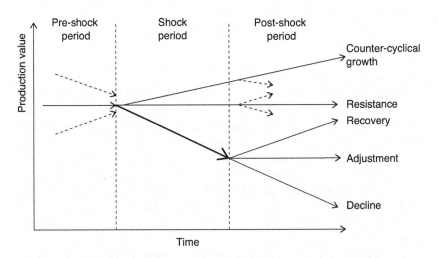

Figure 4.1   Potential SME development paths through a shock period

the external shock. These are (1) decline, (2) adjustment, (3) recovery, (4) resistance and (5) counter-cyclical growth. When the shock period begins, the development path of SMEs is dependent on the vulnerability of the firms; that is, their ability to resist the external shock. Most firms are vulnerable to external shocks and so face a decline in the shock period. Other firms have the ability to (4) resist shocks and continue on a stable development path. A minority of SMEs may even thrive in the unstable and hostile environment (Bamiatzi and Kirchmaier, 2014), and manage to follow a (5) counter-cyclical growth path in the shock period. When the shock period ends, the continued development path of SMEs is dependent on their adaptability. Some firms do not manage to adapt to the period after the shock and continue to (1) decline. Other firms adjust to a new production level, for instance by following a preconceived development path, and thus develop in an (2) adjusted development path after the shock. Lastly, some firms are able to (3) recover entirely from the shock, which likely requires the creation of a new growth path within the firm.

A STUDY OF DANISH SMES

The resilience of established SMEs and the development paths described in the suggested model can be studied empirically. In order to do this, in this chapter I examine the development of a sample of Danish SMEs between 2008 and 2013. The focus is on the period from 2008 onwards since the recession following the financial crisis primarily affected the Danish economy in 2009. I can thus study the development of the SMEs through the recession of 2009 and in the four-year period following it.

The sample consists of private limited companies for which public accounting data are available. Danish private limited companies are required to report a number of accounting items to the Danish Business Authority, which makes the accounting data publicly available. The data has been collected through the NN-erhverv-database. Small and medium-sized companies that had between ten and 250 employees registered at the beginning of the investigated period are included in the sample. Further, only companies for which there are full data through the entire period are included. The sample thus excludes companies that went bankrupt or otherwise ceased to exist during the recession and the years following it. Obviously this makes the sample biased towards more resilient companies, which should be kept in mind when interpreting the results. Also companies that showed very extreme accounting item values were excluded in order to avoid outliers that distort the data unnecessarily. The remaining sample includes 7,033 SMEs from different industries with a median size of 20 employees. While it is thus a sample with some potential biases, it should be large enough to make conclusions that are fairly robust.

Two primary accounting items are of interest for the analysis, namely, gross margin and net profits. Gross margin is the difference between revenue and cost of goods sold. Even if accounting practices differ from firm to firm to some degree, it serves as a solid indication of the production value in the firms. Firms' net profit, on the other hand, is used to calculate the yearly return on equity (ROE), which serves as an indicator of profitability for the SMEs. In order to adjust for industry differences, an additional industry-adjusted indicator for profitability is calculated, which is merely the ROE for the individual firm subtracted by the industry mean calculated at the three-digit level of the NACE industry classification. I removed 180 SMEs with extreme ROE values from this part of the analysis and, although the standard deviation of ROE for the sample remains relatively high, a sensitivity test showed that the results depicted here are relatively robust.

It is not the purpose of this chapter to provide an advanced statistical analysis of the development of the firms in the Danish sample. Rather, I wish merely to point to some simple trends among the firms and their development through time. In order to operationalise the possible SME development paths during and after the shock, I apply a working definition for the development paths of the SMEs in the investigated period, which is displayed in Table 4.1. The focus is on the production value of the firms and their relative changes during the shock period of 2008 to 2010 and the post-shock period of 2010 to 2013. The working definition applied can naturally be discussed, but it allows for a meaningful differentiation of the different development paths conceptualised in the previous section.

Table 4.1   A working definition for development paths

Development paths	Change in production value during shock period (2008 to 2010)	Change in production value in post-shock period (2010 to 2013)	Share of sample
Counter-cyclical growth	Min. 10% growth	All changes	21.8%
Resistance	Max. 5% decline	All changes	15.8%
Recovery	Min. 5% decline	Returns to min. 2008 level	13.4%
Adjustment	Min. 5% decline	Returns to max. 2008 level and max. 5% decline	24.7%
Decline	Min. 5% decline	Min. 5% decline	24.3%

The shares of the sample that followed the different development paths are also displayed in Table 4.1. The first result that can be observed is that, surprisingly, 21.8 per cent of the sample managed to grow more than 10 per cent during the shock period, thus following a counter-cyclical growth path. Further, 15.8 per cent of the SMEs did not experience a drop of more than 5 per cent in their production value in the shock period, and hence proved relatively resistant to the shock. In total, 37.6 per cent of the sample thus appeared not to be very vulnerable in terms of the development of their production value. Still, 62 per cent and hence the majority of the SMEs did face a decrease in production value of more than 5 per cent. Vulnerability to the recession of 2009 thus did appear to be a trait of the majority of the SMEs, in spite of the ability to resist the shock among a large group.

That said, approximately one-fifth of the companies that faced a decline of more than 5 per cent, and 13.4 per cent of the entire sample managed to recover completely in the investigated post-shock period from 2010 to 2013. It is not possible from the available data to analyse whether this is a result of an ability to create new growth paths, or merely a result of following an older preconceived growth path. But it is clear that a substantial group of the vulnerable SMEs did have the ability to recover and hence have somehow adapted in the post-shock period.

Following an initial decline in their production value of more than 5 per cent during the shock period, 24.7 per cent of the sample of SMEs continued to enjoy relatively stable development in the post-shock period with less than 5 per cent decline, although they did not recover completely to the 2008 level. The last 24.3 per cent of the sample faced continued decline of more than 5 per cent in their production value in the post-shock period. For around half of the sample, the shock and the recession of 2009 thus marked the beginning of a more permanent reduction in their production value.

When looking at the profitability of the firms as displayed in Table 4.2, it is clear that the entire sample of SMEs had a very high mean ROE in 2008. While the mean ROE in 2008 was 30 per cent, this decreased considerably after the shock, and in 2010 it was reduced to 13 per cent. Once again this highlights the vulnerability of the SMEs but also indicates a reduction in their financial resources following the shock as profits decrease. Further, the mean ROE for the entire sample recovered to just 16 per cent in the post-shock period as measured in 2013, suggesting a lasting impact of the shock on short-term profits.

Variation among the firms is, however, relatively high. This makes it difficult to draw clear conclusions based on the minor differences in mean ROE that can be observed for the different groups of firms that

Table 4.2   Return on equity for SMEs with different development paths

Return on equity	CCG*	Resistance	Recovery	Adjustment	Decline	Total
Mean 2008	22%	29%	32%	36%	31%	30%
Mean 2010	34%	23%	2%	3%	5%	13%
Mean 2013	23%	18%	29%	16%	0%	16%
Adj. Mean 2008	−9%	−2%	1%	4%	1%	−1%
Adj. Mean 2010	16%	5%	−9%	−9%	−7%	−1%
Adj. Mean 2013	4%	0%	13%	0%	−14%	−1%
Std. Dv. 2008	93%	85%	59%	72%	97%	84%
Std. Dv. 2010	85%	64%	98%	98%	100%	92%
Std. Dv. 2013	89%	69%	78%	78%	103%	86%

Note: The adjusted mean indicates the mean of industry adjusted ROE for the firms in the group, which is calculated as the mean of ROEs of the individual firms subtracted by their respective industry mean calculated at the three digit level of their NACE industry classification.
* Counter-cyclical growth

followed the various categorised development paths. But a few interesting observations can be made. These are also displayed in Table 4.2. The mean ROEs for all groups are relatively similar in 2008 before the shock period. Only firms that followed a counter-cyclical growth development path had a considerably lower ROE in 2008 with a mean ROE of only 22 per cent compared with the 30 per cent average for all firms. These counter-cyclical growth firms, however, reached a considerably higher ROE in 2010 compared with the firms that followed other developments paths. Also, the firms in the resistance group had noticeably higher ROEs in 2010 than the rest of the sample, with a mean ROE of 23 per cent. The firms in the counter-cyclical growth category and those in the resistance category were thus relatively resistant to the shock not only in terms of production value but also in terms of short-run profitability. The same picture remains when looking at the industry-adjusted indicators and this suggests that the specific firms in these groups may have had mitigation strategies in place that reduced their profitability in the pre-shock period, but that at the same time enabled them to resist or even take advantage of the shock in order to remain profitable throughout the shock period.

The firms in the three other categorised groups faced a very low mean ROE in 2010 following the shock, indicating that these firms were vulnerable in terms of both their production value and their short-run profitability. However, in 2013 the firms in the recovery group had the highest mean ROE of the entire sample. The SMEs in the recovery group thus not only were able to recover in terms of production value, but also appeared to have found new growth paths that enabled profitability in the post-shock period. These firms may thus have prioritised adaptability over vulnerability; while being vulnerable in the short run, they were able to create growth and profitability in the long run. The firms in the adjustment group had a mean ROE in 2013 on the same level as the mean for the entire sample thus also showing signs of recovery in terms of profitability. The firms in the categorised decline group, on the other hand, faced continuing decline and a very low mean ROE in 2013, suggesting high vulnerability and low adaptability within this group.

Since I am limited in the empirical part of this chapter by having only accounting data, I cannot identify whether the development paths of the SMEs depicted here and their short-run profit consequences were truly primarily dependent on the management of vulnerability and adaptability within the SMEs as conceptualised in the previous section. The operationalisations of the five types of development path in the working definition remain proxy-indications of vulnerability and adaptability. Still, the empirical quantitative analysis here provides some interesting results that future qualitative research on the trade-off between vulnerability and adaptability could examine further.

CONCLUDING REFLECTIONS

SMEs are important for the economic resilience of regions, and not merely because of their collective size in the economy. While the majority of SMEs are vulnerable to external shocks, many SMEs are also able to resist or to recover from such shocks. Vulnerability and adaptability are essentially different abilities. But both can be managed by SMEs through a series of strategic and operational actions. The primary problem for SME managers is the cost associated with these actions, since most SMEs have limited financial resources and fragile profitability. Thus SME managers are likely to face a series of trade-offs when deciding how to prioritise and deal with the vulnerability and adaptability of their firms.

An important implication from differentiating the vulnerability and adaptability of SMEs is that vulnerability to external shocks and a following decline in production value should not be seen by policymakers as a sign of permanent decline. Rather, it could be a temporary development taking place before a renewed growth period. Thus, the short-term decline of SMEs owing to major shocks should not be taken as a disqualification for policy initiatives. There remains good argument for industrial and innovation policies targeted towards SMEs in order to create resilient regional economies.

ADDITIONAL READING

Bhamra, R. and Dani, S. (2011), 'Creating resilient SMEs'. *International Journal of Production Research* **49**(18): 5373–5374.
Dallago, B. and Guglielmetti, C. (2012), *The Consequences of the International Crisis for European SMEs: Vulnerability and Resilience*, Vol. 27. Abingdon: Routledge.
Sheffi, Y. (2005), *The Resilient Enterprise*. Cambridge, MA: MIT Press.

5. Resilience, adaptation and survival in industry sectors: remaking and remodelling of the automotive sector

Gill Bentley, David Bailey and Daniel Braithwaite

INTRODUCTION

There have been some notable closures of firms in the automotive industry: 2002 saw the closure in the UK of Ford's Dagenham plant as well as Vauxhall's Luton plant, with the loss of 3,000 jobs, and MG Rover closed in 2005 with a reported loss of 6,500 jobs. Other recent automotive closures in the UK include Jaguar at Browns Lane in Coventry (2004), Peugeot near Coventry (2007), LDV in Birmingham (2010) and Ford in Southampton (2013). In Europe, Ford closed its plant in Genk in Belgium in 2014, and GM its Bochum plant in 2016. Meanwhile, in Australia, Toyota announced in 2014 that it would terminate automotive manufacturing operations by the end of 2017, with Ford and General Motors (Holden) having previously announced they would close their operations in 2016. In the US theatre of production, government 'bailouts' saw Chrysler and GM survive. The Chinese automotive industry is growing and Ford has opened a plant for the production of vans in Turkey. These changes affect the regional and national economies of where the plants are located. But, although challenged by overproduction and variable sales, the automotive industry survives. The question is, is it resilient and can it be said that the resilience of the industry is not only founded in a notion of 'bouncing back' after decline but that it is involved in a process in which firms in the industry, as an assemblage, continually reinvents itself? This chapter brings another dimension to the concept of resilience and illustrates how this industry sector can be said to remake and remodel production capability, adapting to changing economic conditions . . . almost reinventing the wheel?

The purpose of this chapter is to examine the resilience of industrial sectors. It situates this in an analysis of the nature of resilience of regions. It begins with a short review of the literature on resilience to set the context for the discussion of research on sectoral resilience. This provides a framework for the study of a case example: the automotive industry. The chapter examines trends in gross domestic product (GDP) and auto sales in the UK to illustrate that the industry has the capacity to respond to outside shocks. It then utilizes secondary sources of information to provide evidence of what action firms take to resist and respond to the challenge of economic shocks. The chapter raises some questions about how sectoral resilience is a contestable concept; the issue being that resilience is seen as the outcome of the actions of individual firms in the sector, rather than sectoral resilience per se. Second, it argues that regional resilience needs to be understood as the interaction of the development of multi-scalar patterns of relational geographies of production in industrial sectors that are of increasing complexity and that require an understanding of this and a policy response to match this complexity: an holistic place-based approach to regional and industrial policy.

RESILIENCE: THE DEBATES

Similar to many terms that are utilized in the analysis of city and regional economic development and policy, resilience is a contested concept. Resilience has been added to a vocabulary that includes terms such as growth, decline, sustainability and survival, concepts that are found wanting, particularly in explaining the impact of major financial crises on regions that those concepts do not entirely capture. Dubé and Polèse (2015, p. 616) consider resilience to be 'an attractive concept, conjuring up positive images of cities and regions able to resist successfully outside shocks and bounce back from the abyss'. In their study of the impact of the 2007–9 recession on 83 Canadian regions, they find it immensely difficult to interpret the findings of their analysis of statistics in the light of a definition of resilience as 'the ability of an entity (being, group, region, etc.) to bounce back from a shock to recover its initial form or pre-shock growth path' (Dubé and Polèse, 2015, p. 616); the interpretation depended on the various possible attributes of resilience being measured. However, the premise of their study can be criticized – that regions bounce back to their pre-shock path – since some regions appear to have the capacity to resist economic shocks and so are not affected, while some regions are affected and do not recover their pre-shock path but change development path.

Thus, the notion of *resistance* to economic shock as well as *recovery* from a shock has entered the debate on how to capture the reality of regional resilience. For Martin (2012), regional resilience is characterized by four factors (Four Rs): resistance (the degree of sensitivity or depth of reaction to a recessionary shock); recovery (the speed and degree of recovery from a recessionary shock); reorientation (the extent of reorientation and adaption in response to recessionary shock) and renewal (the extent to which the regional economy renews its growth path, whether a pre-recession path or hysteretic shift to a new path). Pike et al. (2010) and Simmie and Martin (2010) add to this and emphasize that resilience is related to a region's 'adaptive ability'; a distinction being made between 'adaption' and 'adaptability' of the region. Adaption concerns changes within preconceived paths, while adaptability is about developing new pathways (Boschma, 2015, p. 743). Thus, this would suggest that some regions will experience very little reaction to an economic shock and can be classed as being highly resistant.

Researching Sectoral Resilience

This analysis leads to the question of precisely what factors determine regional resilience and whether the industrial structure of the regions is a factor in determining the resilience of regional economies (Martin et al., 2016). This must include consideration of the role of particular industries in the growth path of regions, which in turn must include the analysis of the adaptive capacity of industries, industrial sectors and the constituent firms (Bailey and De Propris, 2014). Boschma indeed argues that 'structures of industries (e.g. related variety), networks (e.g. a loosely coupled network) and institutions (e.g. a loosely coherent institutional structure) must be seen as the main determinants of regional resilience' (2015, p. 743). Fromhold-Eisebith (2015) contends that true resilience qualities only become apparent when aggregated data analyses that identify adaptive industry sectors (Canova et al., 2012) are combined with qualitative research on the characteristic institutional and location dynamics of sector-related actors. This suggests that sectoral resilience can be analyzed by reference to statistics on sales in relation to general economic trends. A slump and a recovery in sales can be identified.

It can be argued also that sectoral resilience can be regarded as being similar to regional resilience (Fromhold-Eisebith, 2015, p. 1679). However, it is necessary to recognize that, as in the debate about the definition of industrial clusters, the definition of the term 'sector' is problematic (Martin and Sunley, 2003). The notion of automotive *industry sector* serves to illustrate terminological difficulties; it is seen as an industry and a sector. Moreover, the end product is produced by firms in different industries (or sectors): mechanical engineering; plastics; glass and metal manufacturing, among others. Fromhold-Eisebith (2015) provides a working definition and proposes that companies operating in multi-locational production systems, or global value chains, which result in an end product can be characterized by the term 'sector'. She then argues that industry sectors, like regions, will exhibit a reaction to an economic shock, followed by recovery and continuation of the growth path. It can be argued that it is possible to speak of sectoral resilience, since the companies in a sector are bound together in the multi-locational production system, and the development of firms, industries and their relationships can be said to be co-evolving, so firms will similarly reorganize in anticipation of or in reaction to an economic shock to minimize the impact (Nelson, 1994).

Strategies are thus developed by firms to deal with economic shocks, reflecting the adaptive capacity of firms to make changes in production systems in order to sustain and restore a growth path. Firms in a sector will also take action to *avoid* the effects of economic shocks. Martin characterizes resilience as the 'ability of a system to undergo *anticipatory* or reactionary *reorganization* of form and/or function so as to minimize the impact of a destabilizing shock' (2012, p. 5, emphasis added). Fromhold-Eisebith (2015) suggests that a number of sector-specific characteristics of resilience can be identified and that activities in six process fields of adjustment form a conceptual building block to characterize a sector's systemic shock response (see Table 5.1). The focus on the action of firms, however, leads to questions about whether this constitutes sectoral resilience.

This chapter, however, utilizes this framework as a basis to analyze the activities of companies in the automotive industry over various timescales. We begin by looking at trends in GDP and automotive sales in the UK. There is some evidence of a bounce-back after economic shocks.

TRENDS IN GDP AND AUTOMOTIVE SALES: EVIDENCE OF RESILIENCE?

Trends in auto sales are affected by consumption factors and elasticity of demand. Upturns and downturns in GDP in the UK have had significant effect on the automotive industry, through the circular flow of income with negative multiplier effects occurring during periods of recession. During these periods, changes in consumer demand and spending further amplify the crisis or upturn. Policies chosen by governments also have an impact on how UK manufacturers approach the market and, with new products being bought to market, affect consumer demand and firm revenues.

The analysis of the trends and factors affecting market conditions indicates a relationship between UK GDP and automotive industry sales. As

Table 5.1   Conceptual building blocks of sectoral systemic response to economic shocks[1]

Process fields of adjustment	Activities and changes	Sector-specific factors to be taken into account
Market reorientation	Marketing and sales shift away from heavily crisis-affected areas to less affected ones	Consumption pattern and elasticity; size and power asymmetries; location pattern
Value chain optimization	Reorganization of supplier and outsourcing relations for reducing cost and improving the division of labour	Size and power asymmetries; mix of competition and collaboration; location pattern; labour relations and union influence
Strategic corporate reorganization	Mergers and acquisitions, sale of corporate branches to others, strategic alliances with partners and competitors	Size and power asymmetries; mix of competition and collaboration; labour relations and union influence
Focus on innovation and upgrading	Increased R&D/learning efforts and collaboration to support (crossover) product/process innovation, knowledge and skills upgrading; new production technology	Size and power asymmetries; mix of competition and collaboration; location pattern; modes of innovation
Relocation of production	Closing down of 'marginal' production sites and concentration of mandates; opening of new, more efficient plants	Size and power asymmetries; labour relations and union influence; location pattern
Ecosystem dynamics of firm demographics	Various firm exits, changes of operational focus and new enterprises; converging routines and cultures of crisis response	Size and power asymmetries; mix of competition and collaboration; location pattern

Source: Fromhold-Eisebith (2015, pp. 1683–1684).

Figure 5.1 shows, the two variables follow a similar pattern. However, there are some significant differences, noticeably in automotive sales, alongside the erratic trend in GDP. We examine the changes in UK GDP and automotive sales over three specific time periods of economic significance to reveal how GDP and auto sales are intertwined: the 'recession of the early 1990s'; the 'credit boom' and the 'great recession', in the wake of the 2007–8 global financial crisis (GFC).

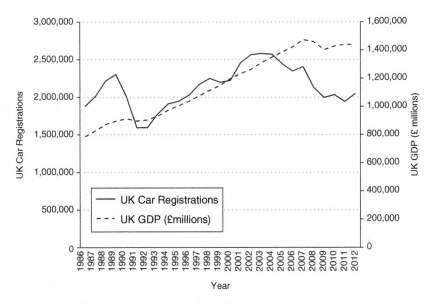

Source: Office for National Statistics (2016) and SMMT (2016).

Figure 5.1   UK GDP and automotive sales 1986–2012

Recession in the Early 1990s

Many factors shaped the recession in the UK in the early 1990s and resulted in a reduction in aggregate demand that had a detrimental effect on the automotive industry. With high interest rates, little affordable credit was available to consumers, who also had little disposable income, due to a rise in mortgage payments. Overall spending in the economy rapidly decreased as well as consumer and business confidence, all affecting the motor industry.

Similar to a recession in the early 1980s, GDP growth was positive every year until 1991 when it saw a 1.3 per cent decrease compared to the previous year. This saw a negative change in the automotive market in the year before as well. Car sales dropped by 12.7 per cent in 1990 from 1989 to decrease once again in 1991 by 20.7 per cent, demonstrating that the automotive market was heavily affected by the downturn in the UK economy. Indeed, in 1989, UK car sales were 2.3 million; during the recession they dropped to under 1.6 million, a decrease of more than 30 per cent. The automotive industry was affected before, during and after the recession.

The 1993 recession, however, was a recession that some manufacturers were not able to recover from. A case in point was MG Rover, which had debts of £1.4 billion and axed nearly 10,000 jobs in the West Midlands in auto manufacturing and its supply chain firms (Tovey, 2015). The loss of jobs in this established motor manufacturer led to a reduction in the circular flow of income, especially in the West Midlands region of the UK, further contributing to the deteriorating economic environment and suggests that there are limits to the resilience of the sector to recover and to bounce back after a recession. The sector subsequently demonstrated a recovery.

The Credit Boom

Indeed, economic growth, in the credit boom period post-1993 recession, shows the extent of recovery in the industry. The UK experienced a rapid expansion in the economy starting from 1993. Low unemployment and pay increases meant an increase in disposable incomes resulting in injections in the circular flow of income in the UK. The high amount of available credit meant consumers could easily access finance to purchase new cars.

From 1992 to 2007, GDP grew every year at an average rate of 2.8 per cent per year. In 1992, the UK generated £1 billion in GDP, with the UK economy rapidly expanding; 15 years later this figure reached £1.66 billion. Similarly, the automotive industry went through a period of growth and expansion, albeit not every year but matching the trends in the economy. Between 1992 and 2005, automotive industry sales grew by 50.9 per cent, at an average rate of 2.7 per cent a year. Both car registrations and GDP in the UK followed a general upward trend.

Sales in the automotive industry, however, did not exactly follow the pattern of UK GDP growth; the recovery phase of resilience in the auto industry is not entirely evident. Car sales in 1999, 2004, 2005 and 2006 fell compared to the previous years, despite growth in the economy. In 2005, in particular, the automotive industry took a 5 per cent drop in sales compared to 2004, whereas there was a 3 per cent increase in GDP. Car sales fell when GDP rose. This can be argued to have been partially due to increasing running costs such as fuel, the price of which was at its highest level ever.

The Great Recession and Recovery

In 2007 the world entered a period of severe economic difficulty, with the UK being affected by the global financial crisis, in experiencing long periods of negative economic growth. The resultant 'credit crunch' and recession lasted for almost five years; it was a prolonged period of low or negative growth and a near double-dip recession. This affected many sectors across the UK, especially the manufacturing industries. In the first year of the 2008 recession, automotive sales fell by 11.3 per cent compared to 2007 and they continued to fall the year after by a further 6.4 per cent, dropping below 2 million in sales for the first time since 1995. GDP followed this trend with a 1 per cent decrease in 2008 followed by a further 4 per cent drop in 2009, falling to an output of £1.44 million for the year, which was the lowest figure in four years.

During this crisis period, there is an apparent relationship between the fall in UK GDP and automotive industry sales. However, the changes in GDP and car sales do not follow exactly the same pattern; auto sales fell at a greater rate than GDP. While there was a small percentage change in GDP, for example, a 0.5 per cent decrease in 2008, there was an 11.3 per cent drop in car sales. Nevertheless, both GDP and car sales recovered in the post-apocalyptic period. Government bailouts and emergency loans were given to car manufacturers and suppliers to stay in business (Holweg et al., 2009). Auto industry firms themselves were taking action to weather the crisis.

SECTORAL SYSTEMIC RESPONSE TO ECONOMIC SHOCKS

Here we utilize the framework of the process fields of adjustment (see Table 5.1) to outline the actions taken by firms in the automotive industry that could indicate the resilience of the automotive sector. As suggested at the outset of the chapter, and as the auto sales figures showed, the automotive industry sector survives. Firms along the value chain respond to economic shocks; firms also carry out activities to resist economic crisis and to remain competitive in the global market; it is an industry that remakes and remodels itself. We look at evidence in relation to each field of adjustment in turn.

Market Reorientation

Business success suggests that a firm will monitor trends in sales and in the different markets it operates in to ensure continuing profitability. Automotive industry firms operate in segmented markets; the automotive industry can be characterized by a set of global region systems of production and consumption. A number of factors, such as consumer tastes, and regulations governing the use of cars, mean that cars are produced for the different market areas. The industry is sensitive to economic conditions in its various markets. The volatility in the global economy and in the different global regional theatres of production and consumption in recent times since the GFC has seen sales fluctuate.

A key strategy for dealing with a downturn in sales in one market area is to reorient sales to other markets, and by developing new markets. This is facilitated by the fact that the auto sector is dominated by a few large multinational companies that run factories in various countries. This makes it fairly easily for the original equipment manufacturers (OEMs) to redistribute sales and marketing efforts across the globe. The United States has long been a market opportunity for British-built autos, such as Jaguar cars. Despite fluctuations in GDP in the US economy, exports to the United States rose from 550,879 units in 2009 to 994,487 units in 2014, a rise of 80 per cent (ACEA, 2015). There is also evidence that European based auto firms have been breaking into the Chinese market[2] for some time (Bentley et al., 2013); exports of autos from the EU to China rose by 251 per cent between 2009 and 2014 (ACEA, 2015). The market reorientation strategy can enable firms to bounce back after a recession such as the 2007–8 GFC but also, as noted above, in anticipation of a downturn in sales and profitability, as a means of resistance to crisis, so displaying resilience.

Value Chain Optimization

A further resilience strategy is the optimization of the value chain. A crisis response requires all supplier and outsourcing relations to be scrutinized and reorganized to achieve greater proficiency (Cainelli et al., 2012). Such action would involve the search for cheaper supplies of parts and services; the integration of low-cost locations and producers into rationalized value chains by the exploitation of competence advantages, such as through the use of high skilled labour, in less-developed countries. The automotive industry value chain is complex; a multilayered, multi-locational production system. Successful functioning of the system would suggest that ideally firms in the first tier of the supply chain would be located in optimal position in relation to a number of the OEMS.

Lagendijk (1997) found that automotive component producers such as Bosch were dispersing production throughout Europe, to serve several OEM national markets. Such firms will supply a number of OEMs, with the companies in their supply chain in turn clustered, in principle, in optimal locations in relation to upstream companies, this changing the spatial organization of the industry. Bosch operates in more than 50 countries and employs over 290,183 people, in supplying a complex distribution network of new products and parts, with economic success. Following the GFC, from 2011 onwards, the company saw profits after tax rise year on year

(Bosch Worldwide, 2016).[3] This suggests that the company strategy was instrumental in contributing to sectoral resilience in the industry. Arguably, however, it is not clear whether this was a grand plan at strategic level for the whole sector or the action of one economic actor.

Strategic Corporate Reorganization

Fromhold-Eisebith (2015, p. 1686) points out that strategic corporate reorganizations take place in the face of crisis, involving mergers and acquisitions, where companies sell divisions to other players within or outside the industry (Filippov and Kalotay, 2011). Strategic alliances occur and might even be with competitors. Such actions reduce risks and are not only a reactive response to crisis but one of resistance; companies are able to resist a possible downturn in business. As Fromhold-Eisebith argues, the purpose of a strategic corporate organization is 'to sculpture less vulnerable, more robust or more flexible corporate structures' to face an uncertain future (2015, p. 1686). Corporate reorganizations, in short, enable companies to maintain profitability and survive in the global market. While these activities help firms survive, they also witness closures.

The automotive industry is crowded with successful examples of mergers, takeovers and strategic alliances, demonstrating resilience. The history of MG Rover and its antecedents in the UK reveal a pattern of takeovers, mergers and acquisitions but ultimately with a different outcome: closure (Bailey et al., 2008). The founding company, Morris Motors Limited, merged with Austin Motors to form the British Motor Corporation Limited in 1952, which then became a component of the British Leyland Motor Corporation in 1968. The MG Rover Group emerged later and, subsequently owned by BMW, it was sold onto the Phoenix Consortium in 2000 (Bentley, 2000; Bailey and de Ruyter, 2012). On going into administration in 2005, the assets of MG Rover were purchased by Nanjing Automobile Group, which itself merged into the Shanghai Automotive Industry Corporation (SAIC) in 2008 (Bailey and Kobayashi, 2008).

This example of MG Rover helps illustrate the relationship between sectoral and regional resilience; the loss of jobs in MG Rover had an impact on the economy of the West Midlands region, and raised concerns about the capacity of the region to recover from the economic shock to the regional system of production (Cook et al., 2013). The closure saw the restructuring of the automotive industry supply chain in the region. Some companies closed; others took advantage of schemes of assistance[4] to shift business to companies in industries other than the auto industry (Bentley, 2007).

Other notable examples of mergers and acquisitions are the purchase of Seat (1986), Škoda (1990) and the UK firm Bentley Motors, by

Volkswagen (1998) as well as the purchase of Rolls-Royce by BMW (1998). Volkswagen and Porsche are arguably an interesting case of competitors building in resilience to withstand and respond to economic shocks via strategic alliances and mergers. Volkswagen has had a tradition of working collaboratively with Porsche but it finally merged with Porsche in 2009, Porsche having bought shares in Volkswagen in 2005 and with Porsche buying shares in Volkswagen in 2008. The company is now Europe's largest automaker, with a market share of more than 20 per cent, and the third largest producer in the world, with a global market share of 11.4 per cent. Its consolidation, through takeover of Audi, Seat, Lamborghini, Bentley, Bugatti, Scania and Škoda, has seen sales steadily rise from 6.3 million vehicles in 2009 to 9.7 million in 2015, and has thus demonstrated a capacity for resilience. Other examples of strategic alliances are between Renault and Nissan (1999) and between Chinese and European automakers (Bentley et al., 2013). These changes raise issues regarding the extent to which the accompanying restructuring of the supply chain is managed through deliberative collaborative action or whether it is an outcome of independent processes and thus whether it represents sectoral resilience.

Focus on Innovation and Upgrading

Innovation and upgrading is an essential activity for companies to undertake to remain competitive on the global market; in principle, firms need to be engaged in a process of continuous innovation (a science-and-technology-based innovation (STI) mode) and upgrading (a doing, using and interacting (DUI) approach). Jensen et al. (2007) find that the combination of the STI mode, using codified scientific and technical knowledge, with DUI approaches, which relies on informal processes of learning and experience-based know-how, is most likely to result in the innovation of new products or services. However, firms need to innovate across all components of the production process: products but also, markets; production process technology; supply chain organization; the labour process and management techniques, company structure, in a collaborative relationship with other companies (Cooke and Morgan, 1991). This implies a resistance strategy rather than a reactive approach to economic shock; it also suggests that if companies collaborate, a sectoral scale of resilience exists. Indeed, Fromhold-Eisebith (2015) argues that industry-specific sectoral innovation systems[5] (see Malerba, 2002; Malerba and Nelson, 2011), where a combination of innovation and connectedness exists, are essential for achieving sectoral resilience (Parrilli et al., 2012).

Resilience avoidance and reactive behaviours would include 'joint R&D (as far as competition permits) and academia-industry collaboration, which enhance the externalization of R&D and cross-over innovation' (Fromhold-Eisebith, 2015, p. 1687). R&D activity in the automotive sector nonetheless is marked by being carried out in the OEMs and tier 1 supply firms, 'driven by strong competition and exclusive strategies' (Fromhold-Eisebith, 2015, p. 1688). This suggests that collaboration is limited and calls into question a concept of sectoral resilience.

The means by which the automotive industry survives is by designing and producing new models, and shaping consumer demand by competitive advertising campaigns to tempt buyers. The annual motor shows across the globe are a showcase for the OEMs' latest singularly developed offerings in the drive to enhance market share. Survival strategies also include the development of new environmentally friendly models, electric and hybrid cars, but also new driver mobility options. BMW, Tesla and Google among others are in the process of developing and marketing autonomous vehicles. These do, however, necessitate collaborative strategies to develop the technology as well as the use of technology developed for other purposes. Audi, Daimler and BMW are reported 'to have put their rivalries aside by teaming up to acquire a €2.8bn (£2bn) mapping business from Nokia, in a bid to outsmart tech groups in the race to cash in on the driverless car revolution' (Hellier, 2015). Google has moved into car production in setting up Google Auto LLC and has tested the fleet of driverless Lexus SUVs that superseded the company's first self-driving Prius saloons (Hellier, 2015). BMW's offering has stemmed from academia-industry links via Munich University[6] when pioneering work with Daimler-Benz was carried out, paving the way for such developments (Adams, 2015). The picture on the role of innovation and upgrading is contradictory; whether it relates to company or sectoral resilience.

Relocation of Production

Faced with the situation of an extreme economic shock, when falling sales and a fall in profitability indicate a failure to sustain business operations, one option for firms is to adopt a process adjustment that entails the relocation of production facilities. This can include the closure of marginally profitable production sites with production being concentrated on those that are profitable or by offshoring activities (Moavenzadeh, 2006; Fromhold-Eisebith, 2015). In the attempt to reduce the costs of production and in an effort to bounce back after a crisis situation, and display resilience, relocation is generally to low labour cost locations. Competitive advantage may be gained by opening new plants in localities that offer not only cheaper labour but also a workforce that is skilled, motivated and entrepreneurial. It may also offer the opportunity for a company to be closer to its market.

In the European theatre of production and consumption, the Czech Republic, Poland, Slovakia, Slovenia and Hungary, have presented as low-cost locations. Western European auto companies have closed plants in Western Europe to open up production plants in Central and Eastern European countries for this reason but also to be in or close to new and expanding markets following the accession of these countries to the European Union. As noted, Peugeot (PSA), for example, closed its production plant in Ryton, near Coventry, in the West Midlands in the UK in 2006 and opened a plant in Slovakia to build the Peugeot 206 and the Peugeot 207 for the Eastern European market (Bentley, 2007). Falling demand, high production and logistical costs and intense competition, with underinvestment an issue, PSA's income had fallen from €2.5 billion in 2004 to €1.94 billion a year later; its net profits fell from €1.56 billion to €1 billion. PSA Peugeot Citroen chief executive Jean-Martin Folz was reported as saying that he would not shy away from closing factories that proved too expensive (BBC News Online, 2006). Some 2,300 West Midlands workers lost their jobs, threatening the resilience of the region.

This pattern of closure and opening of OEMs affects companies in the supply chain. Closures alter the spatial organization of the industry and, as Schamp (2005) puts it, it changes weights between locations. It may result in some lower-tier suppliers moving to more optimal locations, also as a cost-reduction strategy. This spatial restructuring is a necessary concomitant to recovery from economic shock and enable the bounce-back and to secure sectoral resilience. However, it may be an outcome rather than a purposive action of companies in the sector to secure sectoral resilience.

Ecosystem Dynamics of Firm Demographies

For Fromhold-Eisebith (2015, p. 1689), industry sectors display 'complex, self-organized and non-linear development trajectories, which are driven by multiple adaptions' (Martin and Sunley, 2007, 2015). She characterizes this as 'an ecological model of "adaptive cycles" in which an "industry-specific ecosystem" of firms in multilayered, multi-location production systems sees resilience behaviours to forestall or react to economic shocks' (Fromhold-Eisebith, 2015, p. 1689). These include firm exits, changes of operational focus and new enterprises; converging routines, as noted in Table 5.1. She argues that this is underpinned by a 'resilience culture' wherein firms know each other and compete and collaborate to survive.

It can be argued that the dynamics of firm demographies in the automotive industry sector stretch to the meeting of automakers and supply chain firms at trade fairs and motor shows, where the key players in the industry sector can glean ideas on possible developments in products and processes.

Protagonists in the industry belong to trade associations that provide the space and place to discuss rules for the terms of trade to be discussed further in political arenas such as European Union institutions and/or the World Trade Organization. This places emphasis on the idea that it is the outcomes of the actions of individual companies rather than it being a function of concerted action that defines sectoral resilience.

CONCLUSION

Martin characterizes resilience as the 'ability of a system to undergo *anticipatory* or reactionary *reorganization* of form and/or function so as to minimize the impact of a destabilizing shock' (2012, p. 5, emphasis added). The analysis of trends in GDP and auto sales, measured by new car registrations, demonstrates the auto industry *sector* in the UK is resilient insofar as sales bounced back after the global financial crisis of 2007–8.[7] There is evidence that the industry sector has the capacity to continually remake and remodel itself, by adaptations and by being adaptable in the process adjustment fields identified in this chapter (Fromhold-Eisebith, 2015). However, while it can be said that companies in a sector are bound together in the supply chain in multi-locational local and global production systems, and firms reorganize in anticipation or in reaction to an economic shock to minimize its impact, evidence bought forward in the chapter concerns the action of individual firms. This is not the same as the sector; the extent to which firms operate *collectively as a sector* can be questioned.

However, the important aspect of the analysis of sectoral resilience is that the development trajectory of an industry sector has a spatial impact; that is, on regions and in localities and this must be accounted for (Bailey and De Propris, 2014; Boschma, 2015). As Fromhold-Eisebith says: 'the interplay of sectoral and regional resilience can further be investigated by analyzing how interregional differences in resilience may be attributed to the sector composition of regions (advancing research by Davies, 2011). These insights pave the way for more adequate policies supporting the resilient capacities of regions through those of industrial sectors, and vice versa' (2015, p. 1690).

Further research is needed. The trajectory of the complexity of actions taken by companies need to be seen as a collective so that the consequence of such changes for the interdependencies between firms can be mapped. It can be argued that intra-sectoral collaboration between firms is necessary to devise a coherent strategy that anticipates and responds to economic shocks. A policy response is required that reflects this complexity and brings together companies to understand the outcomes of their actions for the collective and the implications for regional economies, to ensure that appropriate actions are taken to secure sectoral resilience in the context of the resilience of regions: this can be seen as requiring a more holistic place-based[8] approach to regional and industrial policy.

NOTES

1. For simplicity Table 5.1 only lists 'Activities and changes'. Fromhold-Eisebith includes analysis of sector-related actors involved, geographical implications and major factors of distinction between resilient sectors.
2. Often through making strategic alliances (Bentley et al., 2013).
3. With the exception in 2013, after new accounting procedures were adopted. Profits continued to rise. Bosch of course is a company that has many different business divisions so it is difficult to disentangle the effects of all the company's activities on profitability.
4. Several schemes were devised to assist firms diversify into selling to companies in other sectors, in anticipation of the possible closure of the OEMs located in the West Midlands region. Among these were the Accelerate Scheme and Rover Task Force Supply Chain Support Scheme.
5. The concept of a sectoral system of innovation and production provides a multidimensional, integrated and dynamic view of sectors. It is proposed that a sectoral system is a set of products and the set of agents carrying out market and non-market interactions for the creation, production and sale of those products. A sectoral system has a specific knowledge base, technologies, inputs and demand. Agents are individuals and organizations at various levels of aggregation. They interact through processes of communication, exchange, cooperation, competition and command, and these interactions are shaped by institutions. A sectoral system undergoes change and transformation through the co-evolution of its various elements (Malerba, 2002, p. 247).
6. Some 30 years ago a German engineer, Ernst Dickmanns, working out of Munich University in association with Daimler-Benz, piloted a project called the 'Programme for a European Traffic of Highest Efficiency and Unprecedented Safety' ('Prometheus').
7. The chapter focuses on demand for vehicles but it should be noted that UK automotive production, which after a major reduction during the global financial crisis, also grew, by more than 60 per cent between 2010 and 2015.
8. See Barca, 2009.

ADDITIONAL READING

Bentley, G., Bailey, D. and MacNeill, S. (2013), 'Restructuring in the European auto industry'. In P. McCann, F. Giarratani and G. Hewings (eds), *Handbook of Economic Geography and Industry Studies*. Cheltenham, UK and Northampton, MA, USA: Edward Elgar Publishing, 67–96.

Fromhold-Eisebith, M. (2015), 'Sectoral resilience: conceptualizing industry-specific spatial patterns of interactive crisis adjustment'. *European Planning Studies* **23**(9): 1675–1694.

Malerba, F. and Nelson, R. (2011), 'Learning and catching up in different sectoral systems: evidence from six industries'. *Industrial and Corporate Change* **20**(6): 1645–1675.

6. The evolution of economic resilience in cities: reinvention versus replication

James Simmie

INTRODUCTION

The recent recession and depression of 2008–9, when gross domestic product (GDP) in the UK fell by 2.7 per cent and 2.8 per cent respectively, was the worst decline in economic growth since the "Great Depression" of 1929–33. The severity of this shock has stimulated current academic interest in the concept of resilience. Much of this has focused on the short-term impacts of individual recessions on regional economies and their different abilities to resist or recover from this type of external individual shock (e.g., special editions of *Cambridge Journal of Regions, Economy and Society* on "The resilient region" 2010 and "Local growth evolutions: recession, resilience and recovery" 2015).

In contrast to concepts of resilience that focus on the short-term ability of a regional economy to bounce back to its previous growth path after a recessionary shock or to absorb the effects of such a shock and to maintain the status quo ante, arguments derived from the theory of complex adaptive systems suggest that economic resilience is based on the capacity to adapt and change over the long-term (Masten et al. 1990; Kaplan 1999; Luthar and Becker 2000; O'Dougherty-Wright et al. 2013; Perrings 2006; Simmie and Martin 2010; Davoudi and Porter 2012). Moreover, there is considerable evidence to suggest that the capacities of urban and regional economies to maintain above-average growth rates and demonstrate overall economic resilience differs significantly (Martin et al. 2013; Gardiner et al. 2013) and that such differences contribute cumulatively to uneven regional development (Bristow 2010; Hassink 2010a) and the long-run divergence of the growth paths of more and less resilient economies (Martin and Sunley 1998; Michener and McLean 1999; Arbia and Paelink 2003; Rey and Janikas 2005; Neven and Gouyinte 2008; Simmie and Carpenter 2008).

In order to explain some of the causes of these observed differences it is argued in this chapter that one of the key causes underlying long-run urban and regional economic resilience is their capacity to adapt to and accommodate repeated technological shocks. These may be negative and destructive in the sense of old technologies and their respective industries becoming obsolete. They may also be positive and creative as new technologies and industries are created for the first time. Accordingly, from this perspective a key element in regional economic resilience is defined as "the capacity of a regional economy to maintain an above average long-term economic growth rate by adapting to the shocks arising from the endogenous or exogenous invention, innovation or diffusion of technological innovations".

Following this definition of economic resilience, the main question addressed in this chapter is, therefore, can we illustrate some of the differences in the long-run growth pathways followed by different British city-regions in terms of their relative capacities to initiate or absorb technological shocks arising from the invention, innovation or diffusion of a radical new technology? The radical general purpose technologies selected for analysis in this chapter are digital information and communications technologies. Data on the current geographic distribution of the new digital economy in the UK is drawn from a dataset put together by Nathan, Rosso, Gatten, Majmudar and Mitchell (2013) as the basis for a study, "Measuring the UK's Digital Economy with Big Data". Data on long-run economic change in English and Welsh cities is extracted from a dataset used to analyse "A Century of Cities: Urban Economic Change since 1911" constructed by Swinney and Thomas (2015).

Following this introduction, the chapter is divided into four subsequent parts. The first provides a brief critical review and development of evolutionary growth theory, its take on technological innovation and the possible explanations of regional and urban economic resilience that it may provide. Second, a method's section expands on the details and nature of the secondary data used in the empirical section. Third, the conclusions of the theoretical discussion are then used to inform an empirical analysis of some relationships between the growth pathways of British city-regions since the 1970s and the technological shock imparted by the invention, innovation and diffusion of digital ICT technologies. A final part draws together some conclusions from these analyses.

EVOLUTIONARY GROWTH THEORY

The continued success of capitalist economies depends on constant change and transformation. In contrast to Marx's prediction of its inevitable collapse, so far at least, capitalism has been marked by the replacement of old and declining technologies, products and firms by waves of new ones. These continual processes of change are famously described by Schumpeter as "gales of creative destruction" instigated by technological and consequential structural change that drive the evolution of the economy "incessantly destroying the old one, incessantly creating a new one" (Schumpeter 1942, p. 83).

According to Schumpeter (1939), the evolution of capitalist economies is a long-run process marked by repeated cycles of prosperity, recession, depression and recovery. These cycles individually and repetitively drive aggregate long-run economic change. Furthermore, Schumpeter (1939) identified innovation as the critical underlying driver of economic change in general and technological innovation as particularly significant in the creation of new products and processes by firms. But, in the context of these changes in the capitalist economy in general, Schumpeter is silent about the impacts of destruction and creation in local economic landscapes. He provides no *a priori* reason why the destruction of old technologies and industries in one locality is necessarily followed by the creation of new ones in those same localities.

In the evolutionary economics literature inspired by Schumpeter there is a long history of studying the shocks imparted by *major changes in technological regimes* that set off "gales of creative destruction" across the economic landscape in general and in different urban and regional locations in particular (e.g. Simmie 2014a). Such shocks can involve major shifts to alternative technological paradigms or general purpose technologies (GPTs). Examples include power looms and the puddling process for the production of iron (1787–1845), the Bessemer steel converter and steam powered ships (1846–95), alternating current, electric light and the automobile (1896–1947), and, more recently, the transistor, computer, communication and information technologies (Hall and Preston 1988, p. 21). Old technologies and the industries based on them can become obsolescent in a relatively short space of time. Shocks of this magnitude can impact on the whole underlying knowledge base of all related industries in an urban or regional economy (Boschma 2015, p. 8).

The reorientation of the underlying knowledge bases of urban and regional economies is a very challenging task. This is not least because the historical trajectories of those knowledge bases are path-dependent. That is to say, the history of their past development "sets the scope for reorienting skills, resources, technologies and institutions" (Boschma 2015, p. 5). Thus, it has to be recognised that the capacities of local economies that have been based on such activities as heavy industries or port activities in the past, to reorient the bases of their economies and create new pathways based on new technologies and forms of knowledge, are constrained by their previous historical pathway developments.

In the context of the shock and destruction wrought by the recent recession/depression the concept of resilience has risen up the academic agenda as a result of its potential for explaining the ability of urban and regional economies to resist or recover from such external shocks. In the Schumpeterian tradition this would be expected to involve a positive combination of the destruction of old technologies and industries, the creation of new ones as a result of innovation and the reorientation of historical path-dependent knowledge bases.

In the contemporary literature that develops the concept of regional and urban economic resilience the focus, so far, has been not so much on the long-term, cyclical evolution of capitalist economies but more on their immediate reactions to recessionary shocks. This is partly a result of their ontological backgrounds. Gardiner et al. (2013), for example, identified four different ontological sources of ideas for conceptualising regional resilience. These include ecology and socioecology, evolutionary developmental biology, economics and psychology.

With respect to economic approaches to understanding regional economic resilience, three different models may be identified. These are the "plucking model", "hysteresis" and "adaptive evolution". Each defines regional economic resilience in a different way. These are summarised briefly below.

According to the "plucking model", the development pathway of an economy can be likened to a tightened string attached to the underside of an upward-sloping board, which is plucked downwards by recessionary shocks (Friedman 1993; Kim and Nelson 1999, Martin 2012).

> The board represents a slowly-rising upper limit or ceiling on output set by an economy's resources, the way they are organised, and their productivity. Though the extent of decline caused by a recessionary shock will vary from downturn to downturn, output is assumed to rebound in each case to the (upward-sloping) ceiling level. In other words, the plucking model predicts that recessionary shocks should be transitory, and should have no permanent effect on the economy's long-run growth ceiling or growth trend.
>
> (Martin 2012, p. 5)

In this case, resilience is defined as the "bounce-back" of an economy to its pre-shock growth path.

The concept of "hysteresis" derives from studies of the magnetic and elastic properties of metals and materials. It was introduced into economics by Georgescu-Rogen (1966), Elster (1976), Cross and Allen (1988), Cross (1993), Göcke (2002) and Setterfield (2010). In mainstream economics the idea is used to describe situations in which an economy is shifted from one equilibrium position or stability domain to another as a result of a major external shock. The concept of equilibrium, however, is not essential to the idea. Romer, for example, defines hysteresis as a situation "where one-time disturbances permanently affect the path of the economy" (2001, p. 471). This involves structural change in the economy (Setterfield 2010). In this instance, resilience is defined as the reaction of an economy to a specific external shock and the nature of the new trajectory of path dependent development that it moves to after the immediate impact of the shock.

The concept of "adaptive resilience" is derived from the theory of complex adaptive systems. It is argued that what distinguishes complex adaptive systems is the way they exhibit self-organising behaviour, driven by co-evolutionary interactions among their constituent components and elements, and an adaptive capacity that enables them to rearrange their internal structure spontaneously, whether in response to some external shock, or in reaction to some from internal emergent mechanisms or "self-organised criticality" (Martin and Sunley 2007). From this perspective, regional economic resilience may be defined as "the capacity of a regional economy to reconfigure, that is adapt, its structure (firms, industries, technologies and institutions) so as to maintain an acceptable growth path in output, employment and wealth over time" (Martin 2012, p. 10). This is the definition of regional economic resilience adopted in this chapter.

Urban and regional economies are clearly complex systems and so this is the approach this chapter will use. From this perspective, the relative adaptive capacities of local economies are critical in how they respond to external shocks. The adaptive capacities of local economies evolve over time and are dependent on such phenomena as the rate of entrepreneurship and new firm formation, on the innovativeness of existing firms, on access to venture capital, on the diversity of a region's economic structure, and on the availability of appropriately skilled labour (Martin 2012). In this sense, urban and regional economic resilience is a dynamic evolutionary and path-dependent process.

In developing the concept of adaptive capacity in explaining economic resilience, evolutionary economic geographers have tended to fall back on the distinction between adaptation and adaptability (Grabher 1993; Grabher and Stark 1997). For the use of these concepts see, for example, Christopherson et al. (2010), Pike et al. (2010) and Bristow et al. (2012). In this work:

> *adaptation* is defined as a movement towards a pre-conceived path in the short run, characterised by strong and tight couplings between agents in place. (In contrast) *adaptability* is defined as a dynamic capacity to effect and unfold multiple evolutionary trajectories, through loose and weak couplings between

social agents in place, that enhance the overall responsiveness of the system to unforeseen changes.

(Pike et al. 2010, p. 62, emphasis in original)

It is argued in the resilience literature that there is a trade-off between the two (Hassink 2010a; Pike et al. 2010). This is said to be because regional economies that favour adaptation of their existing industries can be blind to possibilities for creating new industries based on innovations developed elsewhere (Malmberg and Maskell 1997; Boschma and Lambooy 1999). Adaptation on its own can lead to path-dependent economic trajectories and ultimately to the lock-in of historically outmoded technologies, industries, institutions and organisations. In these circumstances, a locality's potential economic growth path may become weakened, leading to long-run relative economic decline.

But the definitions of both adaptation and adaptability focus exclusively on the strength or weakness of the linkages within *local* economic networks. It is clear, however, that local economies are not isolated islands and "are always characterised by a high degree of openness to external events and forces" (Martin and Sunley 2015, p. 12). Globalisation is one of the most significant of these external forces. This has involved, since around the 1970s, the growing interconnectedness and networking of the world's national and local economies. In the UK, for example, globalisation has increased the competition for local mass production manufacturing and low-cost services. It has led to structural changes in the UK economy with mining and manufacturing, for example, declining from 43 per cent of all jobs in England and Wales in 1911 to less than 10 per cent today (Swinney and Thomas 2015, p. 8). Therefore, a focus exclusively on the nature and characteristics of purely local economic networks can only offer a partial explanation of local economic growth pathways. For this reason, the concept of "replication" is adopted in this chapter in preference to that of "adaptation".

The concept of replication (Simmie 2014b) recognises the significance of the myopia of tightly coupled local economic networks in driving local industries along path-dependent trajectories but, in addition, argues that these local networks are also forced to interact with other geographically defined networks both at home and abroad. This means that they are unable simply to continue indefinitely adapting their pre-existing industries. But, instead of responding to globalisation and technological change by starting "new economy" activities appropriate to the new international division of labour in advanced economies, such local economies have a tendency to replace or "replicate" their declining industries with similar modern equivalents. Thus, "they have replaced jobs in declining industries with lower-skilled, more routinized jobs, swapping cotton mills for call centres and dockyards for distribution sheds" (Swinney and Thomas 2015, p. 1).

The concept of "reinvention" (Simmie 2014b) is also preferred to that of adaptability in this chapter. This is again because an exclusive focus on loosely coupled local economic networks does not explain how radical new leading-edge knowledge is generated or acquired and forms the bases for the creation of new economic pathways. Such knowledge is only generated in the first instance in a select minority of states (Audretsch and Feldman 1996) and regions (Hilpert 1992). This suggests that a significant proportion of new leading-edge technological knowledge needs to be acquired from sources external to any given local UK economy. Simmie (2003) and Bathelt et al. (2004), for example, have argued that cities and regions are nodes in their respective national and the international economies and that a combination of both local "buzz" and multiple global networks or "pipelines" are required for the transfer and acquisition of both new leading-edge tacit and codified knowledge.

Local new path creation and long-term economic growth is therefore argued to be based on the capacity of local economies to reinvent themselves in line with global and national "new economy" industrial and commercial change. In short "contemporary regional economic [growth] . . . is driven by specialisation in those sectors that are undergoing a structural wave of expansion and growth" (Martin and Sunley 2015, p. 34; see also Lindqvist 2009). The challenge for local economies in the UK over the past 100 years has been to replace declining industries with new more knowledge-based economic activities (Swinney and Thomas 2015, p. 9). This requires the continual reinvention of the local economy. The processes driving such reinvention form the bases of the long-run resilience of local economies in the face of global changes in knowledge, invention and technological innovation. Local economies with strong inherited entrepreneurial cultures, histories of innovation and new firm formation are better equipped to achieve such resilience than those without these characteristics. These arguments are summarised in Figure 6.1.

Figure 6.1 sets out a systematic approach for the analysis of the long-run emergence of possible combinations of the economic reinvention or replication of urban and regional economies. The approach consists of dividing the possible combinations of the reinvention or replication of local economies into a two-way matrix consisting of high and low levels of both phenomena. It is hypothesised that the combination of high replication with low reinvention is likely to lead in the long-run to path-dependent development and lock-in of old industries. There will be an overreliance on existing local sources of knowledge. The result will be that the resilience

Reinvention

		Low		**High**
High	**Q1**	Path dependent development andlock-in of old industries. Reliance on existing local sources of knowledge. Resilience very low. Long-term economic decline.	**Q3**	Combination of continued path dependent development of historical industrial and commercial sectors with some new path creation. Resilience moderate. Moderate long-term economic growth.
Replication **Low**	**Q2**	Less history of old industrial sectors. But lacking in dynamic entrepreneurs. Slow development of modern economy sectors. Resilience low. Slow long-term economic growth.	**Q4**	New path creation. Entrepreneurial culture seeks out new knowledge from external sources. Resilience high. High aggregate long-term economic growth.

Figure 6.1   Reinvention, replication, resilience and long-run economic growth in local economies

of such local economies will be very low when exposed to external shocks. This combination of factors is likely to lead to long-term economic decline.

In contrast, a combination of high reinvention and low replication is likely to be marked by new path creation stimulated by an entrepreneurial culture that seeks out new knowledge from external sources. In such circumstances, resilience capacity is likely to be high. Such local economies are likely to be characterised by high aggregate long-term economic growth.

A combination of both high replication and high reinvention could lead to both the continued path dependent development of historical industrial and commercial sectors with the addition of the creation of some new pathways. The balance between the two will influence the resilience capacity of the local economy. If some of the traditional industries begin to decline while at the same time new economic pathways are being created then the aggregate outcome could be moderate long-term economic growth.

Finally, a fourth possibility is the combination of low reinvention and low replication. Such local economies are likely to be characterised by a long history of slow economic growth. Lacking in dynamic entrepreneurs the development of modern economic sectors will also be slow. These may be the type of local economy that time has forgotten. As a result, external economic shocks that affect traditional industries or contemporary knowledge-based industries may not have such a severe impact in such localities because they lack both types of industry. Nevertheless, their resilience capacity is likely to be relatively low in the case where external shocks impact the whole national economy or where they affect the particular industries in those areas.

METHODS

In order to explore the relationships between replication, reinvention, resilience and long-run urban economic growth, two secondary datasets are used to analyse performance of the economies of English and Welsh cities. The first dataset used in this chapter has been constructed by Swinney and Thomas (2015) as the basis for their analysis of urban economic change in major English and Welsh cities since 1911.

This analysis uses a fixed geographical definition of cities based on their current boundaries using their Primary Urban Areas (PUAs). Where possible the PUA boundaries of today were matched to local authority boundaries for 1911 (Swinney and Thomas 2015, p. 3, see also www.centreforcities.org/puas). This provides a sample frame of 57 cities across England and Wales. Among this list, Milton Keynes and Telford were excluded because they were not established until the 1960s. The total sample size of this dataset is therefore 55.

This dataset provides information on long-run employment and sectoral change within PUAs between 1911 and 2013. Growth or decline in total employment over this period of 102 years is used to indicate the relative resilience capacity of cities. Sectoral changes over the same period are used to indicate the degrees to which cities have reinvented or replicated the structure and knowledge intensities of their local economies. The dataset shows the share of jobs in extraction, manufacturing, docking and general working in the major English and Welsh cities in 1911. In this chapter, changes in the sectoral structures of urban economies from these traditional industries to more knowledge-intensive activities are used to illustrate the relative capacities of cities to reinvent their local economies over the past century.

Contemporary participation in the digital economy is used as a key example of a twenty-first century knowledge-intensive sector. In this instance a dataset provided by Nathan et al. (2013) study entitled "Measuring the UK's Digital Economy with Big Data" identifies the geographic distribution of the new digital economy in the UK. In this study, the original dataset was provided by Growth Intelligence. This dataset comprises 3.07 million companies registered in the UK. From this dataset Nathan et al. (2013, p. 15) identify 269,695 companies constituting some 14.4 per cent of total UK companies that made up the digital economy in

Table 6.1   Digital economy firms by sector, UK 2012

Sector	Per cent
Information technology	39.38
Architecture	17.64
Telecommunications	10.79
Electrical/electronic/manufacturing	6.56
Printing	4.66
Entertainment/film/production	4.60
Marketing/advertising	4.41
Semiconductors	3.19
Photography	1.62
Publishing	1.16
Financial services	1.10
Other	4.89
Total N	269,695

Note: Using Growth Intelligence sector-product classification.

Source: Nathan et al. (2013, p.14).

2012. The resulting sectoral definition of the digital economy in the UK in 2012 is shown in Table 6.1.

In this study, a different geographical definition of cities is used from that of Swinney and Thomas (2015). In this instance, cities are defined according to their Travel to Work Areas (TTWAs). In this case, TTWAs containing a core city of at least 125,000 were selected for study. So the two datasets are not directly comparable geographically. Nevertheless, the same cities can be identified according to both their PUAs and the TTWAs that over-bound them. There are 53 cities, excluding Milton Keynes and Telford, where the PUAs from the first dataset form the core areas of the same TTWAs in the second dataset.

A comparison of the 1911 sectoral composition of the PUAs identified in the Swinney and Thomas (2015) dataset is made with the degree to which these had been changed by the introduction of digital firms in their TTWAs by 2012 in order to illustrate the relative degree of the reinvention of their local economies by the latter date. It is argued that higher degrees of the introduction of digital firms indicates higher levels of the reinvention of local economies while lower degrees suggest, at best, higher levels of replication. In addition, these results are compared with the long-run rates of employment growth or decline in the cities studied. It is argued that higher rates of employment growth indicate higher resilience capacity while lower rates and employment decline suggest a lack of economic resilience capacity over the long term.

ANALYSIS

Following the argument that the economic resilience of urban and regional economies is indicated by their ability to maintain above-average long-term economic growth rates (Martin et al. 2013; Gardiner et al. 2013) in the face of continual shocks such as major recessions or the endogenous or exogenous invention, innovation and diffusion of technological innovations, the analysis turns first to an examination of long-run economic growth in English and Welsh cities. This is indicated by the rate of employment growth from 1911 to 2013 (Swinney and Thomas 2015).

Figure 6.2 shows that during the course of the century starting in 1911 the mean employment growth in 53 English and Welsh cities was 59 per cent. This was comfortably exceeded by cities in the top quartile. In this group, employment growth varied between 598 per cent in Crawley to 173 per cent in Southend. All of these cities are located in the south of England. They include four – Crawley, Peterborough, Swindon and

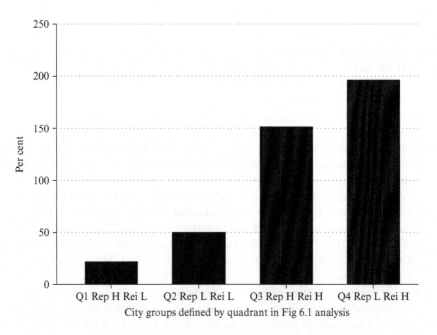

Figure 6.2   Employment growth English and Welsh cities, 1911–2013

Northampton – that have been the subject of major public policy initiatives in the form of comprehensive town expansion schemes. With respect to the concepts of reinvention and resilience, these cities have experienced a number of advantages. First, they inherited a limited number of industries from the Industrial Revolution. Second, as their planned expansion took place, their developing industrial structure benefited from the planned objective of introducing new and contemporary industries to their respective economies. As a result, their local economies were being reinvented on a continual basis as each new phase of town development was introduced.

In contrast, at the other end of the scale in the bottom quartile, employment growth varied between – 51 per cent in Burnley to 15 per cent in Newcastle. All of these cities are located in the north of England. They include some of the largest cities in the UK such as Liverpool, Manchester and Newcastle. While none of the cities in the top quartile participated to any significant degree in the Industrial Revolution, most of those in the bottom quartile were involved in the manufacture of textiles or pottery or in port activities. These industries have left a path-dependent legacy of declining industries in those cities.

Overall it is argued that cities in the top quartile have demonstrated higher levels of resilience in the face of continual external shocks resulting from such phenomena as globalisation, national recession/depressions and technological change than those in the bottom quartile. In contrast, the level of path dependence and lock-in of the industrial structures and trajectories of those in the bottom quartile has been high.

This is illustrated in Figures 6.3 and 6.4. Figure 6.3 shows the correlation between those cities that started with the highest levels of employment in traditional extraction, manufacturing, docking and "general working" in 1911 and those that 100 years later had innovated economic activities based on the new digital technologies. The figure is divided into four quarters corresponding to those shown in Figure 6.1, suggesting that cities in Q1 have been less resilient in dealing with technological shocks and their attendant industrial change than those in Q4.

Overall Figure 6.3 suggests that cities that started with the highest levels of traditional industries in 1911 have been subject to strong path dependence and lock-in as suggested by Boschma (2015). There is a week correlation ($R^2 = 0.1656$) between these cities and those that had created new technological pathways by starting up digital firms by 2012. Again, most of the cities that started with the highest levels of employment in "old economy" industries and have had the lowest rates of digital firm start-ups are to be found in the north of England. Some 17 out of the 20 cities in Q1 of Figure 6.3 are to be found in the north of England. Half of them are also to be found in the bottom quartile for employment growth as shown in

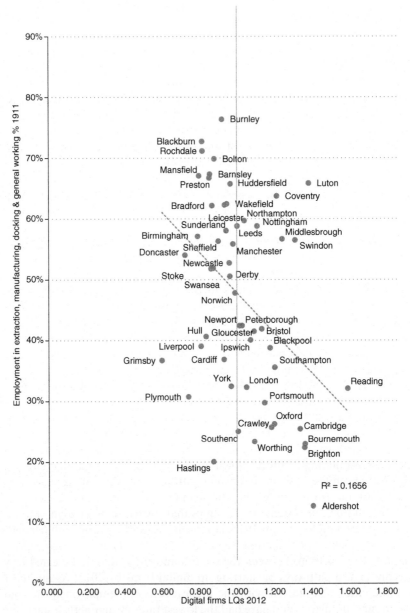

Source: Swinney and Thomas (2015), Nathan et al. (2013).

Figure 6.3 *Replication, reinvention and long-run city employment growth rates*

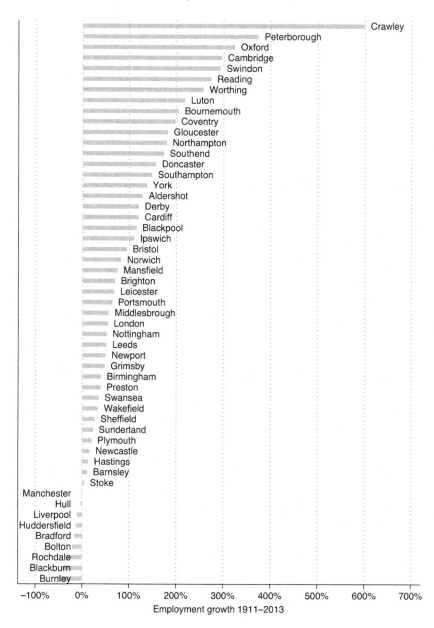

Source: Swinney and Thomas (2015).

Figure 6.4 *"Old economy" employment 1911 versus the development of digital firms in English and Welsh cities by 2012*

Figure 6.2. Starting from above-average levels of employment, particularly in manufacturing and general working, these cities have been the least resilient in reinventing their local economies in response to the shocks imparted by the Digital Revolution.

In contrast, among the cities located in Q4 of Figure 6.3, 15 out of 17 are located in the south of England. These are the cities that generally have the lowest historical legacies of old industrial activities combined with higher than average concentrations of digital firms. Nine of them are to be found in the top quartile of employment growth over the past century. This quadrant also includes the so-called "golden triangle" of London, Cambridge and Oxford with its significant concentrations of research and development (R&D) in general and the Thames Valley where the UK computer industry is particularly concentrated. This supports the views of Martin and Sunley (2015) and Lindqvist (2009) that regional (and urban) economic growth is driven by specialisation in those sectors that are undergoing contemporary waves of international and national growth. The ability to do this underpins the resilience capacities of cities.

Q3 of Figure 6.3 contains a select few cities that actually started with above average levels of "old economy" activities in 1911, but have also demonstrated a capacity to reinvent their local economies in respect of the introduction of new digital economy firms. The significance of public policy in the form of the town expansion schemes in Northampton and Swindon is shown in the possibilities afforded to innovative entrepreneurs to start up digital firms of the "new" economy as those cities were developed. In addition, this quadrant contains five other cities, mainly from the midlands, with a history of light rather than heavy manufacturing industries. The only exception to this is provided by Middlesbrough.

Finally, Q2 contains a small group of mainly port and coastal cities. Although these cities started in 1911 with lower levels of "old economy" industrial employment, they have also made less than average progress in adopting the new digital technologies. In five out of eight cases, they have also experienced lower than average or negative growth rates in total employment since 1911. Overall, therefore they may be considered to have demonstrated low levels of resilience to technological shocks over the past century.

It has been argued above that long-term resilience capacity is based, to a significant degree, on the ability of a local economic system to reinvent itself over time (Simmie 2014b; Swinney and Thomas 2015) and that new expanding specialised economic sectors drive economic growth in the localities where they develop (Martin and Sunley 2015; Lindqvist 2009). It is therefore to be expected that those English and Welsh cities where their local economies have been reinvented as a result of the development of new sectors such as digital firms will have had higher long-term economic and employment growth rates than those that have not. Figure 6.4 shows this to be the case across the groups of cities identified in the four quadrants of Figure 6.3. Thus, with respect to the average total city employment growth over the century from 1911 to 2013, there is a linear relationship between the group of cities with the highest rates of replication combined with the lowest rates of reinvention through the four quadrants to the cluster of cities with the lowest rates of replication and the highest rates of reinvention. The average total employment rate in the former Q1 was 22.5 per cent. In contrast, the average in Q4 was 195.88 per cent.

Taken together, these analyses suggest that if the ability of urban economies to maintain long-term growth rates, at least in employment, is an indicator of their economic resilience in the face of the local impacts of sudden and unforeseen external shocks imparted by such phenomena as recessions, globalisation and the Digital Revolution, then a key basis of their resilience capacity is the long-term and continual reinvention of their economies. From this perspective, resilience capacity is developed over the long term. It includes the ongoing development of local social capital in the form of an entrepreneurial culture, the development of loose knowledge networks particularly with localities where leading-edge knowledge is being developed outside the local area and the absorptive capacity to understand the significance of such knowledge and to deploy it in the creation of new technological pathways.

The long-term development of social capital for the reinvention of local economies has proved to be a difficult task in the face of the path-dependent trajectories followed by those cities that started with the highest levels of employment in 1911 in extraction, manufacturing, docking and general working. With a few notable exceptions, these cities have tended to replicate the modern equivalents of those lower skilled jobs. In contrast to Schumpeter's (1942) argument, many of their local economies have been characterised by more destruction than creation over the past century. Conversely, those that historically had a greater share of more knowledge-based industries have generally found it easier to move in to the new knowledge-based economy in the face of multiple external economic shocks occasioned by globalisation, technological revolutions and recession/depressions.

SUMMARY AND CONCLUSIONS

In this chapter, it has been argued that the concept of resilience should be focused on the long-term development of the capacity to develop and maintain long-run economic growth trajectories in the face of periodic and repeated unforeseen external shocks. In the context of recent history, most of the analytical focus has been on the kinds of shock imparted by national recession/depressions. But there are other types of shock with economic repercussions that impact on urban and regional economies, whose effects may also be magnified by recessions/depressions in "gales of creative destruction". These include the rapid development of globalisation and its consequential effects on the international spatial division of labour and radical technological change such as the Digital Revolution.

Explanations of the bases of resilience in the literature, up until now, have been based on disputed dualisms (Hassink 2010a; Pike et al. 2010). It has been argued that either Jacobs (1969) variety or MAR specialisation (Marshall 1930; Arrow 1962; Romer 1986; Lindqvist 2009), or Grabher adaptation or adaptability (Grabher 1993; Grabher and Stark 1997) provide the base for the resilience capacities of local economies. More recently the supposed differences between these dualisms have become more ambiguous and it has been argued that combinations of these previously exclusive categories in the form of related and unrelated variety or diversified specialisation form the bases of urban and regional resilience.

In this chapter, the two concepts of replication and reinvention (Simmie 2014b) have been adopted in order to understand some of the underlying differences between cities in terms of their resilience capacity. On the one hand, the concept of replication recognises the significance of the myopia of tightly coupled local economic networks in driving local industries along path dependent trajectories. This has often been the pathway to long-term economic decline.

On the other hand, the concept of reinvention stresses the significance not just of loosely coupled local economic networks but on the need to acquire new leading-edge technological knowledge from sources external to any given local UK economy (Simmie 2003; Bathelt et al. 2004). This can form the basis of the development of entirely new technologies and industries to replace those nearing the end of their life cycles.

With respect to the long-term development of economic resilience, it has been argued in this chapter that local economies with a history of continual reinvention are best equipped to deal with the sudden and unforeseen shocks of globalisation, technological change and recessions. The acquisition of new knowledge from at home and abroad – and its absorption into local economies – is a key requisite of this process. Local economies also have to respond to the general trajectory of change towards more knowledge-based economic activities in the advanced national economies.

Cities that have characteristically replicated rather than reinvented their local economies have limited their resilience capacities in the face of globalisation and technological change. Often the processes of replication are marked by inadequate movement into "new economy" knowledge-intensive activities.

The empirical analysis suggests that there has been a high degree of path-dependence in the trajectories followed by city economies in England and Wales since 1911. Most of the cities whose economies were based on low-knowledge work in 1911 also tend to have fewer digital companies today. In general, the capacity to effect significant change towards more knowledge-based sectors has been lowest among city economies that started with the highest levels of employment in extraction, dock working, light and heavy manufacturing and general labourers in 1911.

There is also a distinctive geography to economic resilience expressed as the capacity to reinvent urban economies. With respect to the new digital economy, for example, out of the 20 cities with the highest levels of "old economy" employment in 1911 and the lowest relative concentrations of digital firms, 18 were located in the north or Wales in 2012. In contrast, of the 17 cities with the lowest levels of "old economy" jobs in 1911, and the highest location quotients for digital firms in 2012, 14 were located in the south of England.

These findings suggest a *prima facie* case for investigating further the significance of the continual reinvention of urban economies in the direction of more knowledge-intensive sectors as the basis of local economic resilience in the face of sudden and unforeseen external shocks. Such investigations would need to conduct intensive historical case studies of the ways in which specific urban economies have accessed and absorbed new types of leading-edge knowledge. They would need to establish the degrees to which these processes have embedded cultures of continual reinvention in those local economies. Finally, they would then need to investigate the impacts of different types of external shocks on those economies and how they had responded to them.

Such further research could provide evidence bases for the development of practical policies concerned to improve the long-term resilience capacities of urban economies. The evidence presented in this chapter has already suggested the success of historical planning policies in the form of large town expansion schemes in, perhaps unintentionally, contributing to the resilience capacities of their respective cities. This has been achieved on the back of long-run and coordinated physical development plans and public funding that have combined planned infrastructure, housing, services and economic development on the basis of attracting new forms of economic activity as the phases of development have been executed. Such schemes combined with an emphasis on new scientific economic activities are quite common in Europe, particularly in France, but noticeable by their current absence in the UK.

A further policy lesson to be learned from such research is the significance of creating new technological and economic pathways based on leading-edge knowledge, imported from wherever that is found, in order to reinvent local economies on a continual basis. Thus the evolutionary study of new path creation could form a productive basis for the development of practical policies to upgrade the knowledge bases of local economies and to serially reinvent them. This would also require the provision of long-run public funding to generate protected niches in which new technologies and industries could be developed before they become commercially viable in competitive world markets.

ADDITIONAL READING

Simmie, J. and Carpenter, J. (2008), 'Towards an evolutionary and endogenous growth theory explanation of why regional and urban economies in England are diverging'. *Planning Practice & Research* **23**(1): 101–124.

Simmie, J. and Martin, R. (2010), 'The economic resilience of regions: towards an evolutionary approach'. *Cambridge Journal of Regions, Economy and Society* **3**(1): 27–43.

Swinney, P. and Thomas, E. (2015), *A Century of Cities: Urban Economic Change since 1911*. London: Centre for Cities.

7. Path dependency, entrepreneurship, and economic resilience in resource-driven economies: lessons from the Newfoundland offshore oil industry, Canada

Cédric Brunelle and Ben Spigel

INTRODUCTION

Economic resilience is a recurring theme in economies dominated by resource extraction activities. The literature has long emphasized path-dependent processes linked with cyclical exogenous commodity price shocks. Along with a greater mobility of workers, resource-driven regions tend to have more fragmented labor market structures, where the dominant resource sector provides high wage employment contrasted by a large number of lower-paid jobs in support industries (i.e., services). Can diversification take place in these regions? Existing research on regional path creation has not adequately addressed the micro forces within a region that create opportunities for diversification or that act as barriers to the creation of new economic paths. Understanding these processes is especially important among contemporary resource-rich regions in the developed world, many of which have experienced difficulty moving beyond providing low-value services to multinationals and are therefore locked in to an existence as price-takers in an increasingly volatile global market.

In the developing world, corruption and poor infrastructure have limited the developmental potential of the wealth generated by resource extraction. However, in the Global North, city-regions such as Houston, Calgary, and Stavanger have been able to transition from low-value-added extraction activities to higher-order economic activities such as technology development and corporate services. Entrepreneurs play a key role in transitioning the regional economy away from pure dependence on extraction towards other functions by acting as innovators and path creators. Extractive activities concentrate a large amount of human and financial capital in regions and create numerous opportunities for new ventures. Entrepreneurs can take advantage of these resources and opportunities and may expand into other resource markets abroad or into related or unrelated sectors. This decreases regions' dependence on local extractive opportunities, making them more resilient in the face of sudden price shocks or other exogenous changes. However, extractive activities can also act as barriers to economic evolution. They create institutional structures that are difficult to break out of, lock-out other activities by driving up wage and housing prices, and can create cultures of dependence that discourage entrepreneurial risk-taking. Therefore, this is a tension between the lock-in effects of resource extraction and the opportunities it creates for path creation in the evolution of resource-driven regional economies towards more resilient and sustainable paths.

Formerly a province in economic decline, Newfoundland and Labrador (NL) has experienced an unprecedented economic growth since the beginning of the offshore oil industry. Oil, gas and mining extraction and supporting activities generate revenues that form a significant part of Newfoundland economy. Most of this growth has happened in the city-region of St. John's, which is also the scene of soaring housing prices. A statistical analysis of the NL economy reveals that while it has enjoyed substantial growth up until the decline in energy prices in 2014, it still remains persistently dependent on resource extraction with limited diversification to either higher-value added resource activities or into unrelated sectors. Interviews with technology entrepreneurs inside and outside of the oil and gas industry reveal the underlying forces behind this lock-in, which include both a cultural resistance to risk, lack of spin-outs from major firms, and a sparse investment environment. This chapter argues that while entrepreneurs are key actors in path creation in resource economies, they encounter significant barriers as a result of existing economic and cultural structures inherent to extractive regions.

PATH DEPENDENCY AND ECONOMIC RESILIENCE IN RESOURCE-DRIVEN ECONOMIES

From "Big Push" Theory to Dutch Disease

Natural resources have long been described as strategic assets that can spur long-term regional economic development. One of the leading arguments for resource development is that extractive activities help develop and reinforce regional exports. Theories such as that of the "Big Push" and economic base suggest that a strong regional export base induces local multiplier effects, offering new opportunities for economic development (North, 1956; Rosenstein-Rodan, 1943, 1961; Tiebout, 1956a, 1956b). This has led several scholars to believe resource extraction is a necessary initial step for lagging regions to progress towards new phases of industrialization and more advanced service activities (Hoover and Fisher, 1949; Perloff et al., 1960).

However, the view of resources as catalysis for growth is challenged by limited empirical evidence of this in resource-rich regions. Paradoxically, extractive industries appear to pose limits to long-term growth and development. Economic historian Harold Innis was among the first to theorize that resource activities create the initial conditions for economic dependency and unequal development. In his Staples Theory, Innis (1933) emphasized that market forces and the cyclical nature of commodity prices play a critical role in shaping local systems of resource extraction. During resource price booms, a "cyclonic fury" develops, diverting investment towards resource production and away from other sectors. When prices decline, that capital quickly flows to other regions, leaving scant new human or physical infrastructure behind that can help move the economy into new avenues for development. Staples Theory highlights that market failures in the form of structural rigidities are the likely outcome of disequilibrium generated by the mobilization and demobilization of resources through rapid periods of growth and decline—a characteristic of the commodity cycle.

In the wake of Innis, other explanations have been proposed for the observed patterns of limited development in resource economies. Corden's "Dutch Disease" (1982) model explores the market mechanisms behind long-term resource dependency. Increases in revenue from the export of natural resources and the inflow of foreign investments exert inflationary pressures on the local currency, which affects the competitiveness of exports in other sectors (e.g., services and manufacturing). The impact can be quite strong. Beine, Bos, and Coulombe (2012) estimate that between 33 and 39 percent of Canadian manufacturing employment was due to oil-related exchange rate development between 2002 and 2007. Economic booms further generate resource movement effects, where demand for labor shifts production toward the booming sector and away from lagging industries, leading to the deindustrialization of the latter over time.

Vulnerability and Resistance to Shocks

Big Push or Dutch Disease dynamics describe two facets of the same reality. While resources represent strategic assets in growth periods, there is a high level of ambiguity on how this force plays in the long run, with regions facing increased risks of commodity-led downturns over time. The recent financial crisis and subsequent period of instability have made scholars increasingly aware that the success of an economy extends beyond growth and relates to its long-term regional capacity to absorb, bounce back, or adapt to such changing economic conditions over time—a perspective best represented by the concept of "regional economic resilience" (Martin and Sunley, 2015; Martin, 2012). Research suggests that economic crises and recessions generate differentiated regional impacts, some of which induce permanent impacts or diverging economies over time (Cerra and Saxena, 2008).

Briguglio et al. (2009) argue that a series of characteristics determine the risk of an economy being adversely affected by external shocks over time. Such risks may be seen as the outcome of the interplay between a region's initial vulnerability and its coping ability or resilience. This raises an important distinction between largely predetermined factors and other characteristics that can be nurtured and changed over time. On the one hand, vulnerability appears as an inherent and unescapable situation that determines a region's exposure to external shocks, such as its degree of economic openness, export concentration, or industrial structure. On the other hand, it is possible for regions to develop new coping abilities over time that will reduce the impact of a shock. Good political governance, social and entrepreneurial development, and other policies related to market efficiency and macroeconomic stability are further factors that contribute to local economic resilience.

BEYOND RESISTANCE TO SHOCKS: PATH DEPENDENCY AND PATH CREATION

While the capacity to resist economic shocks may be an important aspect in developing resilient resource-driven economies, there is growing evidence that this does not constitute a sufficient condition to fully detach from future negative impacts of the commodity cycle. Evolutionary concepts of path dependency (Martin and Sunley, 2006; Martin, 2010) and lock-in (Frenken and Boschma, 2007; Grabher, 1993; Hassink, 2007) are helpful in thinking about the long-term economic trajectories of cities and regions. Path dependency suggests that resilience goes beyond the ability to resist or recover from a shock. Martin and Sunley (2015) argue that responses to shocks occur as a process where the initial characteristics of a region impact a region's vulnerability, resistance, robustness, and recoverability over time. Therefore, resilience is not so much about avoiding change but rather the ability of regional economies to reorient or renew their economic bases over time in response to changes in the global economy. Most scholars agree that economic diversification is key in developing and strengthening the resilience of regions, since a diversity of activities will provide a variety of opportunities to adapt to a shock while sharing the risks among a larger group of industries.

However, developing new products or services is not an easily achievable objective in resource-driven economies. Evolutionary theory suggests that new activities in a region are likely to emerge from related local activities, whether in terms of products, skills, or technologies (Boschma et al., 2013). Processes of diversification, either through "path creation," "branching-out," or "re-bundling," emerge from current local industries and pre-existing regional capabilities (Bathelt et al., 2013; Frenken and Boschma, 2007), conditions that are crucially lacking in resource-driven economies.

Furthermore, uncertainty related to the volatile economic environment and the conditions generated by boom and bust cycles are critical forces shaping the lock-in and lock-out potential of extractive economies. Being locked-in a resource-based activity can have both positive and negative implications for economic development (Simmie and Martin, 2010). Being locked in to a resource-based path does not imply that there is little innovation or diversification. Areas like Houston have been able to become centers of oil and gas corporate services and of drilling, exploration, and processing innovation in addition to moving into unrelated sectors such as life sciences and digital technology. While such economies are still exposed to the cyclical nature of these resources, their related diversification has led to a situation of positive lock-in that contributes to long-term economic growth and competitive advantage.

Similarly, a region can still diversify and grow even if local firms are largely unable to participate in the resource supply chain. The capital and skilled workers attracted to the region by the resource development have the potential to spur unrelated diversification in other areas, decoupling the region from economic shocks related to boom and bust cycles. However, the most common outcome for resource regions is to be locked-in to resource production with little subsequent innovation and diversification, exposing the region to significant commodity price fluctuations with a long-term prospect of decline as the resource depletes. These paths are illustrated in Figure 7.1 and the positive and negative lock-in/lock-out processes are summarized in Table 7.1.

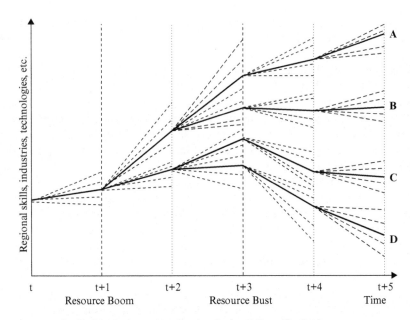

A – Positive lock-out (unrelated and related diversification)
B – Positive lock-in (related diversification)
C – Negative lock-in (stagnant economic structure; cyclic diversification)
D – Negative lock-out (deindustrialization; economic decline)

Source: Adapted from Martin and Sunley (2006).

Figure 7.1   Stylized evolutionary paths of resource regions

ENTREPRENEURSHIP AND PATH-BREAKING IN RESOURCE ECONOMIES

Boom cycles have the potential to create pools of financial and human capital that can be drawn on to diversify a region's economy away from simple extraction and towards more value-added activities such as processing, research, or business services. For example, some resources-driven economies, like Aberdeen, Scotland or Houston, Texas, have been able to leverage early developments in oil extraction to become centers of resource technology development and business services. Scholars describe oil development in Norway and the North Sea as resource-based regional innovation systems (Cumbers et al., 2003; Sæther et al., 2011). Other cases such as mining activities in Australia have showed how knowledge spill-over effects stimulated by resource development offer new opportunities

Table 7.1   *Positive and negative lock-in/lock-out processes in resource economies*

	Regional economic lock-in	Regional economic lock-out (path creation)
Positive	– Related diversification: creation and attraction of new technologies and skills within the dominant resource industry. – Value-chain reinforcement: fast growth and transaction-specific investments lock firms into a given exchange relation within the resource value chain. – Strengthening of institutional and political tissue secures investments in the dominant sector. – Standardization in adoption of local technologies secure local market for that technology.	– Related and unrelated diversification: creation and attraction of new skills and technologies outside the dominant resource industry. – Value chain upgrading: greater cooperation and interactions allow firms to diversify their services and products and reposition in the value chain across sectors. – Sustained growth in resource activities attracts firms and investments into other local activities, which contributes to the development of new institutional and political tissue outside the dominant sector. – Technologies developed for the dominant sectors are adapted and used in other sectors.
Negative	– Lack of local investments and growth opportunities in other sectors creates a barrier for diversification. – Captive value-chain structures make local firms more vulnerable to economic downturn. – Strong social and institutional tissue hinders the sharing of new ideas, learning, and innovation over time. – Technological regimes hamper the development and adoption of novel systems and technologies over time.	– Declining diversification: collapse of the dominant sector leads to deindustrialization and out-migration of skills. – Exit of the resource value-chain: lack of growth in resource industries lowers the opportunity costs for entering new value-chains. – Dissolution of the dominant social and institutional tissue creates a weak base for new investments, while creating new opportunities for new ideas and innovation over time. – Unused capacity of previous specialized resource technological systems creates long-term financial burdens while offering new opportunities for adaptation into other sectors.

for diversification, with the possibility of transitioning the economic base beyond the non-renewable extractive sector (Steen and Hansen, 2013; Steen and Karlsen, 2014; Ville and Wicken, 2013). These industries require highly educated workers to build, maintain, and finance the complex infrastructure necessary to extract oil in hostile environments. Periods of sustained booms in resource prices concentrate these people within the region, creating a population of skilled workers and potential investors that an entrepreneur can draw on. Large resource companies are increasingly externalizing non-core activities such as exploration, research and development, maintenance, and design functions in order to reduce their risk during cyclical downturns, which creates many opportunities for entrepreneurs (Aas et al., 2008; Keogh, 1998). The combination of highly skilled workers, the availability of investment capital, and the presence of multiple unfilled market niches create the conditions for high levels of innovative and growth-oriented entrepreneurship in this industry (Cumbers et al., 2003).

This gives regions experiencing a resource boom the potential to break out of existing economic trajectories and create new paths that are either associated with higher-end business service functions in the resource industry or that are totally unrelated to resource extraction. Entrepreneurs are key actors in this process (Staber, 2005; Stam, 2010). As Wolfe and Gertler (2006, p. 251) argue, "entrepreneurs act as key agents who build on the existing base of institutional assets that provide the local antecedents" for path creation and economic growth. This is due to the entrepreneurs' unique ability to identify new opportunities in the market and to gather the resources, people, and networks they need to exploit it. Entrepreneurs can use local customers as a foundation for developing and selling advanced technologies before expanding to export these solutions to the global market. Similarly, the pools of human and financial capital within these regions can support innovations in new sectors, diversifying the economy away from its resource base and into related activities. Their flexibility in innovation and their ability to identify new opportunities help them induce more structural change than pre-existing firms (Neffke et al., 2014). The potential for diversification through related activities (i.e., related variety) offers an opportunity for resource regions to use the human and financial capital that develop during periods of high resource demand as a platform for diversifying into non-resource industries and therefore establishing new economic trajectories for the region. For example, an entrepreneur might draw on local competencies in subsea remote sensing traditionally used in the offshore oil sector to develop specialized services for the construction of offshore wind farms. Even if local firms are locked out of participating in the larger resource industry, they still benefit from an increase in the availability of skilled workers, investors, and business infrastructure that the resource industry helps to create. Hence, resource booms or busts may be thought of as path-enabling or constraining environments with successive positive or negative impacts at both the firm and regional levels (Martin and Sunley, 2006; Martin, 2010).

PATH CREATION AND PATH DEPENDENCY IN NEWFOUNDLAND AND LABRADOR'S ECONOMY

Economic Decline and Growth

Recent developments in the economy of St. John's, Newfoundland economy highlight the tension between path creation and a path dependency in resource economies and the internal processes that can drive or block the creation of new regional paths. St. John's has historically depended on the extraction and exportation of raw natural resources, beginning with cod in the early seventeenth century, and moving on to timber, nickel, and most recently, offshore oil and gas (Cadigan, 2009). Due to its peripheral location, low population, and lack of capital for infrastructure development, these resources have historically been exported with few localized value-added activities, leaving the region vulnerable to cyclical fluctuations in the price of raw materials. A British colony and Dominion until joining Canada in 1948, Newfoundland has struggled with extreme poverty exacerbated by deep depressions in resource prices and the ultimate collapse of its cod fishery industry in 1992 (House, 1999).

The discovery of large petroleum reserves off the coast of Newfoundland in 1979 signaled a new potential for economic development. Underwater exploration and the construction and operation of offshore drilling and production rigs require large amounts of outside investment and generate significant local employment and economic spillover effects. The Hibernia, the world's largest offshore oil rig began operation in 1997, 315 kilometers offshore from St. John's. Subsequently, three other rigs have come online (Figure 7.2). This activity has had substantial economic impact. While St. John's unemployment rate has historically been higher than the Canadian average, since 2009 it has been lower than the national average. Furthermore, the construction and operation of offshore drilling and production rigs require large amounts of outside investment and generate significant local employment and economic spillover effects. The growth of the region's gross domestic product (GDP) has outpaced the rest of Canada's metropolitan areas over the past decade (Figure 7.3)—the sector

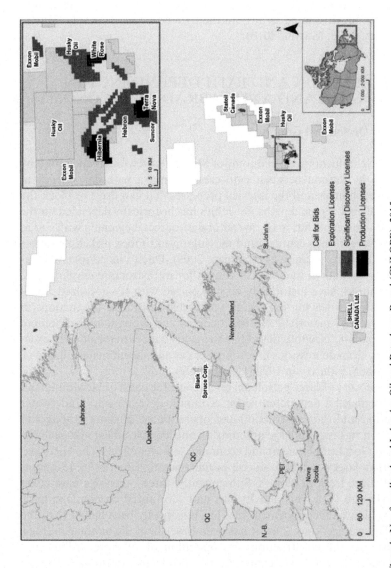

Source: Canada-Newfoundland and Labrador Oil and Petroleum Board (CNLOPB), 2015.

Figure 7.2 Newfoundland and Labrador offshore exploration and production licenses, 2015

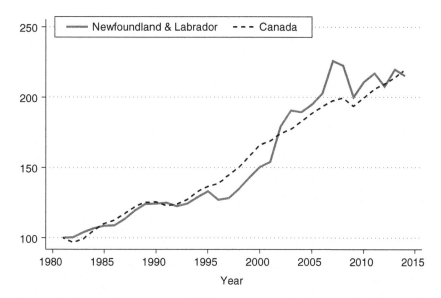

Source: Statistics Canada (2016a).

Figure 7.3　GDP growth in Newfoundland and Labrador and Canada, 1980–2015

accounting on average for 33 percent of the province over since 2007 (Statistics Canada, 2016a).

The government of Newfoundland has fluctuated between interventionist and laissez-faire approaches to the oil industry. Initially the provincial government tried to maximize the local employment impacts of the development through design and local supply requirements (Fusco, 2006). However, for subsequent development, the government took a more hands-off approach, allowing the design and construction of a majority of the infrastructure to be carried out elsewhere (House, 2003). Agreements between the province and the consortiums developing the oil field have led to the establishment of the Petroleum Research Board of Newfoundland and Labrador, which mandates that a percentage of the revenues from oil production be reinvested in local research and development for the oil industry.

Policy development over the past two decades suggest that provincial and federal programs are simultaneous focused to maximizing the economic benefits of the oil and gas industry while also attempting to diversify the economy away from complete dependence on this industry. Agencies such as the Atlantic Canada Opportunity Administration provide substantial grants for research and development to develop export markets and local universities and colleges are expanding their capacities to produce more trained workers for the oil and gas industry. Provincial law has established requirements that offshore producers fund R&D projects carried out by local firms in the hopes that this will improve the innovative capacity of startups and create the potential for knowledge spillovers.

Exposure to Shocks and Vulnerability

The substantial GDP growth of the past decade does not fully reflect broader changes taking place in Newfoundland and Labrador's economy. Important shifts in market structures have made the province increasingly vulnerable to exogenous shocks over the past 15 years. Between 1990 and 2014, the province has seen international trade accounting for less than 8 percent of GDP to more than 54 percent—the highest openness level and relative growth among Canadian provinces. In contrast, the Canadian economy has seen a much more limited evolution, passing from 11 percent to 36 percent over the same period (Statistics Canada, 2016a, 2016b). One implicit consequence of this shift is that a larger share of the province's economy is now exposed to the condition of international market on which it has not direct control. Another interpretation is that this rapid increase in economic openness describes the successful internationalization of firms in the province, with diversified exports across sectors. However, there is strong evidence that exportations are concentrated in only a few industries. To give an order of magnitude, the top two industries in Newfoundland and Labrador (oil and gas extraction; petroleum refineries) represented 75 percent of all exports in 2014, while in Canada, the top two industries (oil and gas extraction; automobile manufacturing) accounted for less than 31 percent (Industry Canada, 2016). This is also reflected in the concentration of employment across sectors, which has remained steadily high in comparison to the Canadian average between 1976 and 2015, providing further indication that the province has overall not decreased its vulnerability to potential future exogenous shocks following the recent oil boom.

Reactions to Shocks and Diversification

Despite increased vulnerability, the positive shock of the oil boom between 2000 and 2014 has been a powerful force, with the possibility to generate early-stage conditions for long-term diversification and regional lock-out. Employment trends provide evidence that the oil boom has indeed acted as a catalyst for the economic restructuring of the NL economy (Figure 7.4).

From a low point in the post-shock impact of the cod moratorium in 1992, employment in the goods producing sector has started to increase as a rapid pace, increasing above its 1976 value as it passed the 2008 crisis. Service jobs have also increased, although more steadily over the period. The fisheries to oil transition, as seen by the steady job decline in extraction industries followed by a renewed growth emerging in the early 2000s, appears as the dominant feature of this transition. One aspect related to the impacts on local activities derived from resource extraction. On the one hand, the emerging oil industry has not been able to provide a substitute for regenerating the pre-1990s fishing and manufacturing jobs that disappeared over the past 30 years. On the other hand, there are clear trends that the oil boom has had an important impact on employment creation in advanced and knowledge-intensive business services (KIBS) as well as business, building, and other support services. Technical, professional, and scientific services related to offshore activities suggest that there have been significant opportunities for technological diversification and entrepreneurship.

ENTREPRENEURSHIP AND THE CHALLENGES OF PATH CREATION IN RESOURCE-DRIVEN REGIONAL ECONOMIES

The previous trends highlight the dynamics of resource dependency taking place in the Newfoundland economy. However, they provide limited insights into the processes through which lock-in dynamics take place and the potential for regional lock-out. To better understand these processes, interviews were conducted with technology entrepreneurs in St. John's, Newfoundland's capital and dominant urban area. Offshore oil and gas activity has created numerous opportunities for entrepreneurs ranging from supplying the offshore rigs with basic services to technological developments to aid offshore oil exploration and production. This creates the potential for entrepreneurs to catalyze new economic trajectories, for instance by using technology used in offshore rig construction for offshore wind development. As argued above, resource booms attract the human and financial capital to a region that entrepreneurs need to innovative and open new markets. However, it also creates barriers to entrepreneurial diversification. In total, 32 interviews were carried out with technology entrepreneurs, local investors and economic development officials in St. John's (see Table 7.2). The interviews focused on how entrepreneurs developed new products and entered new markets, and the barriers and challenges they face in Newfoundland.

The interviews show three interlocking forces underlying the region's

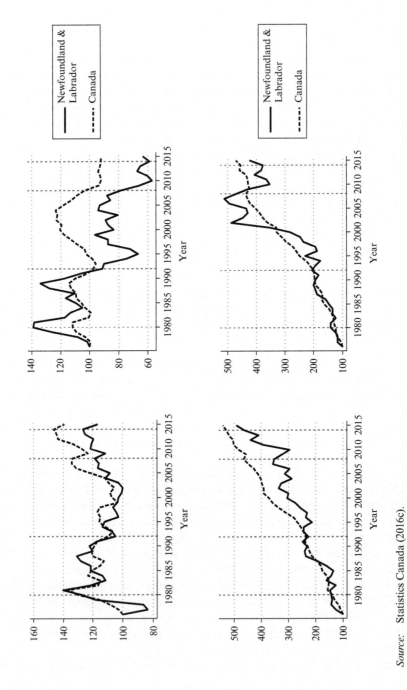

Source: Statistics Canada (2016c).

Figure 7.4 Employment growth, selected industries, Newfoundland and Labrador, 1976–2015

Table 7.2   Interviews in St. John's, Newfoundland

	Entrepreneurs	Economic development officials	Investors	Total
Interviews	20	8	4	32

continued economic lock-in and the challenges of entrepreneurial path creation. These are *changes in the offshore industry* that have progressively shut out new firms from participating in the resource sector, *cultural lock-in* related to Newfoundland's extensive history of poverty that discourages entrepreneurial risk-taking and an *underdeveloped investment environment* that makes it difficult for entrepreneurs to get the capital and assistance they need to achieve substantial growth. While there is substantial technology entrepreneurship activity in the region, these barriers restrict the growth of new ventures and limit their ability to spur long-term diversification of the economy away from extraction activities with little local value-added activities. In essence, St. John's suffers from negative lock-in, where the region cannot shift from its role as primarily a price-taker in the resource extraction industry. As the global oil and gas industry continues to suffer under long-term price declines, the region risks shifting into a more profound negative lock-out cycle, leaving little behind to spur future growth.

Industry Structure

Major oil and gas operators in the 1990s were seen as a key source of entrepreneurial opportunities. Similar regions like Aberdeen, Scotland have seen high rates of successful entrepreneurs who were able to build major international oil and gas service firms by first starting to serve the local producers before expanding internationally (Cumbers et al., 2003). By serving the local market, new firms are able to build up their expertise, capabilities, and their connections within a very tight-knit industry that depends on reputation and legitimacy. However, interviews with entrepreneurs in the oil and gas space and other experts suggest that entering this market has been more difficult than anticipated. The industry has undergone considerable consolidation, and global oil producers like Exxon prefer to work with other global oil services companies such as Schlumberger, who can provide standardized technological services and supplies to all their offshore facilities around the world (Davis, 2006). The major operators prefer to work with large global suppliers rather than smaller start-ups that lack an established track record. In the words of a local investor, while the industry has created numerous opportunities, "those sorts of opportunities are taken up by mostly industry players and not people like us" (SJ23). There is now less opportunity for entrepreneurs to serve the local industry, even for low-value-added activities like catering or maintenance.

Entrepreneurs that have had some success at entering the oil and gas supply chain have been providing solutions that address conditions specific to the Newfoundland offshore industry, such as iceberg detection and avoidance. However, focusing on this area reduces their ability to enter other markets and grow beyond local needs. Currently, Newfoundland is the only offshore oil production zone that requires iceberg detection equipment. Because there are only four production rigs in Newfoundland, there is a limited demand for services, making it difficult for entrepreneurial firms to use their local operations to finance the intensive R&D and marketing necessary for entering the global oil services value chain. Beyond this, as a local economic development official explained: "it turned out the ice wasn't anywhere near as much of an issue as they thought it was going to be . . . [the rig operators] found they could use a lot of off-the-shelf kit, went back to Houston, and brought it all up here" (SJ07).

As a result, the majority of interviewed entrepreneurs who were in the oil and gas sector (five of eight) saw themselves specifically serving the local market with few plans for growth outside the local market in the near term. This reinforces existing paths related to the oil and gas sector. While the expansion of oil exploration into the Arctic may increase the demand for iceberg detection, currently the technology is only needed in Newfoundland. As a result, new firms in this sector have a limited ability to break out of the local market and diversify to meet global needs. As one entrepreneur in this sector said: "I think it's difficult to walk into a different area where you're not from and get the same street cred that we have right here. By the same token, we're only going to be able to leverage off . . . our knowledge and our industry contacts to a certain level before that taps out" (SJ22).

Cultural Lock-in

The second barrier to new path creation is the region's longstanding cultural attitudes towards risk and entrepreneurship. There are very few examples of experienced oil and gas managers or engineers leaving the stable employment of a major operator and creating their own spin-out firms. Other regions such as Aberdeen or Houston have seen high rates of spin-off creation as a key engine of economic development. However, in St. John's, only three of the 20 entrepreneurs interviewed had a background in the oil and gas sector. Many economic development officials suggested that few if any senior managers or engineers in the offshore industry had any interest in leaving the stable employment and high pay of the major operators for the risks of developing a new start-up. They "like the comfort of a nine-to-five job for the government or for Exxon Mobil" and see no reason to take on the risks of entrepreneurship (SJ1). Some interviewees suggested that the high wages in the industry and lack of a pre-existing entrepreneurial culture in the region decrease the economic and social incentives for creating a new start-up. An economic development officer suggested that it would be "highly unusual for someone to say 'well I'm going to quit my $200,000-a-year job' to start a new venture" (SJ4).

There is clear evidence from the interviews that local culture acts as a barrier to entrepreneurship for those with established careers in the oil and gas industry—what can be described as cultural lock-in. Numerous interviewees in both the local government and industry associations commented on the lack of an entrepreneurial and risk-taking culture in the community. The traumatic impact of the collapse of the local fishing industry in the 1990s, in which 40 percent of the workforce—including a large contingent of self-employed "entrepreneurial" fishermen—lost their employment, has also contributed to a risk-averse culture that discourages highly paid workers from leaving stable employment for the extreme risks of entrepreneurship. The director of a local angel investment syndicate commented that "there's a risk aversion here" (SJ24) and a former technology transfer officer at Memorial University suggested that "no one has any tolerance for failure at all in Newfoundland" (SJ19). This is exacerbated by the lack of a history of entrepreneurial success stories in the region to encourage new generations of entrepreneurs. The relative lack of social legitimacy of entrepreneurship as part of a normal career path and the lack of successful entrepreneurial role models in this sector reduces the supply of potential entrepreneurs in this sector. This is evidenced by the lack of serial entrepreneurs in the region. Only four of the 20 entrepreneurs interviewed had previously started and exited previous start-ups. As a result of this cultural lock-in, there is a lack of entrepreneurial skill and experience both inside and outside the oil and gas industry.

Sparse Investment Environment

Many interviewees cited the lack of investment capital in the region as a major barrier to any kind of entrepreneurial expansion or diversification efforts. Without investment, it is difficult for start-up firms to finance the type of R&D or market development activities required to avoid being locked in to their current markets and territories. Interviews with entrepreneurs, economic development officers, and investors confirmed that there are only two technology angel investors in the region. Both investors commented in interviews that they have experienced difficulties recruiting other local business people in the region to invest in technology startups instead of more traditional and safer investments such as real estate. A city economic development official summed up the situation simply: "The city does not do any kind of angel investment and I don't even foresee that ever occurring" (SJ12). Similarly, the leader of a local investment group asked "how do you get [these investors] to move beyond bricks and mortar?" (SJ24). While many potential investors are happy to hear pitches from entrepreneurs, few outside of the two leading angels have invested substantial amounts without first waiting to see if the region's two lead investors are also interested.

This creates several challenges for technology entrepreneurs in St. John's looking to diversify their products or markets. Firms require outside investment to introduce new products and undertake the travel necessary to develop partnerships and sales in other regions or industries. Without investment, firms need to rely on internal revenues to fund both their day-to-day operations as well as their long-term product development plans. But beyond simply supplying financial capital, early-stage investors are important sources of mentorship and industry contacts. Because there have been so few entrepreneurial exits, there is not a pool of successful entrepreneurs who can act as advisers and investors in new start-ups. An entrepreneur in the green energy sector commented: "investors here are, you know, your local brick-and-mortar investors who might have made a lot of their capital through running a grocery store or construction company [but] there's definitely a lack of understanding of high-tech" (SJ17).

The underdeveloped angel investment community reflects absence of a local entrepreneurial culture that legitimizes the risks of angel investment. Angel investors in St. John's are motivated as much by a desire to give back to their community as much as they are interested in the potential profits from their investment. One angel investor commented: "I'm not trying to be a professional investor here. I don't have the skills or the money or the time for it, so I'm, you know, part of the motivation is my wife and I want to do a good thing here, and we can't do good for the entire world; we've got to pick a spot, so Newfoundland is our spot" (SJ23). While in one sense this is a positive element that demonstrates the importance many investors attach to supporting their local community, it depends on the goodwill of investors and is ultimately not sustainable in the face of low returns. A local culture that supports and legitimizes entrepreneurial risk-taking helps justify the decision to invest and support an entrepreneurial venture over what may be a more prudent investment decision. While these two major investors are trying to encourage others in the business community to act as angel investors, they have been unsuccessful thus far. The lack of such a culture in St. John's has made it more difficult to attract high-net-worth individuals in St. John's into its small investment community.

CONCLUSION

The experience of Newfoundland's economy is an example of how difficult it is for regions to embark on new economic paths. The province's economy has undergone profound changes in the past two decades: the discovery of offshore oil and gas reserves has resulted in billions of dollars of investment in the region that have helped to attract skilled workers and created numerous new opportunities in the economy. Until the sudden decrease in oil prices in 2015, the province had emerged from decades of population decline and economic shrinkage to become a center of development in the Canadian economy. However, there are still substantial barriers to creating new economic paths that either build on the extractive industries (by developing new technology and selling it to new markets) or in completely unrelated areas. The interviews with entrepreneurs suggest that the region's existing economic trajectories are difficult to break out of due to both the changing structure of the global energy industry as well as the cultural lock-in that discourages risk-taking, investment, and innovation. As a result, Newfoundland's economy has remained extremely vulnerable to external shocks despite its substantial economic growth. The region's entrepreneurs are locked out of both participating in the oil and gas industry—which would help spur higher-value added exports that would detach the region from depending entirely on local production levels—as well as in unrelated markets that would help reduce dependence on global energy prices. As a result, the province's economy suffered a substantial contraction in 2015–16 as a result of falling oil prices, leading to a downgrading of its credit and drastic cuts in public and private investment and spending.

This suggests that resiliency and new path creation do not come from economic growth alone. Rather, they require a more fundamental change in the underlying social structure and networks within the region to empower entrepreneurs and other actors to explore new markets, technologies, and organizational forms. Resources attracted to the region during a boom time will quickly leave it when the immediate opportunity evaporates, requiring that the region's political and business community help create their own unique assemblage of resources and competencies that can power more sustainable economic development.

ADDITIONAL READING

Dubé, J. and Polèse, M. (2016), 'The view from a lucky country: explaining the localised unemployment impacts of the Great Recession in Canada'. *Cambridge Journal of Regions, Economy and Society* **9**(1): 235–253.

Eriksson, R. and Hane-Weijman, E. (2015), 'How do regional economies respond to crises? The geography of job creation and destruction in Sweden? (1990–2010)'. *European Urban and Regional Studies* **24**(1): 87–103.

Martin, R. and Sunley, P. (2016), 'How regions react to recession: resistance, recoverability and the role of economic structure'. *Regional Studies* **50**(4): 561–585.

8. Resilient regions and open innovation: the evolution of smart cities and civic entrepreneurship

Jennifer Clark

INTRODUCTION

Resilience, and particularly the resilience of urban and regional economies, depends on underlying innovation capacities in those cities and regions. In an era of rapid technological change and devolved governance, innovation occurs both in policy design and policy implementation as well as in the more familiar domains associated with new products, processes, materials, and markets. Innovation is a factor in how resilient firms, intermediaries, and supply chains face shifting market conditions and absorb new technology. And institutional innovation is critical to the resilience of governments and institutions as they create responsive policies and policy frameworks to adapt to rapid change.

Resilience, in other words, has a complex relationship with innovation rather than a clear one (Clark et al. 2010). In recent years, resilience became a core concept in understanding the long-run viability of economic, political, industrial, and environmental systems including those systems that sustain cities and regions. Along with sustainability, resilience entered the lexicon not only as a normative value but also as a variable to operationalize and assess the relative merits of everything from economic policies to infrastructure investments. Resilience speaks to the viability of complex systems to withstand and adapt to change.

Resilient systems are aggregations of private, public, and third-sector actors capable of adaption to changing circumstances (Andres and Round 2015). This adaption is understood to be inherently dynamic although the timescale is often uncertain. Resilience in the face of "exogenous shocks" can range from sustained challenges like climate change to medium-term challenges like economic recessions to short-term crises like earthquakes or hurricanes. And herein lies one of the first key connection between innovation capacity and resilience—the ability to reconfigure organizational designs to respond to specific challenges.

In an expansive definition of innovation, there is a deep connection to resilience. A renewed emphasis on "open innovation" underscores this connection and its meaning in the resilience context. In the context of resilience, innovation is not principally proprietary. Capacity is iterative. It is not an inevitable element of any given system but an intentional outcome of its design. Ultimately, investments are required by institutional actors capable of ongoing adaptation and diffusion to ensure consistent systems upgrading. Crisis response alone is almost always insufficient. Just as a single disruptive innovation brings temporary success to a firm, it is persistent institutional innovation that associates closely with resilience.

This chapter focuses on two examples of intersections between innovation and resilience. The first intersection highlights the innovations observed in policy design and diffusion associated with distributed networks active in governance. The Rockefeller Foundation's 100 Resilient Cities project is one example of this new model of policy design and diffusion aimed at thematic approaches to urban challenges rather than siloed or functional distinctions.

Specifically, innovation in governance and policy models by the public sector and among non-governmental institutions can promote or inhibit resilience in regional economies. In this first case, the public and private institutions engaged in service delivery show greater resilience—the ability to adapt to significant changes—when there is an ongoing and conscious integration of "design-thinking" in policy development and investments. The current discussion of how to understand and prioritize—and subsequently fund and implement—"smart cities" technologies is a case in point (Kitchin 2014, 2015).

The second key intersection between resilience and innovation concerns the regional economic ecosystem. And here, open innovation becomes a critical factor. At issue is the capacity of firms or networks of firms to undertake technology-diffusion both internally and across supply chains in order to adapt to dynamic market conditions. This conceptualization of resilience as an indicator of robust "innovation + production" regional economic ecosystems underscores the real opportunity costs of path dependencies that postpone the adoption of new materials or processes when short-term economic shocks shift the competitive balance and reveal the inefficiencies (Clark 2013).

METHODS AND APPROACH

This chapter describes the two key intersections between resilience and innovation: (1) innovative governance characterized by policy diffusion networks, and (2) regional economic ecosystems characterized by open innovation. The discussion of policy diffusion networks is based on an analysis of the scope, character, and geographic distribution of such networks since 2011. Although many of these networks are international in scope, the analysis here primarily relies on US-based networks including the IBM Smarter Cities Challenge, the Code for America fellowship program, Bloomberg Philanthropies' Innovation Delivery Teams and WhatWorksCities programs, the City Energy Project, the MetroLab Network, and the AT&T Spotlight Cities initiative. The discussion of policy diffusion networks focuses in on one of these networks, the Rockefeller Foundation's 100 Resilient Cities program, and one city's experience (Atlanta) in joining that network.

Similarly, the discussion of open innovation and regional economic ecosystems relies on an industry case study of "smart cities" as an enabling industry defined by the integration of information and communications technologies (ICT) with urban infrastructure deployment (Kitchin 2014). The industry study follows a methodological approach familiar to most economic geographers with an emphasis on identifying producers, customers, markets, and products. The complexity, of course, is that—as with most emerging industries engaged in defining new markets rather than expanding into existing ones—the boundaries of the industry are dynamic and contested. The combination of these two empirical cases of evolving mechanisms of and for technology diffusion into cities—as places and as institutions—highlight the intersections between resilience and innovation.

INNOVATIVE GOVERNANCE: DISTRIBUTED NETWORKS FOR POLICY DIFFUSION

In 2013 the Rockefeller Foundation announced its intention to develop a "100 Resilient Cities" program (100RC).[1] The stated goal of the Rockefeller Foundation's investment is to help cities identify and plan for responses to infrastructure, social, and economic "shocks" and "stresses." The project, in its current form, provides cities with the resources to hire "Chief Resilience Officers" who then work to connect the selected city in which they work with the assets, resources, and networks of best practices available through the 100RC project and partners.

In May 2016, the 100RC project named its final cohort of member cities after three rounds of competition (Herd and Mutiga 2016). Atlanta (USA) was among this final cohort. Atlanta has previously applied to the 100RC program in the first round, awarded in 2013, and the second round of applications in 2014. It was not until this third round that Atlanta was selected as a member of the program. It was in the final round that Atlanta's capacity to identify its own unique set of shocks and stressors and its ability to leverage partners and make plans to further its own regional resilience compelled inclusion. And it was in this final iteration that Atlanta shifted away from innovation and towards sustainability and preparedness to articulate a vision of resilience

The progression of City of Atlanta's resilience planning illustrates the contested intersections between resilience, innovation, and sustainability—as a matter of conceptual clarity, policy design, and governance (Christopherson et al. 2010). This is not, of course, a challenge unique to Atlanta or to US cities. For several decades, academics, policymakers, and research agencies have worked to articulate cross-cutting organizing themes that better assemble local and regional capacities and resources and provide a framework for responsive policy going forward. Terms like *innovation* and *sustainability*—as well as *resilience*—have often been invoked. However, the domains these terms specify have rarely been broadly understood. The MacArthur Foundation supported a network of academics working on regional resilience in the 2000s. Their work resulted in a set of efforts to articulate the connections between community development and regional resilience (Foster 2006; Swanstrom 2008; Pendall et al. 2007).

Here the case of Atlanta's experience with 100RC is instructive. The internal teams involved in responding to the Rockefeller's 100 Resilient Cities call for proposals, at various times, included the Bloomberg Foundation seeded-Innovation Delivery Team, a subsequent iteration known as the Mayor's Office of Innovation Delivery and Performance, the Mayor's Office of Sustainability, and the Office of Emergency Preparedness. In the final (successful) articulation of the 100RC challenge, it was the Offices of Sustainability and Emergency Preparedness who partnered to take the internal lead. In addition to bringing leadership grounded in emergency response and sustainable systems, these offices also brought in external partners from leading area institutions (such as the national Center for Disease Control headquartered in Atlanta) and research universities to advise and support the resilience planning. In other words, in its final iteration, the City of Atlanta shifted away from innovation and towards sustainability, preparedness, and partnership to articulate a vision of resilience.

Although innovation is most often invoked in an economic context with an emphasis on technology diffusion, institutional innovation is increasingly understood as essential for cities and regions. Since 2011, there has been a proliferation of distributed networks as a means to replicate and scale innovative policy ideas and models in the US and international context (Peck 2002; Peck and Theodore 2015). These policy innovation networks have often mapped on to discourses about technology diffusion—notably "smart cities" (Rossi 2015; Buck and While 2015).

These policy diffusion networks can be broadly divided into three categories: third-sector networks, public-sector networks, and private-sector networks (or corporate consortiums). Interestingly, all three types of networks are actively engaged in the construction of markets for smart cities technology and the commercialization of smart cities services and products. In the case of the third-sector and public-sector networks, this market-making is underpinned by discussions of the immediacy implied by values such as resilience and sustainability and the subsequent need for investments in innovation and technology that expands or optimizes institutional capacities now rather than later.

However, these policy models are not exclusively or even primarily about technology—they are about institutional change and expanding capacities. The rationale for this institutional change is the dynamic ability to respond to "exogenous shocks." And within this discourse is the often-implicit recognition that change will come at a rapid pace due to climate change and the resulting uncertainties that challenge the traditional planning practices of incumbent institutions (like cities).

What is common in this innovation discourse across institutions and economies is that time horizons matter. As the proliferation of the distributed networks highlights, partnerships matter as well. Economic and environmental resilience count on independent, individual actors iterating off a shared platform informed by open data. The language around crowdsourcing, crowdfunding, hack-a-thons, "ideation," and civic innovators (innovation) points directly to this fundamental premise that "solutions" are generated through participation rather than being driven by technocratic specializations (Shelton and Clark 2016; Townsend 2013). Among the operating assumptions is that that broad engagement leads to faster problem-solving, not just better solutions.

This emphasis on participation rather than technical competence creates a clear tension between the insights of the citizen and the expertise of the domain specialist. It is often the "new" offices in city governments like Innovation Delivery Teams or Offices of Sustainability with their new Resilience Officers that tap these civic innovation and "design-thinking" forums like Code for America, or develop their own citizen engagement formats using social media and new kinds of public meetings designed for generating ideas from the public rather than hearing public views on previously developed alternatives or vetting policies in a public forum.

This is not a new tension. There is a long history documenting the pendulum swings between technocratic solutions to urban challenges and community engagement. One recalls the robust response to urban renewal of participatory planning scholars and activists (Clavel 1994; Forester 1982) and the emergence of community development as a domain of its own in urban planning practice. There are two key differences in this new iteration of civic engagement and both depend on the role of new technologies: time and expertise.

First, new technologies are redefining expertise. New technologies allow for a broad access to data once only available through specialized sources or privileged interfaces. New technologies also allow for much more effective dissemination of information as well as legible presentations. In other words, the availability of data, dissemination, and display tools redefine the boundary between the expert and the amateur.

It is no longer general technical competence that defines the expert but rather more complex, specified, and localized knowledge. The unfolding story of how and why administrators overseeing Flint, Michigan's water supply chose to switch water sources is a case in point. What appeared to be a "system optimization" solution to save money by switching the water supply (essentially saving money with an alternate vendor) was clearly counter-indicated by deep, specific, and long-term water supply and systems management expertise. Innovative solutions are important. But knowledge matters as well.

It is not surprising that expertise in the public sector is becoming more defined by highly specialized knowledge—and often localized knowledge. This is the case with the balance between firm-specific and industry-specific knowledge in the private sector as well. In the private market, scalable solutions are imperative for effective market-making. Customization is expensive. It is ultimately inefficient to tailor products for individual clients. In the public sector, however, the differences between places are a reflection of the diversity that makes cities so resilient. The tension between scalable and specific solutions is not a problem to be mitigated. That tension is where innovation operates.

Returning to the second difference that new technology brings to civic engagement: time. In past articulations of participatory planning, public meetings and citizen consultation dramatically slowed down decision-making and implementation. In this new iteration, new technologies allow for rapid engagement. This change in the time required for participatory planning means there could be more of it at earlier stages in the policy design process. And indeed, that is what has occurred in recent years. There remains a challenge in assessing how broad and representative that engagement is. And this is where innovation has allowed for a shift in focus from *digital divide*, a concept that leans on lack of assets, to *digital inclusion*, a concept that assigns responsibility to cities to actively involve communities.

Thus, new technologies facilitate innovative policy models. The smart cities discourse is framed around the idea that open data leads to open innovation facilitated by social or civic entrepreneurship. And this is where the dialogue about regional resilience intersects with a discussion about sustainable and robust regional economies.

ECONOMIC RESILIENCE: OPEN INNOVATION, COMMERCIALIZATION, AND SOCIAL ENTREPRENEURSHIP

In a recent article in *Nature*, Martin Curley, the Chair of the European Union's Open Innovation Strategy and Policy Group outlined 12 principles guiding "open innovation 2.0" (Curley 2016). Curley's concept goes beyond Chesbrough's original definition of open innovation by pushing the boundaries of the underlying concept further from the discrete act of invention to dynamic and programmatic acts of innovation (Chesbrough 2006). For example, Curley expands the familiar "triple helix" conceptualization of university, industry, and government collaboration to a "quadruple helix" that adds communities to the discussion (Etzkowitz and Leydesdorff 1997).

The expansion of "openness" as it relates to innovation to include community separate and apart from government parallels the patterns seen in "civic IoT" (Internet of Things) practice. Similar to the crowdsourcing and hack-a-thon processes mentioned above to understand public sector applications of new inventions, open innovation 2.0 looks to includes communities of users in the entire innovation process (Johnson and Robinson 2014). In other words, communities are part of determining what is developed, not just whether to buy a product once it is commercialized.

Recognizing that many organizations still pursue innovation through linear contracts and bilateral relationships, Curley argues for an ecosystem approach in open innovation 2.0. And here the language of innovation returns to the same framework on which much of the resilience discourse is based: a language that favors natural systems and adaption. The proximity between the two concepts—innovation and resilience—seems to shrink in an open innovation 2.0 model.

Economic geographers have long studied innovation within and across industries as part of the broader disciplinary project of mapping and analyzing the spatial distribution of economic activities within and across cities, regions, and nation-states (Glasmeier 2000; Christopherson and Clark 2007; Treado 2010; Feldman 2003; Rantisi 2002). In recent years, technology and innovation gained privileged positions of prominence in industry analyses (Feldman and Florida 1994; Asheim and Isaksen 2002; Cooke 2005). Researchers particularly focused on processes of technology diffusion and how regional economic ecosystems absorb new technologies and incorporate them into existing complexes of firms, industries, and industrial specializations. In other words, how incumbent systems incorporate new processes, products, materials, and actors.

These patterns of technology diffusion and industry change are often responses to emerging new markets as well as the introduction of new materials, processes, or products that enable better, faster, or greener alternatives (Bryson et al. 2015). In other words, new technologies enable optimization—efficiency, sustainability, or increased quality. Resilience in regional economies therefore rests with the ability of institutions and firms to absorb new technologies, not simply invent them (Williams and Vorley 2015a). Economic resilience in this context is about identifying new markets and making new market spaces. The emerging role of the public sector in providing a platform for innovation (through data and access) creates new opportunities related directly to the concept and practice of resilience. The new availability of public data allows innovators (civic, social, private, or public sector) to develop new services or new products (including software, sensors, data, and service subscriptions), develop new processes for performance optimization to more efficiently provision existing public services, and upgrade infrastructure and urban design investments to contribute to either new data or enhanced performance, or both. This is ultimately what is referred to as one of the most popular urban innovation use cases: "smart cities."

In considering smart cities as an industry and not simply as a discourse or movement, it is important to analyze how technology diffusion operates in the context of a city as client and a city as the user location (Paroutis et al. 2014). Cities are tailored in scope and scale to their local contexts. Still, "smart cities" are a market-making enterprise predicated on scalable and commercializable conceptualization of city services and products. That enterprise directly involves social entrepreneurship and relies on open innovation. Smart cities applications allow people and firms to gather information about the conditions of the individual and aggregated lived urban experience, and allow for cities (and other stakeholders) to collect data capable of optimizing services and provisioning enhanced current and future infrastructure(s). These functions have both real and potential value—for the public and the private sectors.

Open innovation also tests the dominance of established and incumbent firms in an emerging market where a new cohort of innovators is becoming increasingly active: social and civic entrepreneurs. Incumbent firms often use privacy debates to justify proprietary platforms and limit open innovation (McNeill 2015). This leads us to a discussion about the covert construction of barriers to entry intended to limit the participants in the smart cities market space. Open innovation platforms ensure interoperability and continuous innovation and competition. Proprietary platforms create barriers to entry into this new market that has potentially broad social and economic benefits. This is why there is a rhetorical emphasis on open data, open innovation, and open access among the public sector actors in the smart cities debate (cities and national governments) but the model itself remains under development.

Thus, urban innovation operates in a contested market space—sitting somewhere between the private, public, and third sectors. Smart cities, as an industry, are focused on the design, development, and deployment of an emerging class of cross-platform, service-integrated, technology products that enhance infrastructure performance. This process of technology diffusion into the public sector is focused on "upgrading," efficiency, and broadening access and opportunity on a platform of open innovation. Despite these promises of more efficient services for a broader public, challenges remain.

To walk through some examples: "the smart city object"—the trash can, the trolley, the streetcar, the light pole, the traffic light—requires embedded sensors (leaving aside the question of what is being sensed for now). Those sensors require connectivity (fiber, wireless, etc.). A service contract is required to maintain and manage that connectivity. A power source is necessary to operate it. Data analytics are required to manage the resulting data. Expertise is required to design and perform analyses. Interfaces and visualization tools are required to make the data accessible to the public or citizen users.

Much of the focus on smart cities and civic engagement concentrates on these last stages: interfaces and visualization tools to make data accessible to communities or customers. This final stage is also where the commercialization opportunities are most robust, especially for social entrepreneurs and civic start-ups. The deployment of smart cities infrastructure—the platforms upon which open innovation relies—faces the same constraints as all other city infrastructure. Those constraints implicate all the existing challenges of capital and operating finance, zoning, legal jurisdiction, public versus private ownership, easements, right of ways, and overlapping authorities. In other words, to get to open innovation and the promise of commercializing technologies with broad and scalable applications, one must first navigate complex, and highly specific, legacy conditions.

And in this, urban innovation is no different than innovation in any other sector. The same is true in the energy sector, for example. It is necessary for emerging and enabling technologies to navigate legacy conditions. It is also typical for industries to remain reticent to deploying new infrastructure for those technologies. If there is a broader public purpose, then there is often public investment. It is no surprise that established firms are less than eager to deploy assets that may make their incumbent technologies more rapidly antiquated or open the market space to a diverse group of more nimble innovators.

However, returning to the concept of resilience, there is the notable potential for smart cities technologies to expand participation and shorten time horizons—for gathering citizen input and making decisions. For resilience, time and participation both matter. If smart cities technologies also provide a platform for regional economic resilience—firm creation, entrepreneurship, and growth—then the case for public investment in necessary infrastructure is fairly straightforward on economic development as well as public safety grounds.

Unfortunately, this has not proven to be the case. The public sector remains reticent to make significant infrastructure investments in the US at the federal, state, or local level. The smart cities industry itself remains focused on the design, development, and deployment of an emerging class of cross-platform, service-integrated technology products to enhance service performance—particularly for citizens, workers, cities, or for those with the ability to pay for that increased service performance. And here lies the particular challenge: who pays? The next step for smart cities may not be enhanced quality and coverage of public services but instead further public service privatization. This would drive the process further from the open innovation 2.0 model and closer to the closed innovation model Curley identifies as antiquated and path-dependent.

In observing who is promoting smart cities, it becomes clear that the stakeholders involved underscore the complexity of the private market versus public-sector debate. As these private, public, and third-sector networks evolve, sets of privileged places have also emerged. These places are the recipients of the demonstration project grants and resources coming through philanthropic investments, private-sector partnership, and federal government competitions and challenges. In the absence of a broad commitment to infrastructure, these are all efforts to implement some smart cities technologies in the hopes that the innovations that occur through successful demonstration projects will compel investment.

There are a few "public sector networks" undertaking or supporting demonstration projects that incorporate resilience. These networks are largely operating at the federal or national scale in the US. The third-sector networks are more numerous and include the resilience efforts of the Rockefeller Foundation and the MacArthur Foundation as well as targeted sustainability and civic innovation research and/or implementation projects through foundations such as Kresge, Doris Duke, the Bloomberg Philanthropies, and numerous local philanthropies and foundations. These organizations employ an incremental, scale-up approach. They set priorities in terms of use cases (bicycle crowdsourcing or urban agriculture). They emphasize "partnerships," "networks," and "convenings" arranged and organized for diffusion of best practices and the brokering of project partnerships. And there is a necessary unevenness that emerges in the implementation. Public services and IoT infrastructure investments are landing on an uneven landscape.

And, as in the case of the 34-city Metro Lab Network that coordinates city–university partnerships to design, develop, and deploy "smart cities" solutions focusing on "urban infrastructure systems, city services, democratic governance, and public policy and management," many of these networks provide a platform rather than resources. Federal agencies such as the US Department of Transportation, the National Science Foundation, and the National Institute for Standards and Technology have initiated challenges or competitions around specific use cases. These agencies emphasize projects that promote open innovation and open data and the development of interoperable standards. However, the investments tend to be far more narrowly tailored to commercializable use cases.

An example of how these competitions often emphasize use cases rather than programmatic infrastructure investments is the recent US Department of Transportation Smart Cities Challenge.[2] Although the Department of Transportation emphasized a programmatic or systems approach with its portion of the challenge (a designated US$40 million), the corporate partner contributing and additional US$10 million identified autonomous vehicles as the critical use case.

From an industry studies perspective, this use case is effectively the "upgrade" of conventional automobiles to autonomous vehicles. Again, the specific application (cars) underscores the difficulty of moving away from legacy conditions: existing technologies, industries, institutions, and infrastructures. As is typical with this sort of incremental innovation—an underlying manufactured good receives an upgrade using new technology. And in this case, like many others, a traditional manufactured good becomes a service-embedded good. In this case, the individual auto remains the fundamental platform but it becomes extensively interconnected through the addition of ICT that takes driving out of the hands of individual, human drivers.

This use case has gained prominence not because it can demonstrably save commuting time or improve safety (although it may). It does, however, create an important new market: a customer base captured in a location with embedded connectivity—people riding in their cars on a commute or errand and now with reliable connectivity and without the distraction of driving as a task. This is a whole new, undistracted, audience to view advertising, use software, and consume media content during a part of the day now largely lost to the ICT industry. Precursor products include the radio, XM radio, and even way-finding applications, but all limit the interactivity of the user with the technology.

Autonomous cars may also have an effect on urban form—there may be less need for convenient parking places and more places for cars to wait on curbs rather than parking garages. But it is likely this new array of captive consumers that presents a strategic opportunity for ICT firms will drive investments. And, the promise of a more resilient urban form will lag behind.

CONCLUSIONS: REGIONAL RESILIENCE THROUGH URBAN INNOVATION NETWORKS

Resilience, at its core, emphasizes capacities. As such, resilience and equity are deeply interrelated concepts. Uneven investments lead to uneven capacities to respond and adapt to exogenous stocks and localized stressors. The creation of a core and periphery of places through the pattern of uneven investments in urban innovation has deep implications for the future spatial distribution of economic activities and the resulting *relative* resilience of regional economies. The core and periphery investment strategy adopted by the test bed and competition approach creates uneven capacities across cities to design and absorb new technologies relevant to both performance management and optimization.

There are also clear issues for regional economic competition. Differential infrastructure and services mean that not only (some) citizens will select places based on smart city endowments, but so also will firms. The uneven distribution of technologically embedded infrastructure affects the economic competitiveness of cities both inside and outside the core. And finally, peripheral cities are obligated to adopt the designs and models developed and tailored for leader cities—causing a convergence towards the needs, priorities, and circumstances of core cities reflected in the design of "smart city solutions" and resilience strategies. The ad hoc implementation of the use cases and capacities produces a complex and uneven landscape with the potential to reshape regional competition and shift the focus away from enhanced quality and coverage of public services and towards increased privatization.

It is worth noting that there are some observable absences in the discussion about producing and deploying smart city technologies. First, there is almost no talk of regionalism or regional governance—the city is the actor of interest in this discourse. This is atypical in the US and leaves open a longstanding question about the management of equity and inter-jurisdictional competition (Clark and Christopherson 2009; Malecki 2004). Second, there is no explicit discussion of economic development strategies, although clearly the differential investment in these technologies changes the calculus for locational choices (Feldman 2000).

In thinking about the intersections between resilience and innovation, one might speculate about whether there is a parallel to "incremental innovation" in the resilience discourse. Is there an incremental approach to resilience? And in what sense is that incrementalism incomplete or uneven rather than simply iterative? Is it possible to view resilience as a process of adaptation with the goal of expanding adaptive capacity?

In returning to the example of Atlanta, we are reminded that cities, all cities, are inherently complex and unique—and in that complexity lies much of their resilience (Shelton et al. 2015). In fact, the City of Atlanta itself holds onto the formal Latin motto, *resurgens*, meaning "rising again." Amid the renewed interest among planners, policymakers, and academics in modeling the resilience of urban and regional economies both as environmental systems and as economic entities, Atlanta has become a case of some interest. Indeed, Atlanta is a city with experience adapting and responding to economic transformation and social change (Etienne and Faga 2014).

One of the great challenges facing diverse regional economies is how to build and maintain sustainable and resilient cities. For several years now, people have recognized the critical and expanding role of "global cities." Although Saskia Sassen's initial conceptualization focused on leading financial centers—London, New York, and Tokyo—the notion has developed to encompass broader ideas about how diverse metropolitan economies serve as regional nodes in a global network (Sassen 2001). These *global cities* serve as the engines behind national and regional economic growth.

Increasingly, academics and policy advocates have argued that global cities constitute *the most important* interconnected network of economic, cultural, and social ties and relationships—a network far more critical to understanding and engaging the economic challenges of the twenty-first century than the national boundaries that set the stage in the nineteenth and twentieth centuries (Storper 1997; Christopherson and Clark 2007).

Purely technical solutions to urban challenges rarely measure up to the promises of their advocates. The diffusion of urban innovations—in policy and planning—requires adaption to local contexts and communities (Shelton et al. 2015). Each city has its own unique quirks and its own embedded norms and values—its own peculiar way of "getting things done." And in this sense, Atlanta is no different from its peers. Whether the challenge is developing new financial models for infrastructure investment as in Chicago, figuring out how to deploy public transit in low-density environments as in Denver, or finding ways to reinvest in neighborhoods and communities overlooked or underappreciated by previous generations, it takes diverse stakeholders within and across cities collaborating on innovative solutions to a wide array of interdisciplinary challenges.

For Atlanta, and the cohort of 100 Resilient Cities, the starting point is the creation of such a network aimed at building dialogue, fostering relationships, and sharing knowledge about what works and what does not. To the broader question of how cities as places and as institutions manage their own resilience in the face of a dynamic technological environment the two empirical cases here provide some potential guidance. Perhaps understanding urban governance and regional economies as open innovation systems would be a step toward both economic and institutional resilience.

NOTES

1. For more information on the 100 Resilient Cities project: www.100resilientcities.org.
2. www.transportation.gov/smartcity: "The USDOT has pledged up to $40 million (funding subject to future appropriations) to one city to help it define what it means to be a 'Smart City' and become the country's first city to fully integrate innovative technologies—self-driving cars, connected vehicles, and smart sensors—into their transportation network."

ADDITIONAL READING

Andres, L. (2015), 'The role of "persistent resilience" within everyday life and polity'. *Environment and Planning A* **47**: 676–690.
Clark, J. (2013), *Working Regions: Reconnecting Innovation and Production in the Knowledge Economy*. New York: Routledge.
Kitchin, R. (2015), 'Making sense of smart cities: addressing present shortcomings'. *Cambridge Journal of Regions, Economy and Society* **8**(1): 131–136.
Peck, J. and Theodore, N. (2015), *Fast Policy: Experimental Statecraft at the Thresholds of Neoliberalism*. Minneapolis: University of Minnesota Press.

PART II

The Resilience of Local and Regional
Economies

9. Governance, civic leadership and resilience

Chay Brooks

INTRODUCTION

The concept of resilience has gained significant traction in recent years, traversing numerous geographical scales from countries and regions to firms and individuals. In particular, this work has tended to focus on the capacity of regions to absorb, adapt and recover from exogenous shocks and managing uncertainty (Bhamra et al., 2011; Sullivan-Taylor and Branicki, 2011: Welsh, 2014). An important aspect to this capacity is the role of local institutions in mediating and negotiating the complexities of sustaining community resilience amid economic and political change (Williams et al., 2013; Williams and Vorley, 2015a). Pike et al. (2010) note that political concerns have been largely neglected in existing work on resilience, with little research on how governance affects regional resilience. Civic leadership provides a lens to think about the minutiae of governance in shaping the contours of regional resilience.

This chapter defines civic leadership as 'the combined connections between political, bureaucratic and business leaders in shaping regional economic policy and the strategic goals of social and economic development' (Brooks et al., 2016). Civic leadership provides the basis of harnessing and steering the collaborations and strategic elements that constitute complex local governance regimes. As Dawley et al. state:

> [P]olitical leadership is clearly of paramount importance at the time of disruption or crisis ... the cross-cutting challenges of adaptation and adaptability imply institutional coordination of multiple actors vertically across and horizontally between multiple spatial levels, from the supra-national to the local.
> (Dawley et al., 2010: 660)

Multiple stakeholder governance may initially represent an organisational challenge, but it is a necessary step to address prevailing civic challenges, which the public sector cannot easily solve alone.

Civic leadership is an increasingly common feature within England and Wales, of which the Local Enterprise Partnerships (LEPs) are a particularly prominent example as public- and private-sector partners collaborate to generate appropriate responses to external shocks. As the shift from Regional Development Agencies (RDAs) to the LEPs under the Conservative-Liberal Democrat coalition government was instigated in 2010, holistic and collaborative leadership has become a hallmark of strategising City Region futures (Liddle, 2012). Governance arrangements such as LEPs may reflect Dawley et al.'s (2010: 661) contention that 'intelligent institutional leadership' is a requirement for managing economic resilience, whereby leaders articulate the nature of the external shock and recruit local and regional actors to develop solutions in collaboration. Civic leaders act as agents that mesh together the public and private, and forge cross-sectoral path creation based on 'real economies' and place-based leadership (Trickett and Lee, 2010).

City Regions have become the de facto geographical focus when considering innovation and economic intervention (Soja, 2015). This chapter seeks to explore the relationships between City Region development under the localist agenda, and the praxis of policymaking and policy-doing. Casting light on this requires an understanding of the institutional decisions that shape regional economic policy and the stakeholders involved at the local level. Developing collaborative leadership based within local communities is important for developing the capacity for regions to 'learn' and integrate leadership in order to adapt to changing economic, political and social dynamics (Morgan, 2007; Porteous, 2013).While LEPs represent a situated government policy aimed at recalibrating local governance arrangements, how they interact and function has serious implications for economic resilience.

This chapter focuses specifically on the strategic priorities of LEPs and how these priorities influence the function and perceptions of civic leadership as a means to harness economic resilience. The transition from RDAs to LEPs in particular saw the redrawing of geographic boundaries, redistribution of public financing and rescaling of power to reflect what were considered to be more 'functional economic areas' that in theory are tailored around local strategic priorities and policies. Since the first wave of proposals, which saw 24 LEPs approved in late 2010, the full complement of 39 LEPs now covers the United Kingdom as a patchwork of local associations and partnerships with occasional overlap but no holes. While the geography of LEPs has become normalised since their inception, this chapter focuses on the extent to which in 'enabling places to tailor their approach to local circumstances' (BIS, 2010: 5), LEPs have (re)configured the strategic priorities of their predecessors and shaped the role of civic leadership and, in turn, the resilience of the region.

This chapter combines the concepts of civic leadership and resilience in order to better understand the importance of how local stakeholders working together have attempted to establish a strategy for economic resilience based on reworkings of older governance forms and new emerging priorities of the localism agenda. In doing so, the chapter contributes to the emergent literature on economic resilience and the governance arrangements of City Regions over the past half a decade. Drawing on a case study of the Sheffield City Region, which has sought to emerge from the recent recession through a more diverse and resilient economy (Williams and Vorley, 2014), the chapter considers how the priorities of collaborative governance have contributed to creating a more resilient regional economy.

REGIONAL RESILIENCE AND THE LOCALIST AGENDA: ECONOMIC RESILIENCE WITHIN REGIONS

The concept of resilience has come to provide a signifier of the numerous endogenous regional capacities to cope with exogenous disruption to a community. However, despite its proliferation across numerous academic disciplines and increasingly within policy discourse, its definition has remained fuzzy and open to multiple usages (Martin and Sunley, 2015; Howell, 2015). Dawley et al. (2010: 650) state that 'local and regional development has recently broadened from a preoccupation with growth to one which captures the notion of resilience'. However, as Martin (2012) states, there is imprecision surrounding the definition and conceptualisation of resilience, which weakens its purchase as an analytical or explanatory tool. For example, Simmie and Martin (2010: 28) state that resilience is 'a regional economy's ability to recover from a shock but also to the degree of resistance to that shock in the first place'. Christopherson et al. (2010: 6) state that 'a resilient region is not just economically successful but maintains economic success over the long term in face of the inevitable adaptation required by . . . "shocks" to the system', while Dawley et al. (2010: 651) state that it can be defined as 'the ability of regions to be able to "bounce-back" or "comeback" from economic shocks and disruptions'.

While regional economies have emerged as a preferred unit for researching economic resilience, the empirical focus often examines the institutional arrangements and infrastructure within different regions as a means to analyse economic resilience. However, it is the entrepreneurial and strategic acumen of economic agents (i.e., firms and individuals), which affects their dynamism and responsiveness in relation to the adaptive cycle. This in turn determines the resilience of regional economies. When an exogenous shock occurs, there is a threat that economic development will stall and firms will close or move out of the region. As such, the resilience of a region has come to be regarded as dependent upon the performance of its firms, and the ecosystem in which entrepreneurial activities are constructed (Ponomarov and Holcomb, 2009; Demmer et al., 2011).

The notion of external shocks affecting firms is not new, and they are often linked to other traditional challenges facing firms such as resource scarcity, cash flow and dependence on infrastructure. Recent debate has emphasised the implication of shocks in relation to organisational resilience and how firms adapt to these shocks in order to remain competitive and resilient (Burnard and Bhamra, 2011). Firms have the dynamism to process environmental feedback that will overcome external shocks, whereas more rigidly organised firms were found to be more exposed. This then contributes to levels of entrepreneurship at the regional level (Huggins and Williams, 2011).

Within England and Wales, the region has been a major focus for policymakers looking to create supportive entrepreneurial ecosystems. The Regional Development Agencies (RDAs) formed a core of Labour policies towards the region during the later 1990s and first decade of the twenty-first century (Huggins and Williams, 2009). The remit of the RDAs was to further economic development alongside promoting business efficiency, and competitiveness, promoting employment and supporting the development skills as well as contributing to sustainable development. An important part of the strategic plan of the RDA was based around helping to increase entrepreneurship in the region by providing support to business start-ups and taking action to ensure more young businesses survived and creating the necessary conditions for a resilient regional economy. Robson (2014: 3) argues that the 'RDAs proved singularly ineffective at the tricky task of prioritising, opting instead to spread resources too thinly and too evenly; they massively expanded their bureaucracy to take on-board endless rafts of new responsibilities'.

In 2010, the Conservative-Liberal Democrat coalition government restructured these arrangements and introduced Local Enterprise Partnerships (LEPs) in an attempt to reallocate resources according to smaller geographical areas centred on city regions. There have thus been corresponding changes in the ways that economic resilience has been harnessed through the impacts of governance that these changes have wrought. Seeking a transition from the existing RDAs, the government sought to use the proposals as a means to reorder the delivery of local growth and enable 'local elected-leaders' to make decisions in a devolved way. The logic of this was to re-territorialise the map of local governance according to a tripartite model incorporating local stakeholders, local economic geographies and the formation of a collaborative public–private civic leadership (SQW, 2010).

In the search for some form of regional competitiveness, the LEPs have sought to thread together public and private sector actors to pool regional knowledge and pursue a common agenda towards local economic development (Quinn, 2013). According to Meegan et al. (2014: 149), this situation has created a 'conditional and fragmented localism' in which local authorities are buttressed in a system of multilevel governance and interlocking forms of leadership. Moreover, 'regionalism' and 'localism' have become geographical buzzwords within policy circles as a means to connote devolved policies and the responsibilisation of local authorities for economic growth (Jonas, 2011; Goodwin et al., 2012; Clarke and Cochrane, 2013).

Economic resilience is moulded by the decisions made by local bodies such as the LEPs that can overcome or reinforce path dependency (Goldfinch and Hart, 2014). However, the LEPs have been noted for their frequently idiosyncratic boards and, as such, have been challenged on their effectiveness as nodal sites of social networks (Brooks et al., 2016; Deas et al., 2013; Pugalis and Townsend, 2013). Conjoined with this has been the pressure to develop regionally distinct cases to distinguish one LEP region from another in the competition for resources. By and large, the LEPs have privileged a business approach to local development and work within a sectoral model of the economy with a mandate to explore intra- and cross-sectoral collaborations. The development of sector groups has formed the most prominent strategic approach towards investment by the LEPs. While the RDAs were part of a 'regional legacy' of the New Labour era (Ayres and Pearce 2013), the LEPs are strongly embedded within the discourses of enterprise and growth and of backing 'winners' that will deliver increasing returns to the region. Within the confines of a discourse of greater effectiveness and local scale accountability, the LEPs must compete with each other for resources and inward investment (Huggins and Thompson, 2013). With the combined pressures of competitiveness at a national level and the localised economic and social issues that LEPs have been tasked to address through enterprise, there are significant questions over the effectiveness and capabilities of such arrangements to harness resilience within regions.

CIVIC LEADERSHIP AND RESILIENCE

With its roots derived from the Latin term *civicus* meaning 'of a citizen', the notion of civic leadership is not new, although the term itself only really emerged during the 1950s and 1960s and really became popular over the past decade or so (Hambleton, 2009; Hambleton and Howard, 2013). Despite the idea of civic leadership being a comparatively longstanding one, there is no universally agreed definition, although in broadest terms it is understood to refer to the work of civic-minded individuals who assume a purpose and responsibility in leading local and regional agendas.

Where civic leadership differs from more traditional forms of public leadership is evident in the distinction that Jessop (2004) draws between government and governance. The former embodies a hierarchically led, top-down mode of governing whereas the latter is a heterarchically led participatory mode of governing comprising political and non-political actors. More specifically, civic leadership can be understood in conjunction with this definition of governance as a network of collaborative governing stakeholders from the public, private and third sectors. A shift from government to governance has occurred over the 25 years, with devolution and decentralisation occurring at an ever-increasing pace. This process of degovernmentalisation has seen a wider network of stakeholders drawn into a more collaborative system of governance, which entails sharing power in the design and delivery of policies and programs (Callahan, 2007; Page 2010). Boyte (2005) describes this transformation in government as amounting to a paradigm shift in the meaning of democracy and civic agency.

Today, the relationship between civic leadership and governance is somewhat unclear. For the purpose of this chapter, civic leadership is viewed as a particular form of governance, which is legitimised in being identified in the rules as stated by meta-government. It should be noted that our contemporary understanding of civic leadership differs significantly from the original civic leadership programmes in the US. Azzam and Riggio (2003) identify *Leadership Inc.* to be one of the earliest recorded programmes, founded in Philadelphia in 1959 as a way to bring the community together and overcome the socio-economic challenges facing the community. Like many other civic leadership programmes established during the 1960s in the US as a means to manage social unrest, *Leadership Inc.* was a government-planned programme aimed at incorporating the citizens (i.e., the *civicus*) into the policy process. Whereas early examples of civic leadership were top-down initiatives, in accordance with the principles of heterarchical governance, civic leadership has increasingly become bottom-up, grassroots initiatives driven by individuals from the public, private, and third sectors through their participation in governance. Both the 1960s organisation of leadership programmes and heterarchical model share the epistemological outlook that economic capacities are shaped through a topology of key stakeholders rather than through a top-down model of governance (Bailey and Pill, 2015).

In addressing the conjoined issues of governance and resilience, it is imperative to stress the means by which the relational aspects of resilience are arranged around historical and geographical articulations. The literature on evolutionary economics – with its accompanying notions of 'path dependency' and 'path creation' – makes this point with regard to how resilience is shaped through complex interactions in heterarchical ways (Martin and Sunley, 2006; Martin and Simmie, 2008). Wolfe (2010) demonstrates this in the Canadian context by arguing that regional and public infrastructures are assembled by decisions made through heterogeneous and diverse stakeholders. Regional strategies are satiated by place-based decisions, which 'lock-in' (and 'lock out') particular capacities for governance and investment (Bailey et al., 2010).

Another point of distinction is in the formation of civic leadership. Drawing on the framework of civic leadership provided by Hambleton (2009) and Hambleton and Howard (2013), shown in Figure 9.1, three forms of leadership can be distinguished and the complex hybrid of what Alinsky (1971) refers to as 'community organising' better understood. *Political leadership* refers to those who have a political responsibility for governing (i.e., councillors or members of parliament), although work within a heterarchical system of governance as a dimension of civic

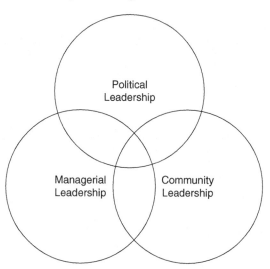

Source: Adapted from Hambleton (2009); Hambleton and Howard (2013).

Figure 9.1   A conceptual framework of civic leadership

leadership. *Managerial leadership*, which is closely tied to political leadership, refers to those individuals who work as public servants, and have professional and managerial expertise in public planning and strategy management. As part of the formal system of the government system, it follows that political leadership and managerial leadership both represent dimensions of civic leadership.

Community leadership comprises representatives from business and higher education, as well as members from religious, community, and voluntary organisations. However, its formation is more complex than 'heroic leaders' who act to shape civil society as recourse to a civic ideal (Liddle, 2012: 37). As opposed to political and managerial leaders, which are elected or employed with the remit of governing, community leadership is a secondary and predominantly unpaid role. It is beyond the scope of this chapter to distinguish whether these individuals act out of civic morality or self-interest; however, both represent valid forms of community leadership. In sum, there are immanent and diverse rationales which, while potentially unquantifiable, provide the motivation for an engagement in civic leadership.

Civic leadership is integral to understanding the ways in which regional capacities are connected in the topologies of governance and politics of localism. Hambleton and Howard (2013) note the importance of considering exogenous factors and the institutional structures that shape the capabilities of civic leadership. Civic leadership is mediated by immediate and long-range concerns for regional growth, but also by the coda and expectancies of the economic, political and social context in which is practised (Yamamoto, 2011). Responsibilities are situational and defined according to the arrangement of political, policy and personal motivations to shape economic strategies. Rossiter and Price (2013) develop this point through a 'multiple streams framework' to place local economic strategy within the streams of policy, politics and expertise. They argue that developing solutions to regional problems is dependent on the crossover of knowledge and practice from myriad organisations into the decision-making strategies of the LEP. In this sense, Rossiter and Price (2013) suggest that the ability to forge policy is shaped by contingency and the 'messiness' of practice. As the LEPs tap into the expertise of civic leaders, there is a potential disjuncture between the ideals of long-term strategising for purposes of resilience, and the realities of engaging across local and regional actors.

If civic leadership is to be effective then these three forms need to be both collaborative and coordinated if they are to develop the necessary power to serve as a purposeful mechanism of governance. Civic leadership provides a useful theorisation with which to deconstruct the institutional, managerial and political streams that underpin those who are imbricated in networks of responsibility and the direction of capacity-building.

THE INSTITUTIONAL AND POLITICAL PARAMETERS OF CIVIC LEADERSHIP IN THE SHEFFIELD CITY REGION

The Sheffield City Region (SCR) covers a broad urban milieu, which includes the city of Sheffield, Barnsley, Chesterfield, Doncaster and Rotherham, and small pockets of north Nottinghamshire. The SCR has a mixed economic history. Through much of the twentieth century, the SCR was at the fore of British industry and became an internationally renowned centre for coal, steel and manufacturing. Yet, the deindustrialisation that occurred since the 1970s has challenged the supremacy of the SCR as an industrial centre (Etherington and Jones, 2009) and also led to the stagnation of the regional economy in the 1980s (Sheffield City Region, 2006, 2010). The desire to maintain 'continuity and evolution' (Dawley et al., 2014) within an industrial region has meant that Sheffield, like many parts of the United Kingdom, has sought to regenerate its economic and social environs. It was not until the 1990s that the regenerating SCR displayed signs of economic recovery as a result of significant infrastructural investment from the public sector and European Union (EU), coupled with sustained economic restructuring premised on promoting the diversification of the economic base and promoting the SCR as a knowledge-based, economy.

From the early 1990s onward, a shift in government policy came to favour the decentralisation and devolution of government. Throughout the 1990s, the prevailing system of collaborative public management represented the interests of an increasing range of genuine public–private partnerships (Dabinett and Ramsden, 1999; Crouch and Hill, 2004). As such, the key governance challenge facing the SCR now is the development of the LEPs to enhance the industrial profile of the region and to work within a model of 'smart specialisation' that has become an accepted synonym for developing a regional niche (Peck et al., 2013; Sheffield City Region, 2013).

One of the major issues facing the strength of the civic leadership to promote economic resilience has been the institutional ecosystem in which the SCR LEP has begun to operate. The SCR has particularly struggled to define its specialist sectoral advantages. The SCR LEP has been caught between need for prioritisation (and its associated risks of picking 'winners') and a general economic and social prescription (which has the potential to test thinly spread resources and local capability) (Williams and Vorley, 2014). The SCR economy includes 54,000 small and medium-sized enterprises (SMEs) without a clear dominant sector. The LEP's own Growth Plan notes its desire to push the region's economic trajectory 'over and above specific sectors' and recognises the relative lack of clear sectoral levers (Sheffield City Region, 2014: 11). The top three priority sectors in the SCR identified by the Growth Plan were creative and digital industries (CDI), advanced manufacturing and healthcare technologies, and logistics (or 'design, develop, distribute') (Sheffield City Region, 2014). Each of these sectors, as acknowledged in the SCR LEP Growth Plan, differ in the contribution to gross value added (GVA) and employment but are seen as central to a non-sector based approach that emphasises business-to-business linkages and knowledge-based economy.

One of the striking issues stemming from the SCR's economic position is the lack of sector specialisation compared to both the former RDA region and other Yorkshire LEPs. Table 9.1 shows the priority sectors of the former Yorkshire and Humber region (Yorkshire Forward) and those LEPs that cover the former RDA region. There is understandably some overlap between the four LEPs in the former Yorkshire and Humber Region; since their formation the Leeds, York and Humber LEPs have refined the focus of their priority sectors compared to the former RDA. Of the four LEPs in the former Yorkshire and Humber region, this could be argued to be the result of the former RDA being dominated by the economic priorities of Sheffield and what has become the SCR. However, the reality – consistent with Robson (2014) – is that, much like the RDA that preceded it, the SCR LEP has failed to prioritise and continues to spread its efforts too thinly.

A significant problem for the SCR LEP is in its capability to influence long-term changes. Many of the support networks for business and skills that were coordinated by the Yorkshire Forward RDA have been lost, meaning that it is harder for the SCR authorities to act as drivers rather than as catalysts for economic development. Although LEPs potentially have the flexibility to be more effective than their RDA predecessors based on a smaller geographical location, due to their nature and form there is equal potential for problems around their capacity to influence public and private bodies, in particular in their roles as regional civic leaders and as place marketers. For example, LEPs are not defined in legislation and have no statutory role. They must work with the UK Trade and Investment (UKTI) and Chambers of Commerce, as well as local business and potential investors. Balancing these connections and actors in harmonious and functional relationships presents significant challenges for the capabilities of the LEPs to establish sustainable dialogues with other civic leaders and to present a coherent and manageable regional strategy.

Table 9.1   Priority sectors for Yorkshire LEPs and the former Yorkshire Forward RDA

Former RDA	Local enterprise partnership region	Biotechnology, pharmaceuticals inc life sciences & healthcare	ICT including software	Aerospace and defence	Manufacturing, engineering, materials, ceramics	Automotive	Chemicals	Environmental inc low carbon & energy	Marine technologies	Finance and business services	Textiles and clothing	Retail Tourism and Hospitality	Food and Drink	Construction	Logistics
Yorkshire Forward (YF)	Sheffield City Region	░	░		░		░	▓		▓		░		░	░
	Leeds City Region						░	▓		▓				░	░
	York, North Yorkshire and East Riding						░			▓			▓	░	░
	Humber						░	▓						░	░

Key:

░ Former RDA Priority Sector

▓ Current LEP *and* Former RDA Priority Sector

▒ Current LEP Priority Sector

REGIONAL RESILIENCE: LEADING LONG-TERM PLANNING AND COLLABORATION

A core element of the LEP's strategic priority for the SCR has been to encourage the proliferation of the private sector and to support small business formation. According to the strategic vision for the region noted in the Growth Plan (Sheffield City Region, 2014: 6), 'there are only three ways to create private sector growth: (1) more start-ups, (2) help grow indigenous firms, (3) attract in new firms'. However, as one respondent noted, local small firms have tended to be 'pretty much ignored' (Business Community Leader, Sheffield) within the SCR and excluded from the strategic conversations surrounding civic and economic development. The recession and its aftermath have stymied the ability of developing entre-preneurial firms and replaced jobs lost from declining industries with far reaching economic and social effects in the SCR (Sheffield First, 2013). As one respondent noted, 'we previously had a strong manufacturing base, but that is moving away . . . We need to replace those jobs and businesses' (Sheffield City Council Officer).

While the neoliberal policies of Thatcherism in the 1980s put out many of the old fires of Sheffield's manufacturing capabilities, the 'Made in Sheffield' brand has been used as a means to harness civic pride and support new firms around a common goal. Importantly, it has provided a lever for place leadership and the support of long-term policies. For example, the LEP has supported the proposal for a new Advanced Manufacturing Innovation District to be located in the Sheffield Business Park adjacent to the Advanced Manufacturing Park on the edge of the city of Sheffield. This will feature a 1.3 million square metre site for advanced manufactur-ing research. Crucially this has brought together numerous stakeholders, including local authorities, universities and private multinationals such as Rolls-Royce and Boeing. Driving this has been the articulation of a strong strategic vision through civic leadership. As one respondent noted, 'you need strong civic leadership to make things happen. You need the vision and the strategy from the top and then everyone can contribute to development . . . I think that has been pretty successful [in City Region] in the last ten years' (Economic Development Officer, Urban Area 1).

Stakeholders in the SCR place considerable emphasis on political leaders for shaping the economic resilience of the City Region. In this sense, har-nessing resilience is dominated by the 'political leadership' dimension of Hambleton and Howard's (2013) framework. Despite this emphasis, to some respondents the potential of civic leadership was overstated. Four stakeholders stated that rather than viewing leadership as the key role of public sector stakeholders, they should instead view themselves more as 'enablers', thereby allowing other stakeholders and the private sector to lead on economic development:

> Leadership is really about empowering people. We need the people of the City Region to be empowered to drive the economy forward by setting up businesses creating jobs, innovating etc.
>
> (Economic Development Consultant, Urban Area 1)

> To me, leadership is about getting out of the way and letting the private sector work. That would be really effective leadership.
>
> (Economic Development Consultant, Urban Area 4)

Typically there has been frustration with regard to how political ambitions – such as regaining office or appealing to short-term goals – has hindered an effective civic leadership and the support of economic stability and resilience. As one business official noted, 'it is still the politicians who are driving decisions, whether they are locally informed or not'. The majority of the stakeholders felt that civic leadership in SCR had a critical role in bringing different groups together and ensuring that visions are realistic and that they are delivered against. As such, a key aspect of leadership was seen to be the ability to foster effective partnership arrangements spanning across local politicians, administrators, business and the third sector. The majority of the stakeholders felt that collaboration in the SCR had been effective at points, but that more could be done to ensure that each of the Local Authorities worked together on shared strategies. As one respondent noted, 'we are looking to facilitate more collaboration. I think it works well but there are obviously ways we can improve it . . . We need to make sure that we are focused and all of the stakeholders are moving in the same direction' (Investment Manager, Urban Area 3).

The resilience of a region requires long-term policy objectives and strategies (Dawley et al., 2010), and the stakeholders all stated that long-term planning and partnership was required in order to make SCR economic development strategies effective. The short-termism that troubled the process of securing economic resilience under the RDAs (Huggins and Williams, 2011) has been a focus for LEP thinking within the SCR. With the public and private sectors working together effectively, stakeholders stated that better long-term planning would be enabled: 'the large private sector employers want to know what the long-term strategy of the city is. We have to get the leadership and vision right, and make sure that we are communicating the right messages that support our desire to grow the private sector' (Economic Development Manager, Urban Area 1).

The changes in governance brought about by the introduction of LEPs mean that long-term strategies have been disrupted with potential consequences for regional resilience. As Huggins and Williams (2011) state, continual changing of the geographic scale of intervention with every change of political administration negates from the policy patience that is vital if economic development is to be successfully nurtured. Mouawad (2009) states that City Region-level policy frameworks must be long-term in nature so that they provide certainty and stability to the range of stakeholders involved, including the private and public sectors, as their investment is essential to future economic development. The respondents noted difficulties in finding the right people to include within policy discussions but representatives from public, private and third-sector organisations have contributed to the development of the longer-term strategic plan.

Many of the stakeholders felt that the LEP would provide a test for how effective partnership working is in the City Region, as it requires the public and private sectors to work closely together. As Rossiter and Price (2013: 860) argue, 'the relative absence of executive support within LEPs has tended to mean that local authority officers have, of necessity, assumed this role in a number of LEPs'. The presence of public sector officers, often seconded to LEP teams, has provided a connective field of leadership but also inherent tensions and conflicts.

A central role of the LEP in encouraging economic resilience has been in the removal of barriers, through initiatives such as the launch of a 'Growth Hub' to serve as a facilitator in encouraging the launch of new firms and collaborations. The intention of the Growth Hub is described by the respondents as to draw together business support from the public and private sectors, with a view to provide a sustainable support service to small and large businesses alike. Some of the stakeholders stated, for example, that the LEPs would bring the different local authorities within the City Region together and that this would assist in the development of joined-up economic development strategies: 'whether the LEPs work or not remains to be seen but at least it seems to be bringing the Local Authorities together. Previously I don't think they have collaborated very much so it should help to start to focus people on what strategies are appropriate at the City Region rather than just in the individual towns and cities' (Investment Manager, Urban Area 2). As is clear from this view, the stakeholders placed emphasis on the importance of different Local Authorities within LEP areas working together to support development of City Region wide projects and opportunities. As collaborative and heterogeneous agencies, LEPs must negotiate the remit of action and present a viable agent in marrying micro- and macroeconomic demands.

Hanson (2009) states that weak business-civic leadership can allow political leaders and near-term political considerations to hold sway. The stakeholders stated that the LEP structure of local public and private sector partnership should help to ensure that long-term strategies are developed. As one stakeholder argued, 'we need to move away from short-term political thinking, and ensure that long-term needs are considered . . . We need to ensure that the next generation of school leavers, the employees and the entrepreneurs, have opportunities in the City Region by getting our strategies right now' (Economic Development Manager, Urban Area 2).

The long-term partnership approach favoured by the stakeholders, which should be inherent in effective LEPs, reflects Dawley et al.'s (2010) view of 'intelligent institutional leadership', whereby leaders can articulate the nature of external shock and enrol local and regional actors to collaborate on solutions, thereby enhancing the resilience of the City Region. Furthermore, it also reflects the need to win strong backing for new visions through effective partnership so that plans can be seen through (Hambleton and Sweeting, 2004).

In addition to the public and private partnership opportunities presented by the LEPs, many of the stakeholders stated that closer collaboration between the public and private sectors and universities was required. The stakeholders stated that links between the City Region's local authorities, chambers of commerce, private businesses and universities had not been adequately developed in the past. As one stakeholder noted 'we don't work closely enough with the universities and facilitate knowledge transfer with local businesses . . . I think the universities could be more proactive in sharing knowledge to benefit the City Region's businesses' (Economic Development Manager, Urban Area 3). Similarly there was a view that the expertise from other institutions could also be more effectively harnessed: 'we need more effective channels for taking academic expertise into businesses. It has worked really well with the Advanced Manufacturing Research Centre, but it would be good to see more going on, particularly in terms of new business sectors like digital and health industries' (Investment Manager, Public Sector Organisation).

These views echoed the perspective that effective mechanisms for transferring university-based knowledge to regional partners can bolster regional innovation and economic development (Benneworth and Charles, 2005). This may be a difficult aim for LEPs to achieve with strategic 'key' priorities having to be supported within limited resources and inter-regional competition. The diversification of stakeholders taking on civic leadership roles is therefore crucial for developing economic resilience. In order to harness these benefits, some of the stakeholders noted that the City Region's universities needed to become better at reaching out to other stakeholders: 'universities need to see the relevance of academic research and knowledge transfer and how it can benefit businesses in the City Region. Universities and other stakeholders need to get together to make it happen more effectively' (Business Development Manager, Chamber of Commerce). Indeed universities were also seen by one private-sector respondent, and echoed by others, as being weak at communicating outside of academia – 'I don't think the universities are very good at connecting with the outside world. That would have benefits for them in terms of applying research and would benefit the local economy through knowledge transfers' (Economic Development Consultant, Private Sector Organisation).

The role of universities as regional stakeholders is well versed (Goddard and Chatterton, 1999); however, in order to create more resilient regional economies, universities need to be more engaged and embedded as civic actors. Moreover, universities have a role not just as a civic actor, but as a civic leader with greater responsibility towards the society they are part of. Therefore, central to realising the wider public good of universities is renegotiating the social contract between universities and society itself (Calhoun, 2011), a social contract that for many institutions means revisiting their civic roots (Bjarnason and Coldstream, 2003). In many City Regions, fostering resilience demands universities providing intellectual leadership in developing a shared vision with other civic partners.

CONCLUSIONS

As Deas et al. (2013) point out, the reliance on subnational economies has created a myriad landscape of economic spaces, encompassing a vast swathe of cross-sectoral, public–private and quasi-state relationships. LEPs are evolving institutions (Etherington and Jones, 2016), whose role as leaders in the City Region is in formation and reliant on developing relations with local stakeholders such as universities and other creative institutions. While the focus and potential benefits of the LEPs will take time to emerge, the stakeholders emphasised that the focus should be on establishing effective governance arrangements and leadership that can address the assemblage of institutions, leaders and strategies of the City Region.

This chapter has shown that civic leadership is considered an important element in economic resilience and the ways in which local stakeholders view their institutional environments and economic cultures. However, the interpretation of what civic leadership means differs between stakeholders, with some arguing for a strong leadership in developing strategy and ensuring that other stakeholders are on-board in meeting visions. Others recommend a more non-interventionist role for local leaders, with leadership being equated with removing barriers to business start-ups and growth and allowing the private sector to flourish. Despite the divergence of views, all stakeholders agreed that whatever role was played, partnerships were key to making strategies work in the City Region, with a requirement for the private and public sector to work together more closely. Indeed, 'intelligent institutional leadership' (Dawley et al., 2010) is clearly required to enable City Regions to become (more) resilient.

In addition to the public and private sectors working together more closely, the stakeholders emphasised the need for the City Region's universities to be more active partners so that knowledge could be spread more effectively in the local economy. With LEPs still defining their role within local economic development, harnessing the full institutional capacity of a region is integral to support a diversified economic base and to support social causes that may be beyond the capabilities of LEPs and local authorities alone. The civic agenda has become more prominent within universities and the inclusion of business and third-sector organisations as leaders is important in releasing the institutional burdens of the localist policy discourses. To be successful in this respect requires the spanning of institutional boundaries across civic society, which in practice means taking a lead in working more closely with public, private and third-sector organisations. By affording opportunities to the communities of which they are part, civic-minded stakeholders are in a position to enhance regional resilience and serve as an engine of economic growth.

ADDITIONAL READING

Clarke, N. and Cochrane, A. (2013), 'Geographies and politics of localism: the localism of the United Kingdom's coalition government'. *Political Geography* **34**: 10–23.

Jonas, A.E.G. (2011), 'Region and place: regionalism in question'. *Progress in Human Geography* **36**(2): 263–272.

Williams, N. and Vorley, T. (2014), 'Economic resilience and entrepreneurship: lessons from the Sheffield City Region'. *Entrepreneurship and Regional Development* **26**: 257–281.

10. Entrepreneurship, culture and resilience: the determinants of local development in uncertain times

Robert Huggins and Piers Thompson

INTRODUCTION

The economic crisis that began in 2008 influenced economies across the globe (Courvisanos, 2009; Paunov, 2012), with certain local economies appearing to have been better placed to withstand it than others (Fingleton et al., 2012). Factors such as the need for a strong local system of innovation, underpinned by an entrepreneurial small and medium-sized enterprise (SME) sector are noted as features of resilient economies (Wennekers and Thurik, 1999; Aoyama, 2009). There is also a growing recognition that culture – both that specifically related to entrepreneurship (Beugelsdijk, 2007) and more generally that underpinning social and community activities (Tabellini, 2010) – plays a role in facilitating economic development. Little attention, however, has been paid to the extent to which entrepreneurial activities are themselves resilient in the face of economic downturns and, in particular, how entrepreneurial activities, attitudes and culture are supported by community culture at local level (Huggins and Thompson, 2016). The reliance of entrepreneurs on geographically proximate factors such as knowledge spillovers (Mattes, 2012), social capital (Davidsson and Honig, 2003; Westlund and Bolton, 2003) and markets (Thomas et al., 2013) makes it important to focus on the local places and regions, which often display considerable heterogeneity in culture, entrepreneurial and economic activities within their boundaries (Huggins and Thompson, 2016).

Persistent differences in rates of entrepreneurship may be explained in part by the underlying culture of places (Freytag and Thurik, 2007; Beugelsdijk and Maseland, 2011; Huggins and Thompson, 2012, 2015a, 2015b). Similarly, community culture may also have an effect on the entrepreneurial resilience of localities, with the prevailing societal traits of localities impacting upon the changing capacity, capability and perceptions of current or potential entrepreneurs. Such community culture refers to the broader societal traits and relations that underpin places in terms of prevailing mind-sets and the overall way of life within particular places. Understanding how aspects of community culture are associated with both the economic and entrepreneurial resilience of localities allows entrepreneurship policy to incorporate the key factors required to sustain entrepreneurial activity when it is most needed. This study, therefore, seeks to answer three research questions:

- To what extent does local entrepreneurial activity increase the resilience of local economies?
- What aspects of the community culture of local economies are associated with greater economic resilience?
- What aspects of the community culture of local economies are associated with greater entrepreneurial resilience?

Data from localities in Great Britain are used to develop a number of indices based on those elements identified within the existing literature concerning community culture (Hofstede, 1980; Schwartz, 1994). To capture the effect of the economic crisis, measures of economic and entrepreneurial resilience are investigated as changes from before the crisis (2004) and after the crisis (2010) using regression analysis.

The remainder of this chapter is structured as follows. The following section examines the literature associated with local economic resilience and the role that entrepreneurial activity plays. To achieve this, a model of the resilience of entrepreneurial activity is developed. The chapter then considers the influence that community culture may have on economic and entrepreneurial resilience. The data and methods used are outlined in the next section, with the results of the empirical analysis presented in the section that follows. The final section summarizes and draws conclusions in relation to local economic policy.

ECONOMIC RESILIENCE AND ENTREPRENEURIAL ACTIVITY

Resilience effectively has three properties in the socioecological context of local economies: the extent to which change can be experienced without the loss of structure; the degree to which an economy can reorganize; and to the degree to which it can create and sustain a capacity to learn and adapt (Hudson, 2010; Thornton et al., 2011). In an uncertain economic environment, innovative activity is likely to be promoted by diversity rather than scale within economies, which may increase the role of the

SME sector in promoting economic resilience in a local economy (Wong et al., 2005; Wennekers and Thurik, 1999; Wennekers et al., 2005). A vibrant SME sector may aid the retention of adaptability, allowing movement to a new growth phase relatively quickly (Martin and Sunley, 2011a). This suggests a positive link between entrepreneurial activity and economic resilience, as outlined below:

H1: Economic resilience will be positively related to entrepreneurial activity.

Studies have found a persistence in the rates of new firm formation linked to factors such as role models and experience of working in SMEs (Fritsch and Mueller, 2005; Mueller, 2006), implying that enterprise cultures are to some extent retained. However, as Figure 10.1 indicates, falls in aggregate demand

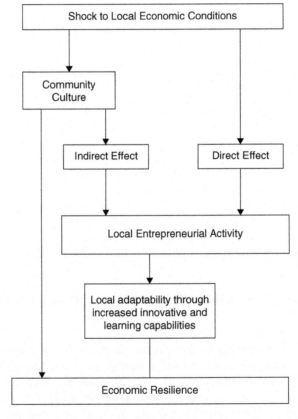

Figure 10.1   Hypothesized relationships between entrepreneurship, culture and resilience

during recessions mean that entrepreneurial activity levels may not be retained (Storey and Johnson, 1987). Culture may influence how economic shocks affect entrepreneurial activity by legitimizing and promoting certain types of entrepreneurial activities and attitudes, which are more or less well placed to withstand this reduced demand, or to exploit the opportunities that arise from the disruption of the status quo (Etzioni, 1987; Spencer and Gomez, 2004; Cowling et al., 2015). The link in Figure 10.1 from local entrepreneurial activity to local economic resilience reflects its role in limiting the employment and income effects of shocks (Simmie and Martin, 2010), and through adaptation and innovation new growth paths may be developed (Wennekers et al., 2005; Williams and Vorley, 2014). The extent to which community culture helps to retain pre-downturn entrepreneurial activity levels, therefore, determines the local economy's ability to withstand negative external shocks. This capability to retain entrepreneurial activity can be described as entrepreneurial resilience. The literature also indicates that local community culture will directly influence economic resilience by determining the level of openness to new ideas and people (Florida et al., 2008), which in turn influences the types of industries attracted and formed (Felton et al., 2010), as well as determining the level of cooperation and collaboration between existing firms and other actors (Raco, 1999).

Prior to a negative external shock, economies can be categorized by their level of entrepreneurial activity, as shown at the top of Figure 10.2. During an economic downturn local entrepreneurial activity may fall, but community culture may play a role in determining the size of this decline (as illustrated in Figure 10.1). Some localities may retain high pre-downturn entrepreneurial activity levels, with the success of the local economy being based on the enterprise culture, captured by arrow (1) in Figure 10.2. These *entrepreneurially driven* local economies are likely to be able to adapt and take advantage of new opportunities (Cowling et al., 2015). Such communities might be associated with well-connected localities in core regions with access to larger markets for both inputs and output (Fotopoulos, 2014). Other local economies, potentially in more peripheral regions, may possess the appropriate complementary community cultures, but lack access to other resources, such as infrastructure and capital (Anderson, 2000). Although some local economies may be less entrepreneurially active in the pre-downturn period, they may also incur a smaller decrease in activity, as indicated by arrow (2) linking low initial activity with high retention. These *high-potential enterprising economies* can adapt to take advantage of opportunities created by the shake-up of the recognized order.

Where entrepreneurial activity is based on strong economic conditions without a complementary community culture, entrepreneurial activity may quickly dissipate as economic conditions become more adverse. This

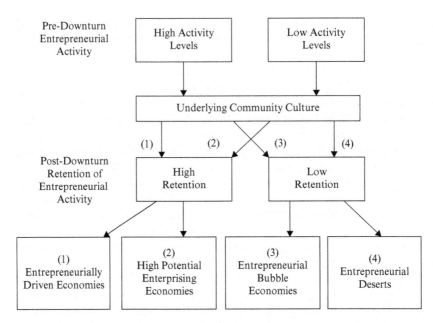

*Figure 10.2   A fourfold typology of the impact of an economic downturn
            on local entrepreneurial activity*

may be linked to the negative impact found by some studies with regard
to natural resource abundance on behaviours associated with innovation
and entrepreneurship, particularly where enterprise is imitative rather than
innovative (Papyrakis and Gerlagh, 2007; Koellinger, 2008). Initial high
levels of entrepreneurial activity in these *entrepreneurial bubble economies*
may not be retained in the local areas, as shown by arrow (3). The final
category of local economies concerns those where there is limited activity
pre-downturn, with this being quickly lost due to the lack of an appropriate community culture to sustain it. Such local areas might be those associated with more deprived neighbourhoods (Thompson et al., 2012), where
entrepreneurs are encouraged by public support and policies, but remain at
a disadvantage in terms of skills, resources and community support (Rouse
and Jayawarna, 2006). These *entrepreneurial deserts*, as shown by arrow
(4), are those economies that are likely to suffer to the greatest extent from
repeated negative shocks.

COMMUNITY CULTURE, ECONOMIC RESILIENCE AND ENTREPRENEURIAL RESILIENCE

Community culture refers to the overarching or dominant mindsets that underlie the way in which localities function; that is, the ways and means by which individuals and groups within communities interact and shape their environment (Huggins and Thompson, 2016). It is associated with the nature of social ties and interaction, as well as the nature of the morality and behavioural norms present and practiced within localities (Hayton et al., 2002). The prevailing community culture may allow the generation of trust (Putnam, 2000), reduce transaction costs (Storper, 1997), alleviate the dangers of opportunistic behaviour (Putnam, 2000), help overcome informational asymmetries (Wade, 1987), and match individual and aggregate interests (Rodríguez-Pose, 2001). Confirming the need to concentrate on the local spatial level, strong communities are often embedded in specific places (Miller, 1992; Storper, 2008; Johnstone and Lionais, 2004).

Community culture can influence entrepreneurial activity when particular characteristics associated with entrepreneurial activities are found in tandem with certain cultural traits in local communities (Spencer and Gomez, 2004; Uhlaner and Thurik, 2007). A second route is the case where a community culture legitimizes entrepreneurial activities (Etzioni, 1987; Anderson and Smith, 2007). A third route concerns a local environment where the prevailing cultural values lead to a minority group becoming excluded, causing them to seek an outlet via entrepreneurship (Hofstede et al., 2004; Noorderhaven et al., 2004). It is also likely that community culture will influence the type of entrepreneurial activity to be engaged in, either promoting or discouraging certain activities.

The community culture measures used within this study are based upon the theoretical literature of prior studies such as those of Hofstede (1980) and Schwartz (1994). Five aspects of community culture are developed below to conceptualize and operationalize the notion of community culture, these being: embracement of employment and investment in education; social cohesion; femininity and caring activities; adherence to social rules; and collective activities and attitudes (for more details see Huggins and Thompson, 2015a, 2016).

Embracement of Employment and Investment in Education

This dimension is based on the engagement of the population with employment and the investment in education required to achieve this, which is linked to Hofstede's (1980) long-term orientation dimension. This element of community culture can be expected to be associated with the resilience of a local economy given its influence on both the capacity of the locality to learn, and the long-term investment required for innovation (Beugelsdijk, 2007; Bénabou and Tirole, 2010). This generates the first hypothesis linking community culture to economic resilience:

H2a: Economic resilience will be positively related to the embracement of employment and investment in education.

Where there is a greater connection to economic production, unemployment will reduce well-being more than where worklessness is normalized (Clark, 2003; Thompson et al., 2012). Therefore, those losing their jobs may be more likely to pursue entrepreneurial activities as a refuge from unemployment:

H2b: Entrepreneurial resilience will be positively related to the embracement of employment and investment in education.

Social Cohesion

Social cohesion relates to the extent to which communities are more homogenous, closely bonded and enclosed, rather than open (Robinson, 2007). Knack and Keefer (1997) and Guiso et al. (2004) have suggested that more homogenous cohesive societies enjoy higher levels of economic development. This is attributed to the greater trust and lower transaction costs generated (Putnam, 1993). However, strongly bonded groups could be too inward-looking, limiting access to new ideas from outside the community (Florida, 2002; Levie, 2007). The importance of new ideas in times of uncertainty may mean the latter dominates in terms of economic resilience:

H3a: Economic resilience will be negatively related to the degree of social cohesion present in a community.

A number of studies have noted the role played by close family and community support in the early stages of entrepreneurial ventures (Davidsson and Honig, 2003), but Levie (2007) finds that outsiders are more likely to be entrepreneurially active. Even so, given the role played by social capital in the earliest stages of entrepreneurial development, the following hypothesis might be expected to hold:

H3b: Entrepreneurial resilience will be positively related to the degree of social cohesion present in a community.

Femininity and Caring Activities

Here feminine and caring activities capture the extent to which family and household production is undertaken by the family itself rather than being purchased through the market. It would therefore be expected that caring attitudes – diverting females away from full-time work – would be negatively linked to economic resilience:

H4a: Economic resilience will be negatively related to the feminine and caring activities present in a community.

Where more feminine and caring attitudes are present, a larger proportion of entrepreneurial activity may be associated with providing a flexible source of employment (Walker et al., 2008). With non-pecuniary motives increasing in importance, these ventures may display greater resilience. However, with alternative demands on the time of these potential entrepreneurs, they may choose to concentrate on other activities rather than start a venture (Thompson et al., 2009), leading to the following hypothesis:

H4b: Entrepreneurial resilience will be negatively related to the feminine and caring activities present in a community.

Adherence to Social Rules

Rodríguez-Pose and Storper (2006) note the importance of adherence to social rules for coordination purposes. Unchecked subversive activities could become the social norm with anti-work and anti-educational attitudes developing (Kearns and Forrest, 2000; Brennan et al., 2000). Therefore, adherence to social rules would be largely expected to boost economic resilience:

H5a: Economic resilience will be positively associated with adherence to social rules.

Entrepreneurs are often pictured as being risk-takers or risk-tolerant (Wennekers et al., 2007; Macko and Tyszka, 2009). Others indicate that entrepreneurship is a mix of science and art (Jack and Anderson, 1999), where a community culture less constrained by social norms may be of benefit (Keeble, 1989). After recessions some of the accepted rules are potentially no longer necessarily applicable (Courvisanos, 2009), so a community culture with less adherence to social rules may facilitate entrepreneurially resilient economies:

H5b: Entrepreneurial resilience will be negatively related to adherence to social rules.

Collective Actions

More individualistic systems may possess a greater propensity toward market activities (Miller, 1992), while more collective systems can create greater trust within groups (Greif, 1994; Ettlinger, 2003). Collective action is linked to a desire for equality or greater equity, which may reduce the legitimacy of activities rewarding particular individuals. More individualistic cultures may yield more resilient economies given their intrinsic capitalist propensities:

H6a: Economic resilience will be negatively related to collective actions.

Community enterprises based in a culture of collective action may be more deeply embedded, and therefore less at risk of failure than ventures whose fortunes are more reliant on global economic conditions (Tiessen, 1997; Wennekers et al., 2007). Such localities may, therefore, retain their entrepreneurial endeavours during economic downturns:

H6b: Entrepreneurial resilience will be positively related to collective actions.

DATA AND METHODS

This study examines the relationship between economic resilience and community culture, as well as entrepreneurial resilience and community culture. This allows the analysis to move one step backwards, since not only is economic resilience examined, but also the extent to which one of the key factors that determines economic resilience, entrepreneurship, is retained. To focus on the local level where community culture is likely to have its strongest influence, data is drawn from 378 of the local authority districts of Great Britain (the Isles of Scilly and the City of London are excluded due to data availability issues). Entrepreneurial activity is measured in terms of the creation of new businesses (Office for National Statistics (ONS) Business Demography publication). This data is scaled by current business stock, and new ventures created per 10,000 population. To capture the resilience of these measures, the analysis is based on the change between 2004 and 2010. Three economic outcome measures are utilized, the change in: gross value added (GVA) per head, median weekly wages and the proportion of the population claiming unemployment benefits.

Each of the cultural components outlined above are formed using the logged terms of relevant indicators to reduce the influence of outliers and skewed distributions (see Huggins and Thompson (2016) for further detail on the indicators used). Indices of each measure are formed on the basis of the UK average value. Weights ensure the main constructs within each cultural aspect are given an equal weighting.

The pre-crisis (2004) levels of entrepreneurial activity are used to consider the standard link between the adaptability of the economy and resilience (change in economic outcomes 2004–10). Second, the study considers the link between the resilience of entrepreneurial activity and economic resilience in times of crisis. Third, the community cultural aspects associated with entrepreneurial resilience are sought.

To isolate the influence of entrepreneurial activity and community culture on economic resilience, regression analysis is used. The economic resilience measures are used as dependent variables regressed upon the 2004 levels of entrepreneurial activity and the respective aspects of community culture. There are three groups of controls included. Business and innovation variables capturing growth potential include employment per 1,000 employees in: high technology manufacturing (HTM), knowledge-intensive services (KIS) and creative services (CS), as defined by van Winden and de Carvalho (2011), using Annual Business Inquiry data. Infrastructure variables capturing localities' domestic and international connections include: gross rail journeys per head (Office of Rail Regulation), being within 25 miles of a major airport (four million passengers in 2008) and within 25 miles of a primary maritime port (handling one million passengers or 25 million tonnes of freight in 2002) (Department of Transport). Industrial and environmental heritage is captured by carbon dioxide emissions per capita (AEA, 2011).

Labour force and population influences include population density, with agglomeration economies providing greater access to information and resources (Martin and Sunley, 2011b). Employment of senior managers or directors, and research and teaching professionals captures key inputs into knowledge production (Huggins and Izushi, 2007). The inclusion of the 2004 median weekly wage allows for catch-up effects.

To explore the factors influencing entrepreneurial resilience, similar regressions are run. Given the persistence of self-employment rates (Fritsch and Mueller, 2005), the proportion of small and medium-sized businesses (10–49 employees) and the self-employment rate are also included. The proportion of the population in the prime age group 35–44 years captures the need to acquire experience but still obtain a return on the investments made (Kim, 2007). Finally, the recession push effect, from the lower opportunity cost of the unemployed (Evans and Leighton,

1990), is captured by the change in unemployment over the average of the preceding five years.

RESULTS

Categorizing localities by whether aspects of community culture are above or below the national average, it is found that falls in entrepreneurial activity are greatest where communities are more homogeneous, display more feminine and caring attitudes, have greater adherence to social rules and a less extensive adoption of collective actions. In terms of economic resilience, localities that are less socially cohesive and display lower levels of femininity and caring attitudes fare more strongly (Table 10.1). GVA per capita is more resilient in those localities with less adherence to social rules and above-average collective action, but unemployment also rises to a larger extent in localities with these cultural characteristics.

Controlling for other factors, both entrepreneurial activity and community culture are found to have little influence on economic resilience as measured by the change in GVA. However, community culture displays a significant relationship with both the median wage and unemployment-based measures; and the unemployment measure is consistently associated with entrepreneurial activity (H1) (Tables 10.2 and 10.3).

When scaling entrepreneurial activity by the stock of firms (Table 10.2), it is negatively related to economic resilience. This is consistent with the importance of having a core of more established globally networked firms to complement newer businesses (Agrawal and Cockburn, 2003), especially through learning and innovation (Grant and Baden-Fuller, 2004). As the results for the other independent variables are similar regardless of the measure of entrepreneurship used, to preserve space only the key coefficients are reported in Table 10.3. When scaling by population, a negative relationship is found with the change in unemployment (Table 10.3), suggesting that entrepreneurial activity enables local economic adjustment through earnings rather than employment (Carrington et al., 1996).

In terms of community culture, economic resilience is stronger when measured by median wages and unemployment where there is a greater attachment to education and the workforce (H2a). Support is provided for H3a, with a negative link to social cohesion, suggesting that access to knowledge is important in an uncertain globalized economy (Atkinson and Kintrea, 2000). Where adherence to social rules is stricter, unemployment remains lower, with individuals potentially seeking to avoid the disapproval of others (Clark, 2003).

Turning to entrepreneurial resilience (Table 10.4), a more self-interested

Table 10.1 Average change in entrepreneurial activity and economic outcomes 2004–2010 by aspects of community culture

	Below or above UK average	Change in firm births 2004–10 (scaled by stock)	Change in firm births 2004–10 (scaled by population)	Change in GVA per capita	Change in median wages	Change in claimant count
Embracement of work and investment in education index 2004	Below	−3.06	−9.97	−0.67	0.18	1.69
	Above	−3.28	−11.32	−0.91	0.18	0.99
	t-test	0.744	1.675	0.765	0.420	11.540
		(0.457)	(0.095)	(0.444)	(0.674)	(0.000)
Social cohesion index 2004	Below	−1.86	−7.26	0.51	0.19	1.03
	Above	−3.58	−11.75	−1.20	0.18	1.40
	t-test	4.919	4.567	3.648	0.785	4.787
		(0.000)	(0.000)	(0.000)	(0.434)	(0.000)
Femininity and caring index 2004	Below	−1.97	−7.68	−0.27	0.18	1.17
	Above	−4.25	−13.40	−1.28	0.18	1.44
	t-test	8.222	7.493	3.206	0.349	4.009
		(0.000)	(0.000)	(0.001)	(0.727)	(0.000)
Risky activities and social rules index 2004	Below	−1.24	−5.85	0.39	0.19	1.55
	Above	−3.83	−12.34	−1.20	0.18	1.23
	t-test	6.889	7.393	3.868	0.780	3.524
		(0.000)	(0.000)	(0.000)	(0.436)	(0.001)
Collective action and equality index 2004	Below	−3.56	−12.32	−1.15	0.18	1.16
	Above	−2.63	−8.41	−0.31	0.18	1.52
	t-test	2.954	4.837	2.600	0.804	5.032
		(0.003)	(0.000)	(0.010)	(0.422)	(0.000)

Note: p-values in parentheses

Table 10.2   Factors influencing economic resilience (entrepreneurial activity scaled by existing business stock)

	Change in GVA per capita	Change in median wage	Change in claimant count
Entrepreneurship			
Firm births as a proportion of the business stock 2004	−0.1027 (0.086)	0.0016 (0.235)	0.0531 (0.000)
Community culture			
Likelihood ratio test	4.0 [5] (0.555)	14.5 [5] (0.013)	56.7 [5] (0.000)
Embracement of work and investment in education	−0.0181 (0.351)	0.0014 (0.002)	−0.0139 (0.000)
Social cohesion	0.0123 (0.633)	0.0010 (0.099)	0.0199 (0.000)
Feminine and caring activities	−0.0585 (0.141)	−0.0007 (0.455)	0.0034 (0.641)
Adherence to social rules	−0.0015 (0.607)	0.0000 (0.466)	−0.0020 (0.000)
Collective action	−0.0023 (0.796)	−0.0001 (0.714)	−0.0013 (0.429)
Business/innovation activities			
High technology manufacturing	0.0016 (0.704)	−0.0001 (0.231)	0.0014 (0.073)
Knowledge-intensive services	0.0098 (0.033)	0.0001 (0.276)	0.0013 (0.113)
Creative services	−0.0018 (0.635)	0.0002 (0.030)	0.0012 (0.083)
Infrastructure and Industry			
CO_2 emissions per capita	0.0217 (0.355)	0.0004 (0.458)	0.0041 (0.338)
Rail connections (journeys per capita)	0.0015 (0.738)	0.0003 (0.002)	−0.0011 (0.173)
Major airport	−0.8539 (0.009)	0.0120 (0.108)	0.1397 (0.020)
Primary maritime port	0.7703 (0.013)	0.0124 (0.081)	−0.1534 (0.007)

Table 10.2 (continued)

	Change in GVA per capita	Change in median wage	Change in claimant count
Population and labour force			
Population density	0.0006	0.0000	0.0000
	(0.000)	(0.953)	(0.703)
Proportion of workforce employed as managers	0.0195	0.0040	−0.0136
	(0.815)	(0.037)	(0.374)
Proportion of workforce employed as professionals	0.0724	0.0045	−0.0311
	(0.134)	(0.000)	(0.000)
Log of median wages	−0.0019	−0.4425	−0.4874
	(0.999)	(0.000)	(0.091)
Constant	4.4224	2.5024	3.2657
	(0.668)	(0.000)	(0.085)
N	378	378	378
*R*²	0.258	0.345	0.490
F-test	7.4	11.2	20.4
	(0.000)	(0.000)	(0.000)

Note: p-values in parentheses.

masculine approach is positively associated with entrepreneurial activity (H4b), especially in periods of economic hardship (Walker and Brown, 2004; Walker et al., 2008). Adherence to social rules potentially restricts creativity (Keeble, 1989; Jack and Anderson, 1999), so entrepreneurship may be an outlet for the dissatisfied (Hofstede et al., 2004; Noorderhaven et al., 2004) (H5b). However, a collective, rather than an atomistic, culture also sustains entrepreneurial activity (H6b).

There is no support for H3b; that is, social capital aids entrepreneurial resilience (Davidsson and Honig, 2003). Rather, there is weak evidence that new ideas and people are important (Levie, 2007; Florida, 2002). Equally, the absence of an influence from engagement with education and work (H2b) indicates that mainstream labour force investments are less supportive of entrepreneurial activity.

Table 10.3   Factors influencing economic resilience (entrepreneurial activity scale by population)

	Change in GVA per capita	Change in median wage	Change in claimant count
Entrepreneurship			
Firm births per 10,000	−0.0012	0.0000	−0.0055
population	(0.926)	(0.988)	(0.025)
Community culture			
Likelihood ratio test	4.4	13.1	49.0
	[5]	[5]	[5]
	(0.499)	(0.022)	(0.000)
Embracement of work and	−0.0138	0.0013	−0.0164
investment in education	(0.473)	(0.004)	(0.000)
Social cohesion	0.0186	0.0009	0.0152
	(0.471)	(0.139)	(0.002)
Feminine and caring activities	−0.0690	−0.0005	0.0105
	(0.081)	(0.575)	(0.157)
Adherence to social rules	−0.0010	−0.0001	−0.0019
	(0.740)	(0.417)	(0.001)
Collective action	−0.0001	−0.0001	−0.0029
	(0.987)	(0.587)	(0.078)
N	378	378	378
R^2	0.252	0.342	0.464
F-test	7.2	11.0	18.4

Note: p-values in parenthesis.

DISCUSSION AND CONCLUSIONS

The lack of significant relationships in Table 10.2 suggests that entrepreneurship is only one element of the resources required to develop economic resilience, and may even lessen this resilience if it is heavily relied upon in isolation to other factors. This could have far-reaching consequences for localities that pursue policies to promote entrepreneurship, particularly if not supported by an appropriate community culture. The findings suggest that there is a link between some aspects of community culture and both economic and entrepreneurial resilience. In particular, a negative influence from social cohesion and adherence to social rules means that there is support for entrepreneurs being pattern-breakers, with access to new ideas being of greater significance than bonding social capital.

Table 10.4   Change in entrepreneurial activity

	Ventures created (percentage of business stock)	Ventures created (per 10,000 population)
Community culture		
Likelihood ratio test	45.9	37.1
	[5]	[5]
	(0.000)	(0.000)
Embracement of work and investment in education	0.0242	0.0491
	(0.136)	(0.241)
Social cohesion	−0.0227	−0.1114
	(0.328)	(0.063)
Feminine and caring activities	−0.1619	−0.2018
	(0.000)	(0.038)
Adherence to social rules	−0.0034	−0.0209
	(0.199)	(0.003)
Collective action	0.0308	0.0620
	(0.000)	(0.003)
Business/innovation activities		
High-technology manufacturing	−0.0135	−0.0206
	(0.000)	(0.031)
Knowledge-intensive services	0.0111	0.0167
	(0.008)	(0.118)
Creative services	0.0048	0.0094
	(0.160)	(0.286)
Small and medium-sized enterprises (10–49 employees)	0.0135	−0.0073
	(0.065)	(0.697)
Self-employment	−0.0594	−0.5758
	(0.438)	(0.004)
Infrastructure and industry		
CO_2 emissions per capita	0.0193	−0.0410
	(0.357)	(0.448)
Rail connections (journeys per capita)	0.0023	−0.0230
	(0.574)	(0.028)
Major airport	0.5518	1.8319
	(0.065)	(0.017)
Primary maritime port	−0.0192	1.6297
	(0.944)	(0.021)
Population and labour force		
Population density	−0.0005	−0.0011
	(0.000)	(0.000)

Table 10.4   (continued)

	Ventures created (percentage of business stock)	Ventures created (per 10,000 population)
Proportion in prime age group	−0.2077	0.3947
	(0.182)	(0.324)
Log of median wages	1.8395	11.4647
	(0.196)	(0.002)
Change in unemployment over five-year average	1.4666	4.9294
	(0.001)	(0.000)
Constant	−0.3758	−61.4686
	(0.969)	(0.013)
N	378	378
R^2	0.364	0.436
F-test	11.4	15.4
	(0.000)	(0.000)

Note: p-values in parenthesis.

Positively, for those localities with less market-driven individualistic perspectives (and often perceived to be lagging in development terms), collective action supports entrepreneurial resilience, which means that such localities may not be handicapped in recovering from negative shocks. Feminine and caring activities reduce entrepreneurial resilience, which puts local policymakers in a difficult position as efforts to increase ethical business practices (El Harbi and Anderson, 2011; Paunov, 2012), and build communities may have benefits in broader well-being terms. Such development is often seen as important for less prosperous neighbourhoods and localities looking to recover, but is shown to negatively impact upon resilience.

It appears to be the case that different routes are open to achieving entrepreneurial resilience through risk-taking and creative mould-breaking (Johnstone and Lionais, 2004; Macko and Tyszka, 2009), as well as the efforts of collective, networked and civically engaged entrepreneurs (Guiso et al., 2004). Clearly, it is hard for governments to influence culture (Robinson, 2007; Rodríguez-Pose and Storper, 2006), but creating the correct institutional environment may encourage desired behaviour that becomes reinforced over time within the community culture of localities. The education system will play a key role in generating entrepreneurs and more generally a workforce better placed to exploit new knowledge sources. Part of this process might require the use of role models to increase the exposure of local communities to those with differing viewpoints and ideas. Decision-makers, therefore, should try to develop more open community cultures, as well as allowing local resources to be pooled and accessed for the greatest benefit of the population.

Future research may be able to shed more light on the correct actions to be taken. Ideally, future work will use measures relating not only to actions, but also attitudes. It is unclear whether the Great Recession is typical of previous economic downturns in terms of entrepreneurial resilience and the effect of community culture upon this resilience, so exploring other recessions would help plan for future downturns of differing natures, especially in terms of their duration, primary causes and severity. Some impacts of the recession are still apparent and longitudinal analysis would aid a deeper understanding of underlying causes and connections across these causes.

ADDITIONAL READING

Beugelsdijk, S. and Maseland, R. (2011), *Culture in Economics: History, Methodological Reflections and Contemporary Applications.* Cambridge: Cambridge University Press.

Huggins, R. and Thompson, P. (2015), 'Culture and place-based development: a socio-economic analysis'. *Regional Studies* **49**(1): 130–159.

Huggins, R. and Thompson, P. (2016), 'Socio-spatial culture and entrepreneurship: some theoretical and empirical observations'. *Economic Geography* **92**(3): 269–300.

11. The resilience of growth strategies

Lee Pugalis, Nick Gray and Alan Townsend

INTRODUCTION

Particularly marked since the onset of the global credit crunch, a pervasive economic growth narrative has inflected political and policy rationalities as nations, regions and cities have attempted to 'bounce back' from recessions as well as contend with other crises, such as the European sovereign debt crisis and the Syrian refugee crisis. Given that '[e]conomic resilience research is primarily concerned with how [places] adapt to exogenous shocks' (Brooks et al., 2016: 1), it is not so surprising that the national and international economic shocks engendered by the Global Financial Crisis of 2007–8 have spawned an extensive range of studies investigating the phenomenon of economic resilience. This has stimulated new conceptual debates at the interface between those concerned with economic resilience and economic growth (Cowell, 2013; Dawley et al., 2010). Yet, 'despite this growing interest, there remains a lack of research on the importance of governance for creating and managing more resilient localities' (Brooks et al., 2016: 1). Governing through partnerships – often involving public, private and voluntary sectors actors – with the goal of developing local economies has become *de rigueur* over recent decades (Bailey et al., 1996; Le Feuvre et al., 2016; Pugalis, 2012), especially in a context of fiscal purging and public sector austerity.

One important activity associated with the role of economic partnerships and governance is the production of economic strategies. These strategies typically come under various different labels and guises, such as regeneration frameworks, growth plans, economic development strategies and, more recently, 'economic resilience toolkits'. Such strategies are often deployed by economic partnerships as a primary governance device. They are commonly utilised to help attain broad stakeholder 'buy in' to a strategic vision, through short-, medium- and long-term priorities and deliverable actions. Thus, we take a broad view of economic strategies as being as much about governing processes and ways of working as they are about the documents per se. Put another way, the production of economic strategies is a process that is not necessarily complete at the point at which a plan is published, neither do economic strategies necessarily require the codification of prioritised activities in the guise of a written document. Nevertheless, the instrumental roles often performed by codified statements should not be discounted.

In this chapter we explore the manner with which growth strategies reflect different understandings of resilience through the case of local and regional economic development practice in England since the Global Financial Crisis. In particular, we examine Local Enterprise Partnerships (LEPs) that were established at a subnational level during 2010 and 2011 to plan for growth and lead recovery in their regions and localities. LEPs, intended to be agile, entrepreneurial and 'fleet-of-foot' collaborative entities (Pugalis et al., 2014), are emblematic of a 'rise of fragmentary, impermanent governance and funding structures' (Haughton and Allmendinger, 2008: 138). As key (yet precarious) governance institutions promoting local growth, these voluntaristic, business-led, multi-actor partnerships have recently prepared Strategic Economic Plans (SEPs).[1] These plans are part strategic and part bidding document, driven by a boosterist policy narrative of 'going for growth' (Pugalis et al., 2016). Nevertheless, with many LEPs preoccupied with 'bouncing back' from the job losses and economic contraction experienced under the geographically uneven repercussions of the Global Financial Crisis, the notion of economic resilience has also influenced the thinking of LEPs.

In view of Martin's affirmation that 'economic governance arrangements shape the resistance and response of a region's economy to, and its recovery from, a shock' (Martin, 2012: 13), together with our contention that strategies are a key technique of governance, this chapter provides an examination of the 'resilience' of growth strategies. After Pendall et al. (2010), our purpose is to identify how particular 'regional stresses' relate to and influence the mobilisation and deployment of a particular 'resilience framework'. First, we review resilience as a fuzzy concept and consider its relevance to economic development. Second, we briefly chart the impact of the recession, the nature of the recovery and the emergence of LEP growth plans. Third, we consider how notions of resilience have permeated growth plans, by analysing their foci, priorities and content. This analysis is derived from a larger project, which examined all 38 SEPs produced and involved interviews with key LEP stakeholders (for further details about the research approach and findings, see Pugalis and Townsend, 2014; Pugalis et al., 2015, 2016).

RESILIENCE: A FUZZY CONCEPT

'Resilience' as a concept in the social sciences and regional studies is the subject of ongoing debate (see, for example, Bailey and Turok 2016), particularly in the context of a renewed deeper interest in the effects of economic recession and of recovery in the wake of the economic upheaval over the past decade (Martin et al., 2016). Despite an acknowledged fuzziness associated with the notion of 'resilience', recent research leads us to consider its value in helping us better to understand regional economic change (Martin and Sunley, 2015; Pendall et al., 2010; Williams et al., 2013).

The resilience metaphor is associated with a diverse range of epistemic communities and disciplines, including ecology, economics, disaster studies, geography, political science, psychology and economics (Pendall et al., 2010). Over recent years it has gained scholarly traction in the fields of local economic development, entrepreneurship, planning and regional studies (White and O'Hare, 2014; Williams et al., 2013), among others, and has arguably become a new motif in policy circles. For example, it is now common practice for councils to produce 'economic resilience toolkits' and plans for 'building' resilient communities. Indeed, the rise of a discourse of resilience parallels the demise of a discourse of regeneration (Pugalis, 2016).

A variety of structural conditions and determinants are considered to be important to the resilience of a region, such as the constitution of its business base, sectoral composition, business productivity, technological profile, labour force characteristics and skills base, and inter-firm networking and partnership working (see, for example, Pendall et al., 2010). In policy terms, 'economic resilience' is now regularly invoked in economic development circles and is often utilised in a manner that is consistent with the 'working definition' of resilience employed by IPPR North: 'the ability of an economy to adapt, both to shocks and to long-term changes' (Cox et al., 2014: 1). This would imply that resilience is as much about processes as it is as about determinants. As Dawley et al. (2010) note, regional resilience is not a permanent characteristic but rather a dynamic process.

White and O'Hare (2014) contend that there has been an opaque political treatment of the concept by policymakers, who have generally failed to recognise the nuances that distinguish understandings of 'equilibrium resilience' and 'evolutionary resilience'. The outcome, they argue, is a privileging of a return to the norm (an equilibrist interpretation), which reduces opportunities for a transformative, evolutionary interpretation. The deployment of the new grammar of resilience can also be understood as being framed by broader techno-managerial trends that pursue a narrow range of conservative concerns and reactive measures (Raco and Street, 2012; White and O'Hare, 2014). It is in this sense that the possibilities of a progressive paradigm shift should be tempered by practical experience, which underpins existing behaviour framed by neoliberal ideologies (Raco and Street, 2012; White and O'Hare, 2014). Some refer to this as 'conservative' resilience (Raco and Street, 2012).

Based on a review of relevant literature, we can identify at least three distinctive interpretations of the notion of resilience relevant to the field of local and regional development:

- 'Equilibrium' or 'conservative' resilience – denoting business as usual following the 'bounce-back' from shocks; a return to conditions before a shock (Martin and Sunley, 2015; Pendall et al., 2010; Raco and Street, 2012; White and O'Hare, 2014).
- 'Persistent' and 'resistant' resilience – the ability of people, communities or ecosystems to thrive despite adversity (Andres and Round, 2015; Martin, 2012; Pendall et al., 2010).
- 'Evolutionary resilience' – a complex systems and multidimensional perspective of transformation, adaptation and reorientation (Bristow and Healy, 2015; Martin, 2012; Pendall et al., 2010; White and O'Hare, 2014).

Differing interpretations of the concept lead Martin (2012) to identify and subsequently develop (e.g., Martin and Sunley, 2015; Martin et al., 2016) four interrelated dimensions of resilience. *Resistance* refers to a region's ability to resist disruptive shocks in the first instance. A region's *recovery* from a shock is vital given that a deep downturn may lead to hysteresis effects that prevent *renewal* of trend growth, and result in a permanent post-shock downward shift in a region's growth path. Regional difference in reaction and recovery to recession may have long-lasting effects, with those places that bounce back and ever reorientate their economies in response to a crisis more likely to emerge stronger. In this respect, *reorientation* is crucial, which describes a positive hysteresis effect in which, rather than a simple return to 'normal', a shock accelerates structural change in an economy.

These dimensions raise questions of what accounts for differences across them and across regions' overall resilience. Explanations are numerous but are likely to include endogenous, relational and historical factors – three fields that Martin et al. (2016) identify as key to future research. Endogenous factors are likely to include political/institutional culture and industrial structure where, for example, in the past northern regions of England have been reliant upon sometimes uncompetitive manufacturing and primary industries that have been prone to cyclical fluctuations. A region's relationship to other places in the wider socio-economic system is also vital; for example, in relation to the kind of policy response to recession favoured by national government, or in the sense of a place's functional specialisation within a national economy. History is important in that resilience is a dynamic process – factors that influence it may change – shaped by ongoing structural change in the economy as well as sudden shocks. Importantly, recessions and recovery shape places, thus the study of resilience is vital in understanding spatial disparities.

A key weakness stemming from the fuzziness of the concept is that almost anything other than complete annihilation of a city or region could be interpreted as resilience. Classic economic theory of spatial adjustment would see an economically struggling place losing population until income and employment stabilised, and we can interpret this as resilience (Dubé and Polèse, 2015). In this sense, timescales are important; Polèse (2009) has argued that Detroit is likely to be deemed resilient at some point in the future. Thus, the notion of resilience is situational.

THE EMERGENCE OF LEPS IN RECESSION CONDITIONS

In the midst of responding to the economic crisis starting in 2008, statutory Regional Development Agencies were abolished in 2012, when voluntary partnerships between leaders of place, including elected local politicians and unelected business members, known as LEPs, were created (Bentley et al., 2017). LEPs are part of the institutional and policy architecture that has been re-geared for growth. A premium has been placed on LEPs delivering tangible economic results during austere economic times (Pugalis and Bentley, 2014) entraining the commercial input, business experience and entrepreneurialism of private sector partners. These partnerships were intended to be based on new spatial imaginaries distinct from and smaller than those of the 'redundant' administrative regions of England, together with an explicit preference for partnership configurations to reflect 'natural economic geographies' (Cable and Pickles, 2010). Implicitly, there was an assumption by central government that this would equip places to be more resilient to the vagaries of global capitalism.

Paralleling the demise of RDAs was the revocation of emergent Regional Strategies, which were intended to bring together Regional Spatial Strategies and Regional Economic Strategies. Thus, extant long-term strategies were 'disrupted' (Brooks et al., 2016: 13). Since this time, the development of SEPs provided all LEPs with an opportunity to reflect on their priorities and reformulate existing plans into a long-term, coherent strategy.

According to the government, SEPs are intended to be 'multi-year plans for local growth', which, alongside a vision statement and priorities, should include a 'high-level investment plan' (HM Treasury and Business Innovation and Skills, 2013). Nevertheless:

> It is fair to say that the government has never directed LEPs to address matters of wider economic resilience, but given the permissive nature of the governmental guidance by which they were formed, LEPs have had the freedom to develop growth plans that address both narrow concepts of productivity growth as well as wider ideas of local economic resilience, should they choose to.
>
> (Cox et al., 2014: 1)

Remembering the time lag between devising strategies and the stimulation (or not) of investment and jobs on the ground, a record of the performance of areas of England through the impacts of the full cycle of recession and recovery is primarily of importance in shaping understanding of the issues faced by, and the outlook of, different LEPs. As shown in Table 11.1, employment in England outside London ('Rest of England') was continuing to fall until 2011, which was coincidentally the year of many LEPs being launched; employment recovery that accelerated after that is generally attributed to the cumulative effect of national economic policy interventions, such as ongoing loose monetary policy and assistance to housing finance.

Table 11.1   Typology of LEP areas' experience of recession

Index figures	*All Employment by Workplace, Annual Population Survey*					
12 months ending September	Capital City	Rest of England	Secular Decline	Minimum Rebound	Industrial City	Exit Velocity
2005	94.3	98.3	102.7	95.6	99.5	96.2
2008	100	100	100	100	100	100
2009	100.5	98.2	99.5	96.7	95.8	99.6
2010	101.1	97.5	98.8	91.9	97.2	99.1
2011	102.2	97.4	95.3	94.6	97.1	96.9
2013	108	98.1	98.2	88.5	97.9	94.3
2015	114.4	101.7	98.2	100.6	106.2	107.8
2016	118.6	102.6	97.9	100.2	105.8	107.2

Key: data are for all Employment age 16–64, attributed to Workplaces, and including self-employed, 'flexible' and part-time staff; this is especially important in comparing this record with others for London. Sample error is greater for places with smaller numbers employed, which are shown for the latest available date, year-ending September, 2016.

Previously, the effect of recessions has been assessed only at the regional scale. Martin et al. (2016) show a positive relationship between resistance to and recovery from recessions from the 1970s to 2014, i.e., that there are certain regions – the south-east, south-west and east of England – that tend to recover strongly, relative to the national economy, regardless of their resistance to recession; this was certainly the case in 2008–14, with the addition of London (the Greater London Council area) to the most resilient regions.

This chapter is able to analyse employment over those years by LEP areas from the Annual Population Survey, with its key inclusion of self-employment which became very important in recovery from this last recession (Townsend and Champion, 2014). The data are for 12-month periods for years-ending September by workplace, including the balance of inward commuters: on this basis, London experienced only a heavy slowing of employment growth in the period, and can thus be considered fully resistant to recession, unique among LEP areas.

The full dataset shows much more variation than might be expected from regional data.

The trough levels of employment among the full range of LEPs are spread out over each of the years 2009–15. As might be expected, the number of LEP minima peaked in 2010–11, in 11 areas compared with eight in 2008–9, the first 12-month period affected by recession.

Those LEP areas that suffered most from the first impacts of recession in 2008–9 (but that showed higher employment figures in all later years) included the large south-east LEP, together with those of Greater Manchester and Greater Birmingham with Solihull. Although this category includes two of the seven City Regions of provincial England, there is no evidence for the often-implied suggestion that these latter areas 'performed better' economically than the rest of England (Champion and Townsend, 2013).

Table 11.1 comprises an approximate typology of LEP areas according to their experience of recession, identifying 'Industrial City' with Greater Birmingham with Solihull, with poor resistance to recession but good recovery from it. 'Minimum Rebound' exemplifies the situation of Stoke-on-Trent and Staffordshire LEP, which had barely recovered at all from deep recession by 2015, similar to several LEP areas, a kind of 'conservative resilience'. On the other hand the buoyancy of areas in the south is shown by the high 'Exit Velocity' of the Swindon and Wiltshire LEP, which showed rapid growth over the last two years of the record. It should be noted that the recorded growth of 41,000 jobs in that area over two years is to be regarded as 'complex'; it was spread across the full range of economic sectors, chiefly in services apart from 9,700 in construction and only 2,000 in manufacturing; that is, in sectors which a LEP would not have created or forecast.

Lastly, however, Table 11.1 records areas in 'secular decline', with Tees Valley standing also for the Black Country LEP in ending the whole ten-year period with fewer jobs than it started with, in both cases reflecting the fate of a key type of place, industrial areas that lack a full share of the modern service sector, through location near major service centres. This further supports Martin et al. (2016: 571) in stating there is evidence of an inverse relationship between 'cyclical sensitivity and growth' because those sectors with the highest long-term average growth rates tend to be the least cyclically sensitive.

TREATMENT OF RESILIENCE IN STRATEGIC ECONOMIC PLANS

This section analyses how the geographically uneven experiences of economic crises, alongside the recent popularisation of the notion of economic resilience, have influenced local and regional economic development plans in England. To facilitate an analysis of the resilience of SEPs, IPPR North developed a 'LEP resilience framework', derived from extant theory and research, which was an 'attempt to bridge the gap between conceptual thinking on resilience and local policymaking on the ground' (Cox et al., 2014: 2). Consistent with our own analysis (see, for example, Bulkens et al., 2015), the study 'found huge variation in the nature, length and thoroughness of strategic economic plans and growth plans' (Cox et al., 2014: 2). They conclude that:

> With few exceptions, no LEPs appear to be taking a systematic approach to building economic resilience. A handful have worked up plans around one or two resilience issues; some include a liberal scattering of key buzzwords on the topic; but for most, issues of resilience are of second-order importance to the primary task of driving high-value productivity growth.
>
> (Cox et al., 2014: 39).

While the IPPR North research is limited to a content analysis of LEPs' formative plans, our own body of research, in addition to analysing SEPs, has also investigated the role of LEPs more broadly, including interviews with stakeholders that help to explain the processes that informed the nature of SEPs. In the remainder of this section we analyse the resilience of SEPs in terms of the three distinct interpretations of resilience derived from extant literation, namely 'conservative resilience', 'resistant resilience' and 'evolutionary resilience'.

Conservative Resilience

Interviews with LEP stakeholders revealed the instrumental role performed by central government in shaping the nature and content of SEPs, which was not immediately apparent in the light-touch guidance that they issued (HM Government, 2013). SEPs' focus and content were significantly influenced by departmental contributions to the Local Growth Fund; in particular a large proportion of spend was from Department for Transport and ring-fenced. In some instances, LEPs were dissuaded from being innovative or radical as they were advised and, even, instructed to concentrate on 'shovel-ready' projects, which were available to spend monies set-aside in the Local Growth Fund; 'what about 2015?' was the question asked by civil servants of one LEP in the south of England after it had submitted what it considered a long-term development strategy. Consequently, many SEPs resemble more traditional economic development strategies and make only a very conservative attempt to produce resilient regions and localities. Similarly, many LEPs were preoccupied with pursuing scarce resources, and this is reflected in many SEPs' identity as essentially bidding documents. A private-sector interviewee suggested their local LEP tended just to be reactive to funding opportunities; bidding for whatever funding stream became available irrespective of its fit with stated long-term strategy, resulting in less energy directed towards endogenous growth and small businesses.

Interviewees were critical of the SEP process and time frame, and the limited clarity from central government; 'changing of goal posts' as one interviewee referred it: '[Central government] weren't very clear on the requirements around the SEP, the Strategic Economic Plans, and what was supposed to be in them ... most LEPs were holding back on finalising how they might present some of this stuff' (LEP in the Midlands) until the final government guidance was issued. However, this guidance never materialised.

Most LEPs were concerned with returning to a normal growth trajectory; 'bouncing back' from the downturn rather than the more fundamental transformation conveyed in the notion of 'evolutionary resilience'. The rhetoric of resilience in the majority of SEPs is couched within a growth-first outlook, which 'leaves them open to being subsumed into a definition of economic competitiveness' (Cox et al., 2014: 13).

Given that LEPs are intended to operate within functional economic areas, most SEPs are predominantly inward-looking and concerned with local authority boundaries. Even the 21 SEPs that sought to prioritise locations for growth and development tended to 'share' locational priorities and projects across all the component local authority areas. Thus, it can appear that every location is a priority for growth. Furthermore, the preoccupation with internal matter suggests a narrower, conservative approach to resilience rather than a more relational understanding emphasised by Martin et al. (2016). For example, 11 SEPs made only passing reference to their LEP's place in the wider global economy.

Given that LEPs were asked to devise plans derived from local priorities – ostensibly contingent upon place-based histories and modes of cooperation, assets, opportunities, challenges, barriers and risks – there is a remarkable degree of similarity across SEPs. One LEP officer, who had read several SEPs, described them as 'uninspiring'. The same, generic priorities were evident across the 38 SEPs. For example, improving transport infrastructure and connectivity featured in all, encouraging, stimulating and supporting new enterprises, business start-ups and entrepreneurs featured in all but one, as did increasing the employment rate and upgrading adult/workforce skills. However, there is greater divergence in LEPs' treatment of these priorities. Some SEPs outline priorities in very simple terms and are less concerned with justifications or explanations, whereas others opt for a more nuanced narrative and/or draw upon different strands of evidence.[2] Government guidance set out that LEPs should 'evidence' the deliverability, capacity and risks of their plans. However, central government took an extremely conservative view, particularly in terms of risks.

Resistant Resilience

Some LEPs involve stakeholders that are well versed in the art of development in adverse conditions, for example those northern areas that have had to be 'resistant' to industrial decline over several decades. This narrative of resistance can interact with the more conservative understanding in that policymakers in persistently struggling areas may see more expansive policy as a luxury. In this sense, 'safeguarding' jobs was identified as an objective by some LEPs. Other LEPs demonstrate a 'persistent' form of resilience in their governance and composition. While LEPs were officially established during 2010 and 2011, some of these entities are derived from longstanding partnerships. The cases of the Black Country, Greater Manchester and Tees Valley demonstrate such persistence, and resistance to state-led rescaling.

There was little recognition in SEPs of the benefits and lessons that could be derived from place-based communities and communities of practice that have successfully developed 'resistant' modes of resilience. While central government had been clear that SEPs should identify and set out to address 'market failure', and that plans should be based on a rigorous understanding of the area's competitive advantage and unique combination of strengths and challenges, there was little acknowledgement of the entrenched nature of some 'market failures'. While 36 of the 38 SEPs provide a clear articulation of the economic role of particular places (for example, opportunity areas, transport nodes and strategic employment areas) critical analysis of their resilience was less common.

Some LEP stakeholders were fully aware of the deficiencies of LEPs and attributed this to a combination of factors, including confusion created by central government and limited capacity, expertise and experience. The differences across LEPs – in terms of disparities in staffing levels and expertise, institutional support and partner support – are an important factor that has inevitably influenced the shape and rigour of SEPs. Discussions with stakeholders of one LEP, which to date had 'survived' with the support of one full-time member of staff, indicated that the role of some LEPs is likely to be particularly limited.

Evolutionary Resilience

Perhaps owing to its complexity and multiple dimensions, evolutionary resilience has had limited policy uptake in local and regional development practice to date: while SEPs are fond of identifying 'transformational' projects, these are usually capital-intensive physical development projects, such as major infrastructure improvements. Considering that 'rebalancing' was a key trope utilised by central government, it is surprising that 'rebalancing' is entirely absent in five SEPs. Reflecting their inward-looking disposition, 16 SEPs set out to rebalance development and wealth within their borders. Twelve SEPs referred to a public sector to private sector shift in employment, whereas only one SEP recognised the need to reduce their reliance on the financial sector of their local economy.

Analysing each SEP as a whole, we differentiate between 15 that are more akin to business plans or bidding documents and 23 that are more akin to plans for the area. The key distinction is that the former are a plan for the *LEP*, whereas the latter are a plan for the *area*. The difference between these two predominant types of plans is important for the way in which SEPs will evolve, as they may pass through future iterations that will also influence the precise roles of particular LEPs and how they are perceived. Thus, some SEPs provide a platform to adapt and evolve over time into more nuanced strategies more likely to engage with ideas of economic reorientation.

LEPs, including specifically local authority members, were encouraged to outline their plans for effective pooling of economic development and planning activities, including co-aligned programmes, the alignment of or joint preparation of local plans, and shared teams. Government guidance did specify that LEPs should take account of capacity, constraints, risks and dependencies when preparing their plans (HM Government, 2013), however this was largely read to relate to projects identified in implementation and delivery plans.

From the outset, partnership working has been at the heart of LEPs; as one minister put it, 'Who better to understand the needs of a community than its business leaders, its entrepreneurs and its residents?' (Prisk, 2011). However, a premium has been placed on business 'nous' and commercial acumen, with less emphasis given to broader societal interests. This can be seen in the narrowly designed consultation exercises that may explain, in part, why many SEPs fail to account for social, economic and environmental complexities and dynamic interactions. Thus, while some of the most robust SEPs make reference to environmental factors, these are primarily perceived as 'assets' to be protected or exploited for economic ends.

Clearly guided by central government advice, most SEPs referred to effective LEP partnership working, although only 27 substantiated such claims. Thirty SEPs provided a reasonably strong account of their relationships with local business, whereas less than a third provided a similar account of their relationships with the broader community. Some SEPs and their LEPs appear to be isolated, from other processes. The degree to which SEPs were informed by a broad range of stakeholders is an important feature of resilience, particularly from a process-based understanding.

An ecosystems view of regions, whereby different social, economic and environmental processes and systems interact and relate to one another, was absent in the thinking underpinning the development of SEPs. Interviews revealed central government officials had cautioned against LEPs producing strategies that 'try to be everything to all people'. Ministers were seeking a prioritised list of deliverable projects. While this is not necessarily against features of evolutionary resilience, such a narrow focus is less conducive to transformative thinking and iterative adaptation. Moreover, the need for places to undergo constant transformation, adaptation and reorientation hardly featured in SEPs, although these plans are evidence of LEPs' ongoing transformation, and plans display a reorientation from regionalism to localism.

CONCLUSION

In the wake of the recession, one of the most important questions that must be asked is whether we are now building local economies that are more resilient. If secondary evidence from local economic development plans is anything to go by, then the answer must be a resounding 'no'.

(Cox et al., 2014: 4)

As practitioners contend with recurrent crises against a backdrop of austerity and in a period of renewed uncertainty exacerbated by the UK's referendum result of 2016 to leave the European Union, the concept of economic resilience is set to retain currency in local and regional development debates for the time being at least. Through this chapter, we have examined the 'resilience' of growth strategies deployed by English business-led partnerships that are expected to formulate, lead and govern recovery and development plans for localities and regions. While many LEPs have had a 'slow birth' (Carr, 2015) and some were and continue to be mired by internal conflicts as part of a formative 'storming' phase (Pugalis and Bentley, 2013), the production of SEPs (and the associated Growth Deal process, which provides LEPs with access to significant resources) has helped to codify the role of LEPs in local and regional development.

While economic development debates often take on the notion of resilience (Dawley et al., 2010), we find that a preoccupation with growth persists. We would concur with IPPR North's assessment of SEPs that 'performance was generally best around those resilience measures which align more closely with traditional economic growth drivers. Against other measures, the plans leave much to be desired' (Cox et al., 2014: 2). Hence, this chapter has identified how much of the novel potency conveyed through the concept of resilience has struggled to reframe growth-first economic rationalities informing the economic strategies of LEPs.

The key finding is that, on balance, the economic strategies of LEPs codified through the production of SEPs are largely conservative. LEPs have faced a difficult dilemma: do they opt to champion local priorities (which may not necessarily accord with central government objectives) and risk reduced growth funding, or do they follow the centralist steer ('muscular localism') of government at the potential expense of local priorities? For some LEPs, this has not been an either/or choice, as they have been able to draw upon past experiences and available expertise to deftly mould the objectives of central government in ways that best suit local priorities. For many others, this has proved unfeasible, particularly due to the prohibitive timescales, which afforded LEPs only nine months to produce and submit final SEPs following the publication of guidance in July 2013.

To some extent, SEPs are the culmination of political bargaining and compromises within places and across government, informed inconsistently by research data, business intelligence, expert opinion, stakeholder interests and submissions, and broader 'community' input. Perhaps unsurprisingly, given the timescale, they often attempt to solidify existing as well as emergent priorities, programmes and initiatives. These factors together in part explain much of the weight given to what we have identified as conservative resilience measures in SEPs.

This chapter suggests a number of directions for future research. Our findings highlight the often generic and conservative aspects of SEPs mixed with intimations of a more nuanced approach and academic research could not only follow but also inform successive iterations of local economic strategies. It may also be instructive to examine the place-based factors that influence the varieties of resilience – equilibrium/persistent/ institutional – and resilient tendencies that places display. In this vein, research could begin to uncover some of the social and economic, and political and institutional characteristics that might influence particular places to promote, for example, evolutionary resilience, asking policy-relevant questions about the kind of intervention that could promote a normatively more 'desirable' form of resilience in a given place.

In the ongoing evolution of local and regional development, it is worth noting here that the adaptive capabilities of a region's economy – including its firms, workers, institutions and policy actors – may well depend on the nature of the region's pre-existing economy; that is, that evolutionally resilience, the ability to reorientate, is likely to be a path-dependent process (see Martin, 2010). A key question for resilience thinking and challenge for future research is how to foster evolutionary resilience and the reorientation of economies (Martin et al. 2015). Whether the concept of economic resilience will be as prevalent in scholarly debates and policy arenas over future years as it is now is an unknown, although it is likely to be influenced by prevailing economic conditions. Nevertheless, for those locations and regions in a perennial state of economic duress, especially those places facing cumulative economic crises, a more radical interpretation of economic resilience could be of value.

NOTES

1. Every LEP except London produced a SEP – 38 in total. London opted not to produce one due to its unique governance arrangements and circumstances.
2. For example, few SEPs consider how enhanced private-sector productivity could promote social inclusion. Indeed, many SEPs completely ignore the issue of deprivation. A key implication of this finding is that even if growth targets were realised (which may be unrealistic), then the qualitative nature of growth is likely to be less effective at reducing economic disparities within subnational geographies.

ADDITIONAL READING

Martin, R., Pike, A., Tyler, P. and Gardiner, B. (2016), 'Spatially rebalancing the UK economy: towards a new policy model?' *Regional Studies* **50**(2): 342–357.

Martin, R. and Sunley, P. (2015), 'On the notion of regional economic resilience: conceptualization and explanation'. *Journal of Economic Geography* **15**(1): 1–42.

Pendall, R., Foster, K.A. and Cowell, M. (2010), 'Resilience and regions: building understanding of the metaphor'. *Cambridge Journal of Regions, Economy and Society* **3**(1): 71–84.

12. Local economic resilience in Italy

Paolo Di Caro

INTRODUCTION

One of the few merits of the Great Recession, if any, has been to stimulate further thinking on the place-specific consequences of economic shocks; that is, the way particular geographical areas evolve in times of crisis. In the recent years, significant spatial differences have been registered across and within countries with respect to both the shock-absorption phase and the first instances of recovery. In the United States and in Europe, where the Great Recession produced the main negative effects, local economic conditions varied substantially from 2007 onwards (Fogli et al., 2012): some areas experienced deep employment losses and severe reduction of economic activities, while other areas suffered less and rebounded quickly from the crisis. In Italy, regional inequalities were amplified by contributing to fuelling the rooted north–south economic and social divide (Bank of Italy, 2015a).

To provide a unified framework for the analysis of the local impact of shocks *lato sensu*, the concept of economic resilience – that draws from disciplines such as ecology, engineering and psychology – has been recently proposed for research and policy purposes (Boschma, 2015). From an evolutionary perspective, economic resilience can be defined as the ability of firms and territories to resist and recover from adverse events in order to keep a specific developmental path and/or move towards alternative growth trajectories (Martin and Sunley, 2015). Resilience implies looking at different attributes such as vulnerability and resistance to a particular shock, robustness and recoverability. At a local level, the resilience approach has been used for shedding new light on the factors determining different local economic developmental paths registered across areas in normal and crisis times (see the special issue 'Local growth evolutions: recession, resilience and recovery' in *Cambridge Journal of Regions, Economy and Society*, 2015). On policy grounds, many efforts have been progressively devoted to the identification of the tools that can promote local economic resilience and the long-term adaptability of specific places and economic actors (OECD, 2015).

The main aim of this contribution is to analyse local economic resilience in Italy, by providing novel evidence on the evolution of local labour markets across the 103 Italian provinces (NUTS III level) over the period 2004–15. Specifically, our work has three main objectives that integrate previous research in this area. First, the investigation of employment dynamics among Italian provinces allows for the more in-depth understanding of local labour markets, by complementing existing resilience studies focusing on the regional dimension and more aggregate data (Lagravinese, 2015). Second, the assessment of the place-specific consequences of the Great Recession and the initial years of recovery on provincial employment updates the findings of the analyses covering different periods and shocks (Cellini and Torrisi, 2014). Third, we participate in the current debate on the determinants of economic resilience by questioning the role of local institutions and governance arrangements for explaining differences in resilience observed across Italian provinces. The relevance of institutional factors, which has received limited attention to date, is increasingly attracting the interest of researchers and policymakers (Eraydin, 2016). Moreover, this research brings new knowledge along two additional directions. The focus on the relationships between economic resilience and local development provides new insights on the view that resilience and competitiveness are interdependent concepts that are helpful for understanding local economic performance in the short and the long term (Huggins et al., 2013). The explicit consideration of female employment becomes crucial for pointing out the resilience of a relevant part of local labour markets (Auer and Cazes, 2000) and the effects of the recent crisis on female occupations that are generally at the margin of the Italian labour market.

The remainder of the work is organized as follows: a brief discussion of the literature is followed by the empirical analysis. Then the final section summarizes the main findings and discusses some policy implications.

ECONOMIC RESILIENCE

Resilience and Local Development

Local economic conditions are deeply influenced by the occurrence of unexpected events such as firm closures, recessions and natural disasters that can modify local development patterns temporarily and/or permanently. History is rich with examples of locally defined positive and negative shocks that shaped the evolution of firms and workers localized in particular areas. From the late 1980s to early 1990s, for instance, the abolition of the so-called *Intervento Straordinario* in the south of Italy and the redefinition of local assisted areas in the United Kingdom produced the reduction of public investments in specific territories and contributed to destabilizing these economies. The analysis of local shocks, however, is hard to generalize given the presence of several micro forces that vary across places. At the other end of the spectrum, the contributions of business cycles provide information on the aggregate consequences of shocks by investigating the general behaviour of output variables during recessionary periods. This macro approach is mostly related to national observations and pays little attention to regional and local dynamics.

The resilience framework provides a key contribution to the study of the relationships between economic shocks and local development by highlighting the relevance of investigating the asymmetric impact of common recessions across the space (Martin, 2012). Dawley et al. (2010) pointed out the connections between the adaptive capacity of local systems, which assumes greater importance during unforeseen events, and the economic and social evolutions of particular places. Martin (2016) suggested that three main pillars – namely dynamic competitiveness, business confidence, and institutional support – characterize economic resilience. Looking at Danish towns from 2008 to 2013, Hansen (2016) pointed out the importance of interpreting local socio-economic patterns by adopting the resilience approach. Similar conclusions were proposed by Lee (2014) when focusing on the labour market dynamics of British cities during the recent crisis.

The exact conceptualization and the theoretical foundations of economic resilience, important aspects that are outside the boundaries of our contribution, remain open issues that are currently the object of a vivid debate in the literature (Christopherson et al., 2010). From an empirical point of view, three main topics have emerged in the resilience literature (Sensier et al., 2016): how to identify the shocks, how to measure resilience, which factors explain differences in resilience across firms and territories. The timing of recessionary events has been selected either endogenously or exogenously through the direct observation of the data (Fingleton et al., 2012). Several measures of resilience have been proposed in the literature (Modica and Reggiani, 2014) such as statistical indices, composite indicators and model-based classifications that used different variables (GDP, employment, exports, etc.). Martin and Sunley (2015) grouped the complex set of explaining factors of regional resilience into five macro categories: industrial and business structure, labour market conditions, financial arrangements, agency and decision-making and governance arrangements.

Local institutions – that is, the system of rules, beliefs and organizations – present in a particular territory in a given time period (Greif, 2006), play a crucial role in supporting the resistance, recoverability and adaptive capacity of places, firms and workers in several ways. Supportive and locally committed institutions create a favourable climate for business development, entrepreneurship, innovation and creativity – elements that are fundamental for resilience (Martin, 2016). The place-specific endowment of social and civic capital, trust and mutual confidence contributes to reduce the costs of transactions, mitigate information problems, ameliorate the efficiency in the provision of public goods, and improve government performance and the quality of bureaucracy (Tabellini, 2010). Using data on local economies in Britain over the period 2004–11, for instance, Huggins and Thompson (2015a) highlighted the role of culture and institutions for sustaining the renewal and reorientation of local entrepreneurship, and the enhancement of entrepreneurship resilience.

Italian Economic Resilience

Although economic and social territorial inequalities characterize the Italian economy like other European countries, the very long-lasting origin of the regional disparities in Italy makes the case of this country unique (A'Hearn and Venables, 2013). Since the early 1890s, the differences between the Centre-North and the South of Italy have been relevant and, apart from the period 1950–70, they have progressively widened (Daniele and Malanima, 2007).[1] During the years of the Great Recession, the Italian *Mezzogiorno* suffered more than the rest of the country: in 2013, GDP figures were about 13.5 per cent and 7.1 per cent lower than those registered in 2007 in the South and in the Centre-North, respectively (Bank of Italy, 2015a). Since the start of the recent crisis, regions located in the south experienced significant migration outflows and the deterioration of labour market conditions, with more than one-third of employment losses observed in Italy due to the consequences of the crisis on this macro-area.

In the past three plus-years, the resilience framework has been widely adopted for throwing new light on the Italian regional disparities. Cellini and Torrisi (2014) studied the relation between annual regional per-capita real GDP growth and resilience over the period 1890–2009, without finding any significant relationships. Conversely, Di Caro (2015a) detected spatial asymmetries in local labour markets when analysing the temporary and permanent impact of economic downturns experienced in Italy since the 1970s: regions located in the Adriatic belt such as Emilia Romagna, Puglia and Veneto were more resilient than other regions during both the shock-absorption and the post-recessionary phases. Comparing these two studies, Cellini et al. (2016) highlighted the importance of integrating several pieces of evidence when approaching resilience. Regional differences in economic resilience across Italy have been explained by the combination of several factors: industrial structure, human and civic capital, financial constraints, export propensity (Di Caro, 2015b). Using data on local labour markets during the years 2009–10, Faggian et al. (2016) motivated the presence of different local resilient patterns among the Italian *Sistemi Locali del Lavoro* by means of the asymmetric distribution of specialization and diversification of economic activities across geographical areas.

In addition, we provide further evidence on the study of economic conditions of Italian provinces. By proposing an adaptation of Markov techniques, Ponzio and Di Gennaro (2004) detected divergent patterns in per capita income of Italian provinces over the period 1952–92. Arbia and Basile (2005) provided empirical support on the fact that in the period 1950–70 per capita income of Italian provinces experienced convergence, but the authors did not find any evidence of convergence (absolute and σ-convergence) from 1970 to 2000. Fiaschi et al. (2011) analysed labour productivity on a provincial level from 1995 to 2006 by finding that high-productive provinces are mostly located in the Centre-North and low-productive ones are in the South.

EMPIRICS

Data and Preliminary Evidence

To describe the resilience of Italian local labour markets annual data on provincial employment (obtained from ISTAT) over the period 2004–15 have been used. This sample allows for the consideration of the Great Recession, which in Italy produced the main consequences from 2008 to 2013 (Bank of Italy, 2015b), and the first two years of recovery, namely 2014–15. During the crisis, the Italian labour market deteriorated significantly and registered relevant spatial asymmetries: in 2013, total employment was about 3.1 per cent and 8.8 per cent lower than that in 2008 in the Centre-North and the South, respectively. Variations in local economic conditions across Italy were observed both before and after the recent turmoil. From 2004 to 2007, provincial employment increased on average by about 3.2 per cent (Centre-North) and 0.6 per cent (South). Since the Italian recovery officially started, provinces located in the Centre-North registered +1.3 per cent in employment, while those in the South +0.5 per cent. Similar patterns emerge when looking at female employment: the Great Recession produced a cumulative growth of female occupations of +0.2 per cent (centre-north) and −4.7 per cent (south). During the crisis, the standard deviation of provincial employment increased by about +0.73 per cent (total) and +2.75 per cent (female).

Tables 12.1 and 12.2 report the two indexes of resilience proposed by Martin (2012) for total and female employment. The sensitivity index is defined as the provincial percentage growth in employment relative to the national percentage growth for the years of the Great Recession (2008–13). The recovery index has been calculated in a similar way for the two years of recovery (2014–15). In resilience terms, the former index measures the degree of synchronization of Italian provinces with respect to the national aggregate in terms of positive/negative growth of jobs in times of crisis, with the national economy being the benchmark against which to measure the relative resistance of provinces. A value of the sensitivity index higher (lower) than one denotes the situation of a province showing lower (higher) resistance in relative terms, given that during the period under investigation the Italian employment growth rate (total and female) was negative. A value of the recovery index higher (lower) than one denotes the situation of a province showing higher (lower) recoverability in relative terms, given that during the years of the recovery the Italian employment growth rate (total and female) was positive.

Some comments are worth pointing out. The sensitivity of Italian provinces to the recent crisis varied both across and within regions. Provinces located in the Centre-North were on average more resistant than Southern provinces. In some regions, differences among provinces were relevant. The sensitivity index in the Marche region (Centre-North) ranged from 0.31 and –2.28 (Ancona) to 11.44 and 61.19 (Ascoli-Piceno) for total and female employment. In Sardegna (South), sensitivity varied from 0.39 and –7.51 (Oristano) to 8.27 and 42.08 (Nuoro) for total and female employment. In addition, the uneven weaknesses of the Italian female labour market across territories found confirmation (Ferrera, 2008): both the average and the standard deviation were higher than total employment, namely 1.37 and 10.91. In Italy, and particularly in Southern regions, women encounter several difficulties to access formal occupations and obtain stable career positions, remaining at the margins of the labour market notwithstanding the levels of education. From 2008 onwards, about half of people migrating from Southern regions to the Centre-North were young women (Svimez, 2012).

The two graphs in Figure 12.1 report the combination of the sensitivity index (x-axis) and the recovery index (y-axis) for total (left-hand side) and female (right-hand side) employment for the 103 Italian provinces. Vertical and horizontal lines denote the Italian average. Observe that, the best performers are placed in the upper-right quadrant where we can find provinces showing low sensitivity (i.e., high resistance) and high recoverability

Table 12.1   *Local resilience, Italian provinces, total employment*

Province	Sensitivity	Recovery	Province	Sensitivity	Recovery
Torino	0.57	0.87	Arezzo	0.18	−2.27
Vercelli	0.60	0.13	Siena	0.35	3.79
Novara	0.66	3.22	Grosseto	0.07	2.61
Cuneo	0.51	1.44	Prato	−0.42	−2.03
Asti	0.31	0.59	Perugia	0.49	2.66
Alessandria	0.07	2.15	Terni	0.35	1.43
Biella	1.39	−0.26	Pesaro-Urbino	0.99	−4.24
Verbano	0.84	2.18	Ancona	0.31	2.07
Valle d'Aosta	0.60	0.21	Macerata	1.12	4.90
Imperia	1.55	3.90	Ascoli Piceno	11.44	3.15
Savona	1.02	0.51	Viterbo	−0.89	4.83
Genova	0.58	0.75	Rieti	0.25	−1.60
La Spezia	0.40	0.61	Roma	−0.87	3.27
Varese	0.74	0.06	Latina	−0.35	−0.91
Como	0.01	−0.16	Frosinone	0.90	3.66
Sondrio	0.71	2.25	L'Aquila	0.58	−2.66
Milano	3.87	2.02	Teramo	0.14	−1.36
Bergamo	0.16	0.31	Pescara	−0.63	−7.18
Brescia	−0.28	−1.94	Chieti	1.21	4.78
Pavia	−0.37	2.66	Campobasso	1.92	1.96
Cremona	0.74	1.07	Isernia	1.96	4.60
Mantova	0.24	0.65	Caserta	0.46	−5.41
Lecco	0.27	2.33	Benevento	3.43	3.96
Lodi	0.01	4.00	Napoli	1.57	1.61
Bolzano	−1.01	0.51	Avellino	0.19	−5.61
Trento	−0.52	1.18	Salerno	0.98	0.60
Verona	0.01	0.50	Foggia	2.77	1.00
Vicenza	0.82	3.19	Bari	5.13	1.36
Belluno	0.53	−0.01	Taranto	0.89	−3.67
Treviso	0.58	0.44	Brindisi	0.67	3.75
Venezia	0.78	4.00	Lecce	1.59	−0.17
Padova	−0.01	−4.35	Potenza	1.52	5.37
Rovigo	0.66	−5.06	Matera	0.68	2.41
Udine	0.82	−1.37	Cosenza	3.21	5.03
Gorizia	1.28	2.07	Catanzaro	0.51	−6.47
Trieste	0.87	2.11	Reggio Calabria	2.03	−2.19
Pordenone	0.24	−0.10	Crotone	1.25	0.20
Piacenza	0.10	−0.02	Vibo Valentia	2.10	−5.63
Parma	−0.19	0.04	Trapani	1.93	5.63
Reggio Emilia	−0.07	−0.06	Palermo	2.10	1.07
Modena	0.19	−1.47	Messina	2.44	0.68
Ferrara	2.27	3.62	Agrigento	0.59	−6.66

Table 12.1   (continued)

Province	Sensitivity	Recovery	Province	Sensitivity	Recovery
Ravenna	0.73	−0.27	Caltanissetta	1.90	1.57
Forlì-Cesena	−0.38	1.53	Enna	2.16	3.89
Rimini	−0.70	3.29	Catania	0.98	1.33
Massa-Carrara	0.29	−1.23	Ragusa	1.68	1.18
Lucca	0.08	−1.05	Siracusa	1.06	2.37
Pistoia	1.04	5.24	Sassari	6.96	2.88
Firenze	−0.20	2.16	Nuoro	8.27	−2.98
Livorno	−0.70	0.33	Cagliari	6.52	3.81
Pisa	−0.36	2.06	Oristano	0.39	3.78
				Sensitivity	Recovery
Average				1.04	0.81
St.dev.				1.82	2.83
Min				−1.01	−7.18
Max				11.44	5.63

Note: the sensitivity index reports the average for the years 2008–13; the recovery index reports the average for the years 2014–15.

Table 12.2   *Local resilience, Italian provinces, female employment*

Province	Sensitivity	Recovery	Province	Sensitivity	Recovery
Torino	0.10	−0.09	Arezzo	−0.40	−0.09
Vercelli	−0.25	2.17	Siena	1.42	7.14
Novara	−1.03	3.99	Grosseto	3.55	2.94
Cuneo	2.52	2.01	Prato	−1.56	0.65
Asti	−2.76	−0.52	Perugia	0.89	3.28
Alessandria	−1.49	4.20	Terni	−5.02	−3.49
Biella	5.55	2.32	Pesaro-Urbino	7.22	−3.53
Verbano	−0.45	2.55	Ancona	−2.28	1.40
Valle d'Aosta	−3.02	0.70	Macerata	1.35	3.84
Imperia	9.71	10.36	Ascoli Piceno	61.19	5.05
Savona	3.89	0.10	Viterbo	−16.42	1.52
Genova	−0.05	0.08	Rieti	−4.87	2.02
La Spezia	−0.08	1.35	Roma	−9.33	4.02
Varese	−4.63	−4.40	Latina	−7.22	−0.87
Como	−1.49	−0.93	Frosinone	−6.41	2.41
Sondrio	7.01	1.87	L'Aquila	5.05	−3.87
Milano	19.49	1.11	Teramo	−6.85	−4.70
Bergamo	−5.35	2.76	Pescara	−14.93	−10.35
Brescia	−8.23	−3.26	Chieti	4.80	4.50

Table 12.2 (continued)

Province	Sensitivity	Recovery	Province	Sensitivity	Recovery
Pavia	−9.42	0.39	Campobasso	7.52	0.97
Cremona	3.69	2.85	Isernia	−2.73	0.17
Mantova	0.01	2.25	Caserta	−11.25	−14.88
Lecco	−1.73	1.69	Benevento	28.55	7.44
Lodi	0.22	6.22	Napoli	−5.07	−1.39
Bolzano	−11.35	0.60	Avellino	4.12	−1.89
Trento	−6.78	3.47	Salerno	−1.01	1.66
Verona	−0.79	4.52	Foggia	6.03	−1.29
Vicenza	4.22	3.27	Bari	22.69	2.78
Belluno	1.35	−0.21	Taranto	−12.90	−4.41
Treviso	−3.17	−1.18	Brindisi	−3.10	8.46
Venezia	1.54	5.83	Lecce	5.91	0.99
Padova	−3.74	−4.80	Potenza	1.15	1.46
Rovigo	−3.00	−8.53	Matera	−14.66	−2.59
Udine	0.12	−2.13	Cosenza	17.42	7.38
Gorizia	5.04	−2.70	Catanzaro	−5.82	−8.18
Trieste	5.73	2.92	Reggio Calabria	5.81	−3.30
Pordenone	−2.20	−1.77	Crotone	0.90	4.34
Piacenza	−2.69	1.19	Vibo Valentia	0.07	−12.96
Parma	−5.44	−2.18	Trapani	7.11	9.49
Reggio Emilia	−4.75	−0.78	Palermo	11.79	2.38
Modena	−0.95	−2.75	Messina	10.29	1.48
Ferrara	−2.03	0.50	Agrigento	−7.27	−7.37
Ravenna	7.75	2.33	Caltanissetta	10.02	1.46
Forlì-Cesena	4.04	−4.10	Enna	7.72	8.36
Rimini	−9.95	2.45	Catania	−0.32	1.65
Massa-Carrara	1.68	6.86	Ragusa	1.21	−1.72
Lucca	−2.42	1.07	Siracusa	2.15	9.56
Pistoia	−1.16	0.24	Sassari	25.59	−1.95
Firenze	2.82	5.52	Nuoro	42.08	5.49
Livorno	−6.36	3.48	Cagliari	25.47	6.39
Pisa	−15.08	−2.40	Oristano	−7.51	10.92

			Sensitivity	Recovery
Average			1.37	0.98
St.dev.			10.91	4.56
Min			−16.42	−14.88
Max			61.19	10.92

Note: the sensitivity index reports the average for the years 2008–13; the recovery index reports the average for the years 2014–15.

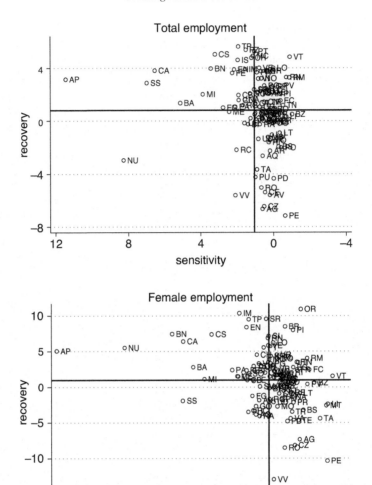

Note: Graphs above plot the recovery index (y-axis) versus the sensitivity index (x-axis) for total and female employment.

Figure 12.1   Local resilience, Italian provinces

with respect to the Italian average. At the opposite (down-left quadrant), we can observe those areas – mostly located in the south – registering low sensitivity (i.e., low resistance) and low recovery. Provinces showing high sensitivity and high recovery are placed in the upper-left quadrant, while

Table 12.3   Ranking of Italian provinces, resilience

Total		Female	
Sensitivity	Recovery	Sensitivity	Recovery
BZ	TP	VT	OR
VT	PZ	LI	IM
RM	PT	PE	SR
RN	CS	MT	TP
LI	MC	TA	BR
PE	VT	BZ	EN
TN	CH	CA	PI
PO	IS	FC	BE
FC	LO	PV	CS
PV	VE	RM	SI
–	–	–	–
FE	NU	CL	RA
ME	TA	ME	VA
FO	PU	PA	TA
CS	PD	CS	TE
BE	RO	MI	PA
BA	CE	CA	CZ
CA	AV	SS	RO
SS	VV	BE	PE
NU	AG	NU	VV
AP	PE	AP	CE

Note: Provinces are ranked on the basis the following criteria. Sensitivity (total and female): increasing values. Recovery (total and female): decreasing values. The abbreviation of provinces follows the ISTAT nomenclature.

provinces registering low sensitivity and low recovery are located in the downright quadrant. Notably, provincial employment dynamics resulted resistant to the recent crisis in many areas, but with different recovery patterns. Table 12.3 reports the top and bottom ten Italian provinces according to the sensitivity (increasing values) and recovery (decreasing values) index for total and female employment. Previous observations, however, allows for the consideration of the shock-specific effects on provincial labour markets, without taking into account the structural patterns registered over different periods. In Italy, the provinces showing better (worse) employment growth patterns before the crisis registered higher (lower) resistance and recoverability in the recent years. Indeed, the average provincial employment growth rate observed before the Great Recession is negatively correlated to the growth rate registered during the crisis, namely

–0.19 and –0.06 for total and female employment, respectively. Conversely, pre-crisis employment growth rates are positively correlated to the variations of employment observed in the recovery phase: 0.06 (total) and 0.21 (female).

Estimates

To explore the role of local institutions as possible determinants of economic resilience, a panel model for the 103 Italian provinces in the sample has been estimated. The dependent variable is the (total and female) annual employment growth rate on a provincial level. The newly released 'Index of Institutional Quality (IQI)' elaborated by Nifo and Vecchione (2015) is used to describe local institutions.[2] For each province, the IQI contains information on five institutional dimensions that include several variables obtained from different databanks: voice and accountability; government effectiveness; regulatory quality; rule of law; corruption. This index takes values from 0 (low quality of institutions) to 1 (high quality of institutions) and covers the years from 2004 to 2012. The geographical distribution of the IQI reflects the presence of spatial differences across Italy: over the sample period, the index registered 0.67 (Centre-North) and 0.34 (South), with a standard deviation among provinces of about 0.22. During the Great Recession, IQI values experienced a slight increase in both areas, becoming 0.71 (Centre-North) and 0.35 (South). In resilience terms, we expect a positive relationship between the quality of local institutions and employment growth, given the influence of institutional and governance arrangements on determining the ability of particular areas to resist to and recover from shocks.

Tables 12.4 and 12.5 report summary statistics and estimation results. The period under investigation covers the years 2004–12 that represent

Table 12.4   Summary statistics

Variable		Mean	Stand. Dev.	Min	Max
TOT_EMP	overall	−0.0029	0.0419	−0.6141	0.1024
	between		0.0116	−0.0633	0.0126
	within		0.0403	−0.5537	0.1160
FEM_EMP	overall	0.0026	0.0566	−0.5887	0.2206
	between		0.0116	−0.0590	0.0226
	within		0.0554	−0.5270	0.2292
IQI	overall	0.5871	0.2182	0.0000	1.0000
	between		0.2152	0.0028	1.0000
	within		0.0414	0.4331	0.7208

Table 12.5   Estimation results

| Dependent variable: Employment growth | | | | |
Variables	(1)	(2)	(3)	(4)
IQI	0.0227***	0.0225***	0.0116	0.0046
	(0.0045)	(0.0060)	(0.0097)	(0.0107)
Constant	YES	YES	YES	YES
Fixed Effects	YES	YES	YES	YES
Observations	824	515	824	515
R^2	0.08	0.02	0.03	0.02
Wald statistics ($\chi^2_{(K)}$)	93.63	14.02	19.53	14.02
	[0.000]	[0.000]	[0.000]	[0.000]

Note: The dependent variable is total employment growth rate (1) and (2) and female employment growth rate (3) and (4). Errors are in parentheses ().* implies significance at 10%, ** implies significance at 5%, *** implies significance at 1%. Figures in brackets are p-values.

the time span when the IQI values are available. Estimation results have been obtained by applying the Prais-Winsten estimator in order to take into consideration the presence of heteroscedasticity, autocorrelation and cross-sectional dependence in the error structure (Beck and Katz, 1995). Models (1) and (3) report the results obtained for the whole period for total and female employment growth, respectively. A time dummy covering the years of the Great Recession has been introduced in order to account for the effects of the recent crisis. Models (2) and (4) report the results obtained for the years of the Great Recession. Provincial fixed-effects have been introduced in all the specifications. The robustness of baseline results has been controlled by introducing additional time dummies, region-specific effects and checking for the initial conditions of local labour markets.

Interpretation of the Results

Estimation results confirm the positive effects of local institutions on local employment dynamics in normal and crisis times. The coefficient of the explanatory variable IQI is positive and significant for total employment growth, but not significant when the dependent variable is the growth rate of female employment. This can be due to the presence of endogeneity issues arising from the connections between female employment and the shadow economy that is part of the aggregate variable IQI. Observe that local institutions play a crucial role when limiting the observation to the Great Recession only. After re-estimating models (1)–(4) by disaggregating the five dimensions of IQI, each institutional dimension has a relevant impact on employment growth. As for model (1), for instance, we find the following coefficient that are statistically significant at 1 per cent level (except from the coefficient of the dimension 'Regulatory quality' that is not statistically significant): Voice and accountability (0.0195), Government effectiveness (0.0199); Regulatory quality (0.0076); Rule of law (0.0276); Corruption (0.0227).

A local context embedded with supportive institutions can experience both long-term social and economic development and register high resilience when facing unexpected events. The presence of cooperation, public trust and sense of community results helpful for reducing free-riding issues, inefficiencies due to lack of coordination and fostering political-economy incentives. In Italy, these factors have been associated with shared attitudes toward industriousness that are particularly relevant in the locations being part of the Italian industrial districts. Although the occurrence of some territorial exceptions, the institutional gap between the Centre-North and the South has implications on the different enforcement of property rights and contracts, frictions in credit markets, and entrepreneurship. As pointed out by Williams et al. (2013) and Williams and Vorley (2014), entrepreneurship becomes crucial in making localities more resilient to shocks and better equipped to undertake positive developmental paths. Not surprisingly, then, it can be interpreted the good performance of the provinces of the so-called 'Third-Italy' in the first instances of the current recovery. In such areas, local institutions operate for creating a favourable environment for entrepreneurship, with positive effects on exports, innovation and labour market dynamics.

The role of local institutions, moreover, allows for the continuous recalibration of local economies in order to sustain the robustness of specific places in an evolutionary process. Three concrete examples are worth illustrating. Since the 1980s, the city of Turin and its surrounding area (Piemonte – North-West) experienced deep employment losses and social instabilities due to the industrial crisis that hit the automotive sector. Yet, this area reacted to the shock by redefining the local identity investing in innovation and creativity. About a decade after the automotive crisis, the survival of the Italian eyewear district in the provinces of Belluno and Treviso (Veneto – North East) was undermined by several factors such as the emergence of new international competitors and variations in consumers' preferences. To resist to the negative pressures, local entrepreneurial forces and institutions cooperated by investing in new materials, valorizing brands, and developing more efficient organization and distribution channels. The province of Ragusa (Sicily – South) provides an example of a resilient territory facing a structural lack of physical infrastructures: this province has the lowest level of infrastructures (roads, railways) among Italian provinces. Local development in Ragusa has to be read as a dynamic process of reaction to its historical constraints. Prior to the Great Recession, this province registered positive economic and social trends notwithstanding the negative effects deriving from the fact that it is located in Sicily and the *Mezzogiorno*. Labour market indicators, including the high participation of women, are in line with those observed in the provinces located in the Centre-North. More recently, the resilience of Ragusa made it possible to respond to the recent turmoil by undertaking important initiatives like international partnerships for improving export towards Russia and North Africa, and the attraction of UK-based tour operators to enhance tourism.

CONCLUDING REMARKS

The Great Recession has emphasized some economic and social challenges in many countries, specifically in some European nations still struggling to address structural problems such as rigid labour markets, international macroeconomic imbalances and large public debts and deficits. Given the global dimension of the current economic situation, suggesting locally inspired analyses can appear *prima facie* inadequate. Yet, the understanding of the place-specific consequences of aggregate shocks and the overall effects on local development is one of the main policy objectives for the coming years. The OECD has stressed the pivotal role of local economies as drivers of national recovery and sources of successful responses already underway (OECD, 2013); the European Union has invested more than €350 billion for enhancing investments in lagging regions and cities to deliver growth and jobs through the next European cohesion policy for the programming period 2014–20. Leveraging on local economies to achieve economic growth and face the challenge of current global issues becomes crucial in order to find new paths of development. As highlighted by Barca et al. (2012), the continuous movement of capital, goods, people and ideas maintains its connections with particular places.

This chapter presented new evidence on the resilience of Italian provinces. An explicit discussion on the extent of and the reasons behind the uneven distribution of economic resilience across provincial local labour markets has been provided. The following main results have been achieved. In Italy, local economic resilience follows strong place-specific patterns: variations in total and female employment are relevant across and within regions. In general, provinces located in the Centre-North of the country are more resilient than those located in the South. The Great Recession contributed to amplifying local labour markets' differences, particularly with respect to female occupations. The quality of local institutions plays a relevant role for explaining the asymmetric distribution of resilience on a territorial level. Supportive local institutions and governance arrangements foster the resistance and the recoverability of particular places during and after adverse events. The impact of local institutional arrangements has important implications on entrepreneurship, local development and local credit markets. Economic resilience and local development are interrelated aspects that need to be investigated in order to understand the competitiveness of particular areas in an evolutionary perspective.

Although our analysis represents a step forward in resilience thinking, further research effort is required for throwing new light on what the drivers are behind the differences in local resilience. The comparison of a large number of local economies in different countries (Crescenzi et al., 2016) is needed in order to advance conclusions that are more robust on the explaining factors of resilience. The investigation of the place-specific responses of local economies to different recessionary events (i.e., financial, industrial, currency) can provide additional insights on resilience as a dynamic process. The assessment of the relationships between policy actions aimed at counterbalancing the negative consequences of shocks and resilience has to be questioned. In the European Union and in Italy, this means studying also the counter-cyclical properties of the regional cohesion policy (Camagni and Capello, 2015; Arbolino et al., 2016). Finally yet importantly, for the Italian case, further analyses shall be focused on the multiple connections among local resilience, local competitiveness and the unsolved regional inequalities.

NOTES

1. According to the Italian Institute of Statistics (ISTAT), the two macro-areas are defined as follows: Centre-North: Valle d'Aosta, Piemonte, Lombardia, Liguria, Trentino A.A., Friuli V.G., Veneto, Emilia Romagna, Toscana, Marche, Umbria, Lazio; South: Abruzzo, Molise, Campania, Puglia, Basilicata, Calabria, Sardegna, Sicilia.
2. The databank is available at https://sites.google.com/site/institutionalqualityindex/empir ics, where a detailed description of the index can be found.

ADDITIONAL READING

Cellini, R., Di Caro, P. and Torrisi, G. (2016), 'Regional resilience in Italy: do employment and income tell the same story?', in R. Huggins and P. Thompson (eds), *Handbook of Regions and Competitiveness.* Cheltenham, UK and Northampton, MA, USA: Edward Elgar Publishing.

Martin, R. (2016), 'Shocking aspects of regional development: towards an economic geography of resilience', in G.C. Clark, M.A. Feldman and M. Gertler (eds), *New Handbook of Economic Geography*. Oxford: Oxford University Press.

Sensier, M., Bristow, G. and Healy, A. (2016), 'Measuring regional economic resilience across Europe: operationalizing a complex concept'. *Spatial Economic Analysis* **11**(2): 1–24.

13. Evolutionary perspectives on economic resilience in regional development

Emil Evenhuis and Stuart Dawley

INTRODUCTION: EVOLUTIONARY APPROACHES TO REGIONAL ECONOMIC RESILIENCE

Within the recent 'evolutionary turn' in economic geography, much attention and debate has focused on the concept of resilience and its application to local and regional economies (Martin and Sunley, 2015). Evolutionary approaches within economic geography have rapidly emerged as one of the hottest areas for social science citations (Coe, 2011). Evolutionary approaches seek to examine "the processes by which the economic landscape – the spatial organisation of economic production, circulation, exchange, distribution and consumption – is transformed from within over time" (Boschma and Martin, 2010, pp. 6–7). On the one hand, they highlight the ways in which such processes are dynamic (instead of stationary or tending to some type of equilibrium), irreversible (they are rooted in real historical time, and hence the order of events is essential), and are the result of novelty (i.e. they take the creative capacity of economic agents as a starting point) (Boschma and Martin, 2007). On the other hand, the geographical context is brought to the forefront. The geographically uneven economic landscape is not just an 'outcome or by-product', but a 'determining influence' in shaping paths of local and regional evolution (Boschma and Martin, 2010).

So far, most studies on regional economic resilience have assessed how various regions have been affected by and have recovered from recessions, particularly the most recent one (see Martin et al., 2016). The focus is then clearly on issues regarding the measurement of regional resilience, and the comparative performance of various regions during and after especially a macroeconomic downturn.

However, applying an evolutionary perspective shifts attention beyond snapshot-type analyses to instead situate a region's resilience and adaptability to shocks as part of its longer-term evolution and character (Martin and Sunley, 2015). Indeed, resilience and adaptability may not only reflect responses to macroeconomic perturbations, but also developments with structural ramifications, such as the erosion of the competitive position of certain key industries, technological changes, demographic developments, etc. In this sense, we understand resilience as being a capacity to bring about alterations within a regional economy to cope with changes in the broader context in which a regional economy operates.[1] In other words, resilience refers to the ability of regional economy to 'adapt'.

Evolutionary conceptions of regional economic resilience are characterised by the fact that they do *not* presuppose a return to some equilibrium or shift to a different equilibrium state, but rather presume continuous renewal in the regional economy (Simmie and Martin, 2010). As such, regional economies evolve through a dynamic process of constant renewal rather than achieving any type of equilibrium (although renewal may at times be more intense). Here then, the emphasis moves from the quantifiable dimensions and outcomes of resilience (such as resistance,[2] recovery,[3] and shift[4]) to the more qualitative dimensions of the process of renewal: the mechanisms and drivers through which adaptation occurs in regional economies.[5] As Boschma (2015, p. 735) notes, the focus in an evolutionary understanding of resilience will be "on the long-term evolution of regions and their ability to adapt and reconfigure their industrial, technological and institutional structures in an economic system that is restless and evolving".

Evolutionary approaches within economic geography have, to date, drawn upon three broadly distinct, albeit partly overlapping, theoretical frameworks: Generalised Darwinism, Complexity Theory, and Path Dependency Theory (Table 13.1). The purpose of this chapter is to review and assess each of the frameworks with regard to their ability to unpack the 'black box' of resilience processes that contribute to the uneven geography of resilience outcomes. In particular, we respond to recent debates within economic geography that argue for a clearer and stronger identification and articulation of agency, institutions (especially governance arrangements), and the multi-scalar and extra-regional nature of evolutionary processes (MacKinnon et al., 2009; Pike et al., 2016). As such, our particular attention in the next three sections is to, in turn, explore and critique the analysis of agency, mechanisms, institutions, and multi-scalar contexts within each approach. In conclusion, we suggest that the Path Dependency framework offers the most advanced account of agency, institutions, and scales in explaining regional resilience and can offer the basis for an overarching evolutionary framework on this agenda.

Table 13.1   Core tenets of the three theoretical frameworks within evolutionary approaches

Generalised Darwinism	• Explanation of evolution through population dynamics, in particular the principles of variation, inheritance and selection (Hodgson and Knudsen, 2010).
	• Following Nelson and Winter (1982), the starting points are 'organisational routines' (see Boschma and Frenken, 2006, 2011). These consist of physical technologies and standardised patterns of social interactions. These routines are relatively stable over time, although firms have some scope in amending them when it is clear they are not working well (Boschma and Frenken, 2006).
	• Within a region different firms with different routines exist within several different industries, and new firms with new routines will appear constantly. There will be a mechanism of selection working as market competition will drive out unfit routines, and cause smart, fit routines to diffuse and spread out.
	• The proposed mechanisms of replication and diffusion are various: firms with fit routines will grow much faster and hence come to represent a larger share of the industry in a region, successful firms will also produce more spin-offs, and some of the successful routines will spill over to other firms through labour mobility, professional networks, and inter-firm collaborations (Boschma and Frenken, 2006). Moreover, routines are further diffused through merger and acquisition activity, and the establishment of new plants and offices by firms in other locations (Boschma and Martin, 2010).
	• The replication and diffusion of routines will have a strong spatial dimension as the growth of a successful firm and the spin-offs and/or spillovers it will generate, will likely be in one geographical location, and hence over time industry clusters will emerge.
	• Through 'co-evolution' also the development of institutions, networks, agglomerations, and other meso- and macro-level phenomena can by analysed (Boschma and Martin, 2010; Schamp, 2010). In this way the 'selection environment' is further endogenised; as from routines and local industry dynamics, higher-level patterns develop, which impact on selection and diffusion on the micro-level.

Table 13.1   (continued)

Complexity Theory	• Sees cities, clusters, or regions and other spatial units as so-called 'complex adaptive systems'. From this point of view, there are a set of components (firms, institutions, infrastructures, individuals, etc.) which, through the outputs they generate (behaviours, knowledge, incomes, etc.), fulfil functions for other components, and can consistently reproduce themselves (Martin and Sunley, 2007).
	• It postulates mechanisms of self-organisation and emergence: the ongoing interactions and dynamics between the individual components at one level 'spontaneously' (i.e., in a way that is not planned or imposed) lead to relatively stable patterns on a higher-level (e.g., at the level of a city, cluster or region).
	• The complexity aspect implies that these components in turn respond to the patterns they create together, and hence the system is not coherent in a fixed manner, and will normally evolve over time as components create patterns, and these patterns impact on the components, etc. (Arthur, 2009).
	• Instead of an ontology of closed, linear, and equilibrium systems (as in neoclassical economics), systems are posited to be open, nonlinear and far-from-equilibrium (Beinhocker, 2007).
Path Dependency Theory	• The 'canonical' model – as based on the works of Paul David and W. Brian Arthur – has three main features (Martin, 2010): a seemingly small event has significant and unpredictable long-run effects ('nonergodicity'); this event becomes progressively 'locked-in' through various self-reinforcing mechanisms (e.g., increasing returns, coordination effects, self-reinforcing expectations, sunk costs, etc.), which limit the scope for alternative development paths; and this pattern is then assumed to remain stable until disrupted or dislodged by an external shock of some kind.
	• Martin and Sunley (2006) and Martin (2010) have argued that – when applied in the context of regional economic development – path dependence should also be able to capture situations which are 'metastable': i.e., regional economies still exhibit continuous incremental development, renewal activity, and the emergence and disappearance of industries and technologies, but in a manner that somehow builds on the assets and legacies of the past. Hence instead of seeing the path a stable state, the path is then seen as an ongoing dynamic process.
	• As a corollary, more far-reaching changes in the way a regional economy develops may be understood as the 'creation' of a new path, the 'branching' of a path, or the 'breaking' of a path (see Garud and Karnøe, 2001).

GENERALISED DARWINISM

To date, Generalised Darwinism has been the dominant framework for evolutionary approaches. With regard to the mechanisms and drivers of regional economic resilience, the framework in its most basic form suggests that regional adaptation is an aggregate of the adaptation processes that relate to firms: firms with unfit routines go out of business, whereas those with good routines grow and diffuse their practices[6] (Boschma and Frenken, 2006). Hence on the short run, resilience will largely depend on the region's portfolio of firms: the more varied and diversified, the more resilient, and the more uniform and specialised, the less resilient. But on the longer run, the framework suggest that resilience depends crucially on the degree to which regions can qualify as appropriate environments to take advantage of new rounds of innovation and entrepreneurship. Supporting structures at higher aggregation levels will 'co-evolve' with the evolution of firms in a region over time: knowledge and competence bases, innovation networks, specific institutions, agglomerations, etc. For the theorisation of resilience in this framework, this will mean two things. First, the framework highlights the importance of 'related variety'. That is, a degree of cognitive proximity between economic activities that is not too large, to ensure effective learning; nor too small, as agents with the same knowledge will have nothing to learn from each other (e.g., Frenken, 2007; Boschma and Frenken, 2011). Related variety between industries within a region will strengthen resilience on the long run, as this will be a crucial factor in generating innovative activity and the development of new industries (also Boschma, 2015). Second, the supporting higher-level structures that emerge (knowledge bases, institutional arrangements, agglomerations, etc.) can over time act as constraining rather than enabling; thus reducing the development of new initiatives and hence the variety available (Schamp, 2010; also Boschma, 2004). Hence for resilience it is important that such constraints are removed and variety-reducing processes are offset by variety-creating processes (Boschma, 2004, 2015).

The framework of Generalised Darwinism has important limitations regarding the role of agency, of institutions, and of multi-scalar processes in regional economic resilience. The basic ontology of the Generalised Darwinism framework is one of methodological individualism, which means that the emergence of phenomena on higher levels of aggregation are to be explained from the population dynamics and interactions between micro-level actors (primarily firms) (MacKinnon et al., 2009). This does indeed leave scope for the incorporation of the emergence and evolution of some types of institutional arrangements through co-evolution.[7]

Furthermore a notion of collective agency of different firms (and other micro-level actors) deliberately working together to achieve common objectives, could also be examined using the framework (Boschma and Frenken, 2009, p. 155; 2015, pp. 9–10). Importantly, however, there appears little room to analyse a role for the state (and its policy interventions) and other more overarching institutional structures (such as industrial relations, or corporate governance), in the resilience of regional economies (see also MacKinnon et al., 2009). These cannot plausibly be explained by the notion of co-evolution with the population of firms, and can thus not be theorised through the Generalised Darwinism framework as such.

COMPLEXITY THEORY

The Complexity Theory framework provides scope for a more holistic approach to regional economic resilience, in which there is an explicit role for agency at the collective level and macro-level institutions, including the state. Complex adaptive systems are believed to be highly resilient because they are characterised by distributed and dispersed (rather than centralised) control, by strong positive and negative feedback loops, and by a degree of redundant variety (Martin and Sunley, 2007). Concerning the mechanisms and drivers of resilience, the main focus in the Complexity Theory approach has been on how resilience will vary with the extent and form of 'connectedness' between various elements of the regional economy.[8] This has been worked out in various ways. Wink (2014) has analysed regional resilience from a Complexity Theory perspective by looking at inter-firm linkages and linkages between firms and other organisations (universities, research institutes, cluster bodies, etc.) in a comparative study of economic crises in Baden-Württemberg and Saxony in Germany. Similarly, Crespo et al. (2014) have hypothesised that regional resilience will vary with different structural properties in knowledge networks, with 'bridging strategies' between the core network and organisations at the periphery of the network enabling a flow of fresh and new ideas and thus averting ossification.

Complexity Theory allows for a much better theorisation of the role of agency at the collective level (and not only at the individual level) within regional economic resilience. Actors may come together in the face of (potential) disturbances, and draw upon their various available resources. Bristow and Healy (2014, 2015) have explicitly conceptualised the role of governance and policy in regional resilience from a Complexity Theory perspective. They have highlighted the interactions and connections between actors to be able to arrive at an adequate response, not only between firms, but also between various actors in the private sector, public sector, and civil society. Bristow and Healy have furthermore drawn attention to the importance of anticipation, information, communication, and narratives for such collective agency. Actors will have to make sense of the outside world and their position in it (which is to an important extent a collective process); and hence there needs to be arrangements in place to develop intelligence, formulate alternative plans and scenarios, and communicate and debate opportunities, risks and options (also Weick et al., 2005).

The state will be a particularly important actor with regard to such collective agency. It is in a unique position to facilitate networking and interactions between various actors, and to put suitable institutional arrangements in place. But through its policies it can also affect regional resilience more directly. Cowell (2015) has explicitly analysed the role of policy in evolutionary resilience from a Complex Adaptive System perspective. She has compared how eight metropolitan regions in the American Midwest have dealt with deindustrialisation. She concludes that regions with policies that responded early to deindustrialisation, and were aimed at diversification into new economic activities, have produced better results than policies that came relatively late and focused on retaining manufacturing. Furthermore, regions in which a diverse set of actors was involved in the decision-making, have generally performed better than regions that lacked such diversity.

Nevertheless, also the Complexity Theory approach has some limitations. Most importantly, the framework does not seem suitable to adequately theorise the role of institutions. Institutions mainly feature as 'networks' in the framework, which highlights the fact whether or not connections between actors exist, but downplays the exact nature of these connections. How does coordination and decision-making take place? How do institutions structure the interactions between actors, and how do they shape the possession and use of certain powers and resources? These questions cannot be addressed very well within this framework. Moreover, the role of relations with actors external to the region is still to be worked out, in particular with regard to connections between policy-actors operating at different spatial scales and the role of macro-level institutions.

PATH DEPENDENCY THEORY

In the literature on regional economic resilience, the potential of the Path Dependency framework to theorise resilience and adaptation has received comparatively little attention so far. However, we argue that Path Dependency not only offers a more holistic approach – similar to the Complexity Theory framework – but also better captures the roles of institutions and multi-level governance contexts in understanding regional resilience.

Within the framework, the idea of 'lock-in' evidently relates to the mechanisms and drivers of resilience. A lock-in in the context of regional economic development can be understood as a 'rigidification' of structures, technologies, networks, ideas, knowledge bases, etc., which will significantly constrain the options available for further development. Hence lock-ins will inhibit adaptation to new and changing circumstances, and diminish resilience. Grabher (1993) – in a study of the development of the Ruhr Area, once dominated by the coal and steel industries – has distinguished between lock-ins at three levels within a regional economy:

- Functional lock-ins: rigidities that inhibit entrepreneurship of people and firms, because a lack of boundary-spanning functions (marketing, research and development, long-term strategy department) as a result of strong and tight relations between firms in the supply chain, and investments in specific assets and technologies within these cooperative relations.
- Political lock-ins: arrangements between local businesses and the political leadership that ensure that vested interests are protected, and policies are enacted that support the status quo and inhibit renewal.
- Cognitive lock-ins: rigidities in the worldviews and ways of thinking of key regional actors, because of complacency and a lack of critical reflection.

As highlighted, however, in Table 13.1, path-dependent development does not necessarily imply a state of lock-in, but may also exhibit ongoing incremental development, new path creation, and path branching. With regard to the mechanisms and drivers of resilience and adaptation, the question then becomes: what determines whether a regional economy comes to be dominated by self-reinforcing processes that increase rigidification, constrain opportunities and produce strong lock-ins; or whether it instead maintains its dynamism and continues to exhibit renewal based on the – enabling instead of constraining – legacies and structures built up in the past (Hassink and Shin, 2005; Martin, 2010)?

To start answering this question, and thus make a start in developing a more sophisticated theorisation of regional economic resilience within the Path Dependency framework, we should – as Grabher did – disentangle the notions of 'regional path dependence' and 'regional lock-in', and instead focus on the constituent components and the interactions between these components. Following Henning et al. (2013), we should be explicit about the level of analysis. Path dependence is most fruitfully applied to the development of specific elements of regional development, such as a specific technological/knowledge base, networks, skills, institutional arrangements, etc. (also Martin and Sunley, 2006). The path dependent evolution of each of these elements will have a logic of their own, based on their own mechanisms. Moreover, there will likely also be interactions between the development paths of the various elements; that is there will be 'path interdependencies' to take into account (Martin and Sunley, 2006, p. 413).

Within the functional, political – or rather institutional – and cognitive domains, we may identify many mechanisms of positive path dependence (ongoing renewal based on past legacies, facilitating resilience) and of lock-in (narrowing the scope of options and thus inhibiting resilience) (see Evenhuis, 2016). Within the functional domain, we may further distinguish between mechanisms that operate in clusters and industries, in the regional labour market, or in the built environment. Table 13.2 lists a number of mechanisms of path dependence and lock-in, as they may operate in these various domains.

While not intending to give an exhaustive account, Table 13.2 does illustrate the potential of the framework to integrate various different aspects of resilience into the overarching framework, and thus develop a more comprehensive theorisation of the drivers and mechanisms of regional economic resilience. By identifying particular mechanisms of path dependency and lock-in within the institutional (political) and cognitive domains (and examining their interactions with mechanisms in the functional domain), a role for collective agency and for institutions can clearly be fitted in. Indeed, several studies have utilised the Path Dependency framework to emphasise the crucial role of institutions and especially the state and in effectuating or inhibiting renewal (see Hudson, 2005; Hassink, 2010a; Morgan, 2013; Dawley et al., 2015). More than in the Complexity Theory framework, path dependency lays stress on the way actors interact with institutions, in order to cope with change.[9]

By being precise about the level of analysis at which mechanisms of path dependence are suggested to operate, we can also be more precise about the levels of scale at which they are to be found. Moreover, we suggest that mechanisms of path dependence and lock-in beyond the region in question (in, for example, national institutions, or ideas and ideologies in national politics) may interact with mechanisms in the region as well. The way mechanisms at different scales are interdependent, and

Table 13.2   *Regional economic resilience understood as interdependent*
mechanisms of path-dependence and lock-in

Functional domain	*Mechanisms of path dependence and lock-in in clusters/ industries, with regard to technology, networks, industrial organisation*	• Continued dominance by the same industries, or alternatively creation of new paths/path branching as a result of dynamism, entrepreneurship and innovation conditioned by existing technologies/ knowledge bases, assets, and capabilities (in particular when the technologies and knowledge bases of prevailing activities exhibit 'related variety') (Neffke et al., 2011; Dawley, 2014).
		• Close relations between firms in a supply chain, and investment in relation-specific assets, through which certain technologies and types of knowledge are favoured (Grabher, 1993; Maskell and Malmberg, 2007).
		• Sunk costs in capital base and infrastructure, which make divestment expensive (Martin and Sunley, 2006).
		• Development of a particular industrial organisation through which there may be too little or too much competition, which inhibits investment in innovation and renewal (Hervas-Oliver et al., 2011; Popp and Wilson, 2007).
		• Development of cluster specific institutional arrangements, such as standard practices, quality certification, registration, skills training, etc., which stifle renewal (Boschma, 2004).
	Mechanisms of path dependence and lock-in in skills and labour market	• 'Low-skill equilibrium' in which only new economic activities emerge or are attracted to a region, which capitalise in on low skills (e.g., Finegold and Soskice, 1988; Dawley et al., 2014); or 'high-skill equilibrium' in which a regional economy can constantly renew itself because of a large subset of population that is skilled and entrepreneurial (e.g. Glaeser, 2005).
		• Dominance of certain industries leads to a prevalence of certain skills in the labour market, and a distinctive culture (e.g. 'culture of dependency') (Cooke and Rehfeld, 2011).

Table 13.2 (Continued)

	Mechanisms of path dependence and lock-in in built-environment	• Lack of attractiveness of urban spaces and surrounding countryside because of environmental degradation, smoke stacks, slum housing, chemical outpourings and waste (Power et al., 2010), which results in a lack of investment because improvements are seen as less viable. Or alternatively attractiveness in this respect may induce more investments, and development of more amenities (new shops, cultural institutions, leisure facilities, etc.).
Political/ institutional domain	*Mechanisms of path dependence and lock-in in institutions*	• 'Local growth coalitions' and urban regimes with tight relations between business and politics, which may result in the protection of vested interests and support for the status quo (Olson, 1982; Grabher, 1993; Safford, 2009). • Incremental institutional change based on existing institutions, through 'layering', 'conversion', 'drift', 'displacement', 'recombination', etc. (Streeck and Thelen, 2005; Martin, 2010).
Cognitive domain	*Mechanisms of path dependence and lock-in in world views*	• Myopia and complacency in 'sense-making' in which only certain pieces of information are picked up and given weight, instead of an ongoing search for alternative options and new possibilities (Maskell and Malmberg, 2007; Weick et al., 2005; Schmidt, 2010). • 'Escalating commitment' in which more and more resources are committed to a certain course of action, even though this has so far been to no avail (or even resulted in negative outcomes), in order to prove the ultimate rationality of that course of action and/or to 'save face' (Staw, 1976; Tuchman, 1984).

Source: Based on Evenhuis (2016).

how multi-scalar processes and structures may feature within this framework, has the potential to be captured within this framework but remains an important challenge yet to be taken up (Martin and Sunley, 2006; Hassink, 2010a).

CONCLUSIONS

The evolutionary conceptualisation of resilience is characterised by its insistence on continuous renewal in regional economies, dismissing the notion of a return or shift to some equilibrium state. This entails that the qualitative processes through which renewal processes in the regional economy take place are foregrounded, rather than the more quantifiable dimensions of resistance, recovery, and shift. The question then becomes how we can best theorise the mechanisms and drivers of resilience, in particular with regard to the role of agency, of institutions, and of processes between various levels of scale. Accordingly we have reviewed and assessed the three main theoretical frameworks within evolutionary approaches. Generalised Darwinism starts from micro-level actors (mainly firms) and the processes between these, and in its account the portfolio of firms in a region, and – in the longer run – related variety and the constraining effects of co-evolving structures, play key roles. Accounts developed on the basis of Complexity Theory, have drawn attention to the connections between actors and the collective agency they develop in this way, and to the key role of government policy in facilitating (or inhibiting) regional resilience. However, it has some limitations in theorising the exact nature of the relations between actors (especially how these relations shape questions of power, and the way decision-making takes place). Moreover, relations and processes between various scales and beyond the region in question, have yet to be worked out.

In response, we think that the Path Dependency framework is most effective in addressing the limitations of existing approaches, offering a framework to better distinguish and connect different actors, structures, processes, and scales of resilience and adaptability (see also Pike et al., 2010).

This chapter has sought to bring together these three theoretical frameworks in discussion as a means towards developing an improved understanding of evolutionary approaches to regional resilience. Rather than seeing Path Dependency purely as just another alternative framework, therefore, we suggest that actually further work is needed to explore the extent to which it can serve as the basis for an overarching framework that can also incorporate mechanisms highlighted by Generalised Darwinism (between firms in the functional domain), and by Complexity Theory (connections between actors in mainly the institutional/political domain).[10] Moreover, as we have argued, while Path Dependency offers the scope to incorporate the multi-scalar dimensions of regional resilience, this remains an emerging research agenda. A key challenge becomes to theorise and examine the interactions (the 'path interdependencies') between the various path-dependent developments operating at various levels of scale (in particular clusters, in a region, at the national level, and even at the supranational level).

NOTES

1. The immediate alterations caused by the change in circumstances are not considered as part of this process, neither are alterations that occur autonomously within the region, and which are hence independent of changes in the broader environment.
2. Initial effect of a shock on output measures, such as gross value added, or employment.
3. Speed and degree of the rebound.
4. Move to a new equilibrium or growth trajectory.
5. As a consequence, evolutionary resilience is much harder to operationalise and measure. But at the same time, the evolutionary conceptualisation may rid the concept of any conservative overtones and the tendency of privileging the preservation of existing social relations (a critique levied by, for example, Swanstrom (2008) and MacKinnon and Derickson (2012)). Maintaining an existing system is then no longer a point of reference; and the processes of reorganisation and reorientation behind resilience are seen as entirely open-ended.
6. In addition, firms may to some extent adjust their routines in case those do not work well.
7. There has indeed recently been an acknowledgement of the importance of institutions (including the role of the state) in the long-run evolution of regions within this framework (e.g. Boschma and Capone, 2015; Boschma, 2015; Boschma and Frenken, 2015).
8. This 'connectedness' is in turn seen as a function of the 'self-organising tendencies' in the system.
9. For example, Strambach and colleagues have highlighted how institutions shape the options available for agents, but how agents work at the same time to actively alter institutions (Strambach, 2010; Strambach and Halkier, 2013). They have introduced the term 'path plasticity' to capture this: 'the dynamics within a path and the way actors use the narrowed down or the limited range of choice [. . .] in creative ways for the development of innovation without breaking out of the path' (Strambach and Halkier, 2013, p. 1).
10. Complexity Theory does not appear to have this same potential to provide an overarching framework that can encompass mechanisms in various domains and at various levels. This is mainly because its most important concepts are about the general structure of systems, and the dynamics within these structures; its concepts seem limited in the way they address the more particular nature of the relations between components and actors, and leave open the question of geographical scale (and more generally the boundaries of different 'systems').

ADDITIONAL READING

Boschma, R. (2015), 'Towards an evolutionary perspective on regional resilience'. *Regional Studies* **49**(5): 733–751.

Boschma, R. and Martin, R. (eds) (2010), *The Handbook of Evolutionary Economic Geography*. Cheltenham, UK and Northampton, MA, USA: Edward Elgar Publishing.

Henning, M., Stam, E. and Wenting, R. (2013), 'Path dependence research in regional economic development: cacophony or knowledge accumulation?' *Regional Studies* **47**(8): 1348–1362.

Martin, R. and Sunley, P. (2015), 'On the notion of regional resilience: conceptualisation and explanation'. *Journal of Economic Geography* **15**(1): 1–42.

14. Regional resilience: the critique revisited

Huiwen Gong and Robert Hassink

INTRODUCTION

One of the most intriguing questions in economic geography is why it is that some regional economies manage to renew themselves or to lock themselves out, whereas others are more locked in decline (Martin and Sunley, 2006). We have just used the verb *to renew*, others have used terms with slightly and subtly different meanings, such as *to adjust*, which refers to an extension of established trends, *to adapt* or *to transform*, which refer to changing structures (MacKinnon et al., 2009; Chapman et al., 2004; Hu and Hassink, 2015).

Several concepts related to evolutionary economic geography, such as path dependence, path creation, lock-ins, co-evolution, sunk costs, related variety, as well as cluster life cycles have been used in order to theorize about this question of regional adaptation. This evolutionary perspective has its roots in economics. Not only have many economic geographers introduced evolutionary thinking into their discipline (Boschma and Frenken, 2006; Hassink et al., 2014), this has also been the case in other disciplines, such as economics, planning and sociology (Frenken, 2007). In contrast to neoclassical theory, this school takes history and geography seriously by recognizing the importance of place-specific elements and processes to explain broader spatial patterns of technology evolution. Evolutionary economic geography deals with "the processes by which the economic landscape – the spatial organization of economic production, distribution and consumption – is transformed over time" (Boschma and Martin, 2007: 539). In this perspective, it is not only firms and industries, but also local and regional development policy, and in a broader sense the institutional environment of firms and industries, that affect the dynamism and adaptability of regional economies. The emergence and persistence of negative path dependence and lock-ins can hinder necessary adaptations (Hassink, 2010a).

The regional resilience framework might be an alternative concept to the above-mentioned evolutionary concepts to explain differences in regional economic adaptability. Studies on socioecological resilience (Agder, 2003), as well as on more or less successful responses to a crisis, such as the financial and economic crisis in 2008–10, have raised the interest in resilience from a regional and metropolitan perspective (Pendall et al., 2010; Swanstrom, 2008; Martin, 2010; Lang, 2012; Doran and Fingleton, 2015; Balland et al., 2015; Bristow and Healy, 2015). The highly cited special issue of the *Cambridge Journal of Regions, Economy and Society* published in 2010 can be regarded as the main conceptual foundation of regional resilience (Christopherson et al., 2010). However, in that special issue, critical voices were also expressed (Pike et al., 2010; Hassink, 2010b). After the publication of that special issue and the critique, a burgeoning conceptual and empirical literature emerged on regional resilience (for instance, Balland et al., 2015; Boschma, 2015; Brakman et al., 2015; MacKinnon and Derickson, 2013; Martin, 2012; Martin and Sunley, 2015; Bristow and Healy, 2014, 2015).

Therefore, the aim of this chapter, which builds upon Hassink (2010b), is to review this recent literature and, on the basis of that, to revisit the critique of the regional resilience concept. In the next section, the regional resilience framework will be further introduced. Then the critical discussion on the regional resilience framework will be juxtaposed with recently emerging conceptual and empirical literature, followed by a discussion and conclusions.

REGIONAL RESILIENCE

Several researchers belonging to a US national research network, sponsored by the MacArthur Foundation, have attempted to transfer the metaphor of resilience from psychology, ecology and disaster studies to regional economic development (Pendall et al., 2010; Swanstrom, 2008). According to Swanstrom (2008), resilience is more than a metaphor but less than a theory, it can be best depicted as a conceptual framework. It helps us to think about regions in a dynamic, holistic and systematic way, rather than providing us with testable hypotheses. A resilient region would be one in which "markets and local political structures continually adapt to changing environmental conditions and only when these processes fail, often due to misguided intervention by higher level authorities which stifle their ability to innovate, is the system forced to alter the big structures" (Swanstrom, 2008: 10). Although resilience is most often used in connection with sudden shocks and disasters, it can be applied to slowly developing challenges as well (Swanstrom, 2008; Pendall et al., 2010). Pendall et al. (2010) refer in this context to "slow burns".

Pendall et al. (2010) have distinguished four common themes in the literature on resilience in several academic fields. First, the studies often presume one or more equilibriums to which the situation will return:

> When we say that a person, society, ecosystem, or city is resilient, we generally mean that in the face of shock or stress, it either "returns to normal" (i.e., single equilibrium, or engineering version of resilience) rapidly afterward or at least does not easily get pushed into a "new normal" (i.e., an alternative equilibrium, or ecological version of resilience).
>
> (Pendall et al., 2010: 2)

Second, the studies take a systemic approach with internal and external factors that can both strengthen the system or put it under stress. Particularly in disaster studies and psychology, the external factors are often the stress-causing factors, whereas internal factors are seen as the strengthening ones. Third, the observed equilibriums have path-dependent elements, that is they are a consequence of cumulative decisions taken over a long period of time. Fourth, the studies stress the long-term view on resilience.

Martin (2012: 10) defines regional economic resilience as "the capacity of a regional economy to reconfigure, that is adapt, its structure (firms, industries, technologies, and institutions) so as to maintain an acceptable growth path in output, employment and wealth over time". According to him, the regional economic resilience in recent economic geography literature is generally interpreted in three different ways: an engineering or neoclassical view that emphasizes the bouncing back to a pre-recessional equilibrium state after transitory shocks; an ecological view that allows "hysteresis/ remanence" and path-switching to another stable state; and an adaptive or evolutionary view that regards resilience as path-dependent process of creative destruction. Recently, it is particularly the latter evolutionary view on regional resilience (see Christopherson et al., 2010; Simmie and Martin, 2010; Boschma, 2015; Balland et al., 2015) that contributes much to the understanding of the concept. When conceptualizing resilience in terms of a region's capacity to develop new growth paths, the evolutionary approach tends to distinguish between adaptation and adaptability (Bristow and Healy, 2015). Adaptation concerns changes within preconceived paths, while adaptability is about developing new pathways. In this framework, scholars argue that there is a trade-off between the two sides. Here, regional resilience has been associated primarily with long-term adaptability, how history can stand in the way of true economic renewal, and how to overcome negative lock-ins (Boschma, 2015; Balland et al., 2015).

In recent years, the notion of resilience has been applied in a broader set of fields related to regional resilience, such as resilience of individuals

(Doran and Fingleton, 2015), sectoral/industrial resilience (Fromhold-Eisehith, 2015), resilience of local knowledge production (Hannigan et al., 2015), local entrepreneurial resilience (Huggins and Thompson, 2015a; Williams and Vorley, 2014) and resilience of the labour market (Ibert and Schmidt, 2014). Although, on the one hand, these studies greatly enrich the regional resilience research, they, somehow, on the other hand, make "resilience" an even fuzzier concept (Markusen, 2003).

CAN REGIONAL RESILIENCE EXPLAIN DIFFERENCES IN REGIONAL ECONOMIC ADAPTABILITY? THE CRITIQUE REVISITED

Having presented the resilience framework; to what extent can regional resilience explain the differences in regional economic adaptability? And how does it compare with existing concepts around evolutionary economic geography (path dependence, lock-ins, cluster life cycle, the learning region) (Hassink, 2010b)?

In Hassink (2010b) it has become clear that there are some overlapping interests between the resilience framework and some evolutionary concepts, such as related and unrelated variety in relation to the diversity of a regional economy and the concept of co-evolution. The regional resilience framework refers to a regional economy that is able to resist external economic shocks. However, the more interesting question is not so much the resilience alone, but the adaption that has taken place and that ensures a long-term growth and prosperity of the regional economy. Resilience in connection with regions might be a useful concept in ecological and disaster studies, it is much less so in connection to regional economies, as has been stated in Hassink (2010b). This is due to three main shortcomings: first, the focus on equilibrium and multi-equilibriums; second, the neglect of state, institutions and policy at several spatial levels; and, third, the neglect of culture and social factors affecting adaptability (see also partly Pendall et al., 2010; Swanstrom, 2008). In the following subsections, these arguments will be juxtaposed by insights from recent regional resilience literature.

Equilibrium Thinking

First, the contingently constructed emphasis on equilibrium and multi-equilibriums in the resilience framework does not fit with the evolutionary theorem of regional economies in a constant state of change. Similar to Martin and Sunley (2010) and Pike et al. (2010), we are sceptical about equilibrium and also multi-equilibriums thinking in relation to regional economic development and path dependence: "we conceive of the idea of path dependence as entirely consistent with patterns of economic evolution in which technologies, industries, institutions, and regional economies adapt and mutate over time without ever reaching or tending towards any equilibrium" (Martin and Sunley, 2010: 84). This has not only been criticized concerning the resilience framework, it is also something that has been criticized concerning the canonical path dependence model (Martin, 2010). "The problem is that retaining notions of equilibrium in defining path dependence and 'lock-in' seems to run counter to the key tenets of evolutionary economics, especially the ideas of endogenous change, constant transformation, and the role of novelty" (Martin, 2010: 13). Socio-economic systems, such as regional economies, cannot be compared with radical technologies, as they are composite, heterogeneous entities which in fact "may never become 'locked-in' to any stable or 'equilibrium' configuration" due to continuous incremental changes (Martin, 2010: 20).

Recently many scholars, particularly economic geographers, have noticed this shortcoming of the regional resilience concept (Balland et al., 2015; Boschma, 2015; Bristow and Healy, 2015; Christopherson et al., 2010; Diodato and Weterings, 2015). Instead of favouring equilibrium thinking, they have emphasized the above-mentioned evolutionary approach. This approach focuses on the long-term evolution of regions and the ability of economic agents to adapt and reconfigure their industrial, technological, network and institutional structures within an economic system that is in constant motion. Resilient regions are capable of overcoming trade-offs between adaptation and adaptability, as embodied in related and unrelated variety, loosely coupled networks and loosely coherent institutional structures. These dynamics are twinned to processes of capitalist competition that continually reorder the competitive standing of technologies, modes of organization and institutions, and in aggregate, the firms and regions within which they are embedded (Balland et al., 2015). In this framework, history is key to understand how new growth paths develop in regions, and how industrial, network and institutional dimensions of resilience come together (Boschma, 2015).

While evolutionary thinking has brought the idea of dynamics to resilience study, this strand of research somehow still remains premature when it comes to issues such as the definition of the notion, the applicability of the concept and the measurement of the ideas. A much more comprehensive framework beyond the equilibrium model therefore is still needed.

Neglecting State and Policy at Several Spatial Levels

Second, and more importantly, the neglect of state and policy at several spatial levels in the resilience framework has been criticized (Swanstrom, 2008; Pike et al., 2010). According to Swanstrom (2008: 20) "the conceptual framework of resilience ignores the role of sovereign authorities in setting the rules for resilience, the need for researchers to make tough normative choices about desired end states, and the inevitability of political conflicts in resilience processes". "Politics cannot be subsumed to a natural order of things", as power and conflict are "present in regional governance in ways they are not present in ecosystems" (Swanstrom, 2008: 3). The state, policy, institutions and agency do play a very important role in explaining regional economic adaptability differences in some of the evolutionary concepts, such as political lock-ins or the learning region. Also Olson's (1982) statements regarding the negative impact of institutional sclerosis on economic development at the national level can be related to economic adaptability and according to Wößmann (2001), Olson's concept of institutional sclerosis can be well applied at the regional level. Not only can institutional rigidities hinder economic restructuring at both levels, also in a worst case scenario these rigid institutions at the regional and national level mutually reinforce each other.

Related to this second shortcoming, the resilience framework stresses decentralized autonomous consensus-oriented decision-making (Swanstrom, 2008; Bristow, 2010). External factors at higher levels of scale are often seen as a threat or causing the shock, but in some cases they can also be a chance for the renewal and transformation of regional economies, as seen, for instance, in the case of the restructuring of the textile cluster in Daegu, South Korea, where the central government initiated the necessary restructuring project (Cho and Hassink, 2009). Similarly, by conducting an employment growth model of all US county areas after 9/11 and the Great Recession, Xu and Warner (2015) find employment growth is positively related to state centralization of fiscal responsibility. According to them, state rescaling has shifted redistributive expenditure responsibility down to the local level, crowding out development investments and undermining local resilience.

The state and policies at several spatial levels, in fact, are of utmost importance in analysing and explaining differences in regional economic adaptability, as has been shown in several case-studies of old industrial areas (for example Hassink, 2010a; Hu and Hassink, 2016) as well as crisis response (Lang, 2012; Bristow and Healy, 2015).

Recently, some scholars have started to pay attention to the role of institutions in regional resilience (such as Balland et al., 2015; Bristow,

2010; Boschma, 2015; MacKinnon and Derickson, 2013). Boschma (2015) argues that institutions are highly related to regional resilience in three aspects: first, institutions are closely intertwined with the two other dimensions of regional resilience – techno-industrial variety, and networks; second, institutional structures that are subject to external shocks might have a direct impact on the capacity of regions to develop new growth paths, and thus on regional resilience; third, institutions can be linked to the trade-off between adaptation and adaptability, as there is a strong historical and path-dependent dimension to institutions. Linking resilience with new institutionalism, Lang (2012) highlights the vital role of a supportive institutional environment for the constant advancement of a resilient system. Resilience could be seen as being linked to a particular culture that constantly advances the key properties of the system and facilitates institutional learning in the long run. Connecting to a wider array of actors and multi-scalar institutional contexts that mediate the emergence and development of growth paths, Dawley (2014) argues that new path creation in offshore wind has to be understood as shaped by political interventions as well as by successive causal episodes of complex and geographically situated social agencies.

While institutions and policies have gained increasing attention, inconsistencies remain concerning the measurement of such factors when analysing regional resilience. Both quantitative and qualitative methods seem to have their own shortcomings; we will come back to this issue below.

The Role of Social Capital and Networks

Third, cultural norms and habits may also be an important source influencing adaptation and adaptability, but they have been largely ignored in previous resilience studies. There are of course both advantages and disadvantages of such social capital. Agder (2003), for instance, is relatively positive concerning the role of social capital. There are, however, legion of empirical studies stressing the weaknesses of strong ties: too strong ties or too much social capital can lead to cognitive lock-ins and thus weaken regional economic adaptability (Hauser et al., 2007; Rodríguez-Pose and Storper, 2006).

In recent years, notions such as cultural norms, social capital, human agency, communities, etc. are becoming increasingly popular nouns in resilience studies. Bristow and Healy (2014), for example, acknowledge the variable capacities of social actors to interpret shocks, make sense of their meaning and act in relation to them. In this ontology of including the human factors in resilience thinking, place and context become inescapable in the understanding of regional resilience. Huggins and Thompson

(2015a) examine localities in terms of the impact of community culture on the resilience of their entrepreneurial activity. They found that local social values play an important role in fostering entrepreneurial resilience. They also suggested that future policy intervention may be best targeted at the educational system, where the tolerance and skill-sets underpinning entrepreneurial resilience can be most effectively developed. Utilizing the case of Wales, Bristow and Healy (2015) explore how a complex adaptive system can be deployed to understand crisis responses of agents and their contingent, co-evolutionary development. The social foundations of economic behaviour, their interactions both with each other and their context, their past experience, and the prevailing norms and expectations, are particularly important in shaping adaptive agencies within regions in response to a crisis. Brakman et al. (2015) suggest that commuting areas near to large cities may have been more resistant to the economic crisis in 2008, because they possess more human capital.

Parallel with this increasing interest in the local social environment, recently, many scholars started to emphasize collective and contextual features, including connectivity and networks in regional resilience studies. Examples of this work are the study by Todo et al. (2015) on supply chain networks and the research by Boschma (2015) and Balland et al. (2015) on regional knowledge networks. Looking at network structures, there are in general two types of trade-offs between adaptation and adaptability: On the one hand, closely linked networks make regions perform better on adaptation but worse on adaptability (Boschma, 2015), as these networks might easily lead to lock-ins. On the other hand, local network structures with many nodes having few connections and lacking proximity between the various nodes in the region score higher on adaptability but lower on adaptation, as these provide opportunities to accommodate shocks, and give access to new and non-redundant knowledge (Boschma, 2015; Balland et al., 2015). Besides looking at network structures as a whole, key agents in networks also play a strategic role in regional resilience. Therefore, how to overcome the trade-offs between adaptation and adaptability at the level of structural properties of networks and how to coordinate different agents in local networks remain interesting questions that deserve more academic attention.

DISCUSSION AND CONCLUSIONS

After the special issue of *Cambridge Journal of Regions, Economy and Society* (2010) on regional resilience, there is an increasing literature exploring the theoretical as well as practical aspects of the notion of regional resilience. By juxtaposing earlier critique (Hassink, 2010b) with recently emerging conceptual and empirical literature on the topic, we find that much of the critique has been taken seriously in recent studies. However, new challenges or deficiencies emerge as more work has been done in the area.

First of all, the concept of "resilience" is becoming increasingly fuzzy, as it has been applied extensively to areas such as economic geography, regional and urban economies, planning, crisis, transportation, climate change, etc. As Martin and Sunley (2015: 1) put it: "There is still considerable ambiguity about what, precisely, is meant by the notion of regional economic resilience, about how it should be conceptualized and measured, what its determinants are, and how it links to patterns of long-run regional growth."

Moreover, policymakers have quickly adopted the resilience concept without clearly defining it. This has been criticized by MacKinnon and Derickson (2013), who have examined how the concept of resilience has been applied to places. According to them, resilience is externally defined by state agencies and expert knowledge in spheres such as security, emergency planning, economic development and urban design. Such a "top-down" road inevitably serves to reproduce wider social and spatial relations that generate turbulence and inequality. This criticism has been underlined by some scholars, such as Martin and Sunley:

> [A]s is often the case with new ideas (others that come to mind are "competitiveness" and "clusters"), the notion of regional and local economic "resilience" is already finding currency among those interested in policy. Resilience is emerging as an imperative "whose time has come" in policy debates around localities, cities and regions, propelling a new discourse of "constructing" or "building" regional and urban economic resilience.
>
> (Martin and Sunley, 2015: 2)

This new discourse has found a ready reception across a variety of policy bodies and scales, from the transnational to national, regional and local economic development agencies. However, "this eagerness to use the idea of regional and urban economic resilience as a policy tool or objective is arguably in danger of running somewhat ahead of our understanding of the concept" (Martin and Sunley, 2015: 3). There are many aspects (such as definition, measurement, theory, applicability, etc.) that need more discussion and exploration before it can form the basis of policy action. Martin et al. (2015) also manifest that it is not only highly necessary for those who formulate local policy to understand the notion of resilience, but core competencies of each local region, as well.

Second, we are critical concerning the methods used to study regional resilience. We have seen a surge in quantitative research on regional resilience looking at the impact of the economic structure, region-specific and competitiveness factors, and state rescaling for explaining differences in resilience (for example, Davies, 2011; Han and Goetz, 2015; Brakman et al., 2015; Xu and Warner, 2015). As pointed out by Wink (2014: 86), indicators of regional economic resilience are usually based on macroeconomic models: "These macroeconomic models, however, still refer to equilibrium, i.e., they consider disturbances to existing equilibriums, adjustment behavior afterwards and a new equilibrium as a result, and measure time and costs for assessment of effects." Although economic geographers tend to refute this equilibrium approach, and recently some of them analyse the resilient processes by introducing complexity theory (for instance, Boschma et al., 2015; Balland et al., 2015; Diodato and Weterings, 2015), such an equilibrium method somehow remains quite popular in resilience modelling, particularly in economics.

Besides this deficiency, macroeconomic approaches also tend to focus too narrowly on "objective" indicators to define vulnerability and resilience (Wink, 2014). Other factors, such as cognitive processes in regions, which affect acceptance of adaptation and adaptability, and psychological concepts related to capabilities of change, have gained little weight in these kind of quantitative studies. As a result of that, Wink (2014: 87) claims: "Concepts of vulnerability and resilience, as social constructs, should look for human perceptions and specificities in recognizing and coping with external shocks and change." We strongly agree with this point, but we think more exploration is needed on where quantitative and qualitative methods could complement each other (Strambach and Klement, 2016). Moreover, as regional economies are composite complex systems, which are composed of numerous heterogeneous firms, workers and institutions, a regional economy might be resilient in one sense but not in another. As a result, how to build such heterogeneity and complexity into the measurements of regional resilience remains a vital issue for regional resilience research.

Third, while the increasingly popular evolutionary thinking has brought the idea of dynamics to resilience study, this strand of research is still far from mature. First of all, the evolutionary literature remains disconnected from the core focus of the resilience literature, namely, the capacity of regions to absorb shocks, and the speed with which they can recover from them (Boschma, 2015). Moreover, there is a tendency in the literature to equate regional resilience with the avoidance of path dependence, as if regions need to escape from their historical legacy to develop new growth paths (Henning et al., 2013). The reality that the legacy of the past has a strong impact on regional adaptation and adaptability, does not necessarily mean that path dependence only causes problems of adjustment, and neither does it imply that developing new growth paths in regions need to break with the past, for history not only sets limits but also provides opportunities for making new combinations and diversifying into new pathways (Boschma, 2015).

All in all, we are consistent with the argument of Hassink (2010b) that we should be careful to take up another fashionable concept without first carefully exploring the value of it in answering key questions of economic geography, such as differences in regional economic adaptability. But on the other hand, after scrutinizing the recently emerging literature on regional resilience, we think that this concept can complement existing theoretical concepts in economic geography to explain differences in regional economic adaptability (see also Strambach and Klement, 2016). Particularly, as elements such as institutions, social capitals, networks and historical legacy of regions are increasingly being taken seriously in resilience studies, we believe that regional resilience potentially will become a powerful concept as long as issues such as the fuzziness of the concept, the way to measure it and the way evolutionary analysis should be carried out, are tackled properly.

ADDITIONAL READING

Balland, P.A., Rigby, D. and Boschma, R. (2015), 'The technological resilience of US cities'. *Cambridge Journal of Regions, Economy and Society* **8**(2): 167–184.
Boschma, R. (2015), 'Towards an evolutionary perspective on regional resilience'. *Regional Studies* **49**(5): 733–751.
Martin, R. and Sunley, P. (2015), 'On the notion of regional economic resilience: conceptualization and explanation'. *Journal of Economic Geography* **15**(1): 1–42.

15. Final thoughts and reflections

Nick Williams and Tim Vorley

Economic resilience is an emergent field in the social sciences, and this unique volume demonstrates that the concept can be applied at individual, organisational, sub-national and national levels. The rationale for this book was to explore and develop the concept of economic resilience in the context of uncertain economic times. Indeed, the contributions serve to highlight the applicability of resilience thinking and its strength as a conceptual lens in examining how to respond and react to external shocks. In this sense, resilience as a concept is used to describe the relationship between a system under observation and externally induced disruption, disturbance, shock or crisis. Consequently, resilience has become a key concept in understanding how individuals, organisations and government institutions respond to shocks and how the effects can be managed and minimised. In this concluding chapter, we emphasise some of the key lessons from the chapters to set out the ways in which the collection provides academic insights as well as implications for policy and practice.

The book has shown how the concept of resilience has evolved from natural and physical sciences to be appropriated and adopted within the social sciences. It is a concept that has taken on multiple courses and trajectories, and inevitably there are myriad ways in which resilience has become important to social science thinking and practice. Central to this emerging research field has been a focus on the determination of how social systems are constructed and understood, to work exploring how these contexts and conditions influence shocks to and the responses of the system. The chapters comprising this collection focus on the shocks as a result of the economic crisis on individuals and organisations as well as the aggregate impact at the local, regional and national scales. In this way, the book responds to the question of how resilient people, organisations and places are, as well as how they can develop greater resilience. Crucially, it approaches resilience as a complex set of arrangements that have impacts that span scales and invokes agency across space. The issues have attracted significant interest, not only from academics, but also policymakers and think tanks. Indeed, resilience has become a persuasive idiom and is malleable enough to encompass a broad range of applications in policy and practice. For policymakers, the emphasis is on the need to foster the resilience of communities, organisations and individuals in the face of multiple potential and realised shocks and crises.

The potential for 'fuzziness' in the concept of resilience, given its nascent nature, has been highlighted by a number of contributing authors, although this is a reflection of the recent development and application of resilience to different contexts. While the book has not sought to constrain authors with a strict definition, the chapters serve to highlight similarities as well as differences concerning how economic resilience can be applied. As we stated in the introduction to this volume and as the contributors attest, resilience serves as an important analytical lens for illuminating and examining the impact and the responses of shocks. The contributors highlight that there is no 'one size fits all' solution to these shocks, and that different approaches in both the private and public sectors must be appropriate to the context in which they are being applied. Consequently, the search for solutions to external challenges is ongoing and can only be achieved through policy experimentation. There is no silver bullet for ensuring individuals, organisations and economies are more resilient, but through the implications provided in each of the chapters it is possible for broad lessons to be provided and recommendations to be integrated into policy frameworks.

Resilience thinking, therefore, offers an opportunity to reframe economic development policy and practice and to provide a clear evidence base of the cultural, economic, political and social conditions that shape the adaptability, flexibility and responsiveness to crises in their many forms. Given the early developmental stage of research on resilience and crises, there is an opportunity to both advance and bring coherence to these debates. The evolutionary approach towards resilience challenges both actors and researchers to explore an evolutionary transition towards more sustainable enterprise and sustainable economies taking into account how conditions emerge and are propagated by stakeholders involved in policy formulation. Harnessing resilience and new path creation do not come from economic growth alone. Rather, it requires a more fundamental change in the underlying economic and social structure within a locality to empower entrepreneurs and other actors to explore new markets, technologies and organizational forms. As resources attracted to a locality during a positive growth phase may quickly leave when the immediate opportunity expires or when a crisis hits, making operations more challenging or less cost-effective. To avoid this there is a need for political and business communities to work to create their own unique assemblage to drive economic growth, and with it promote more sustainable economic development as well as enhancing economic resilience.

The imperative to come up with new solutions so that the impact of crises can be minimised will be particularly acute in areas that are reliant on specific sectors or, alternatively, have a high proportion of public sector employment. While there is evidence that businesses and industries have the capacity to remake and remodel themselves through adaptability and flexibility, the success (or failure) to do so will have a spatial impact on their resilience and the resilience of place. As such, the importance of support for specific industrial sectors must be properly considered by policymakers. This is not to say that direct intervention is always the appropriate course of action, but, more importantly, policymakers should consider the linkages between industrial sectors, firms and places. In this way the interdependencies that affect the resilience of localities can be better understood. Consequently, a systems approach is required that focuses on inter- and intra-sectoral linkages, rather than focusing on support for a specific sector that may be vulnerable to a shock such as economic downturn.

At the same time, the attractiveness of a place to sectors and individual businesses must be considered by policymakers. In the competitive global economy, locations compete for investment by companies, sectors and governments, resulting in winners and losers. With the emergence of the knowledge economy, 'smokestack chasing' of traditional industries is no longer sufficient. Within countries and regions, competition and uneven investment has seen the distinction between core and periphery places extenuated, with deep implications for the spatial distribution of economic activities and the relative resilience of different places. Often, peripheral places adopt the designs and models developed for core cities, aiming for a convergence of economic performance over time. Alternatively, without effective strategies they can become more marginalised from dominant economic centres. However, cities are inherently complex and unique and in that complexity lies much of their resilience. This means that intelligent institutional leadership is required that is able to reflect the strengths and future potential of core and peripheral places so that appropriate strategies can be developed.

Within debates on resilience, the role of innovation and entrepreneurship is often regarded as integral to fostering and sustaining a dynamic and diverse economy, by stimulating competition, driving innovation, creating employment and increasing productivity. The presence of a diverse economic base often serves to lessen the impact of external shocks. While path dependency shapes the development of economies, entrepreneurially engaged economies are more likely to avoid 'lock-in' and exhibit path renewal, extension and creation and with it be more resilient. Consequently, entrepreneurship and enterprise are recognised as crucial to economic resilience. This is in part due to the ability of entrepreneurs and small businesses to respond and adapt to external shocks and crises, which in turn has a positive impact on the resilience of their locality. However, in lagging and peripheral regions, such as traditional industrial areas, the ability to adapt is lower, which – coupled with low levels of entrepreneurial activity – serves to undermine economic resilience.

To this end, two broad lessons can be distilled that have policy relevance. First, while there is a need to identify and build on core competencies of regions, there is a need for strategy to look beyond the extension of existing paths to the renewal and creation of new paths. This is not about picking winners, but rather creating conditions that allow entrepreneurship to thrive and contribute to the diversification of economic activity. Second, there is a need to ensure that any entrepreneurial response both meaningfully combines and is premised upon appropriate public- and private-sector action partnership. While governments around the world have provided an abundance of support for entrepreneurship, this needs to create the conditions for high growth potential activity, flexible and adaptable businesses to thrive, rather than simply increasing the number of start-ups per se. Harnessing entrepreneurship has implications both for individual entrepreneurs themselves, but also the local, regional and national contexts in which they operate. This in turn, will improve the resilience of the local, regional and national context in which they operate if the nature of entrepreneurial activity is productive.

A significant factor determining the adaptive ability (of a region or locality) is the way in which public policy can affect the trajectory of the economy over time by influencing and investing in the business environment, skills profile, institutional arrangements and infrastructure. The role of public policy is particularly pertinent during the initial phases of decline following a shock or crisis, but is also clearly important in the reorganisation and restructuring phase also. In this sense, resilience is commonly an issue of political economy, as the governance and strategies of public bodies will determine what policy objectives are prioritised and how resources are allocated in responding to an economic shock or crisis. Government bodies thus determine the overall approach to resilience; for example, through spending or austerity. The extent to which national governments introduce specific measures to assist localities will cause variance, while the rescaling of regions according to different priorities will inevitably influence the uptake and success of the 'resilience agenda' in different places. Different rates and types of entrepreneurship at the national, regional and local level, and thus how resilient places are, can in part be explained by culture. Depending on the prevailing culture, different routes are open to achieving entrepreneurial resilience through risk-taking and creative mould-breaking, as well as the efforts of collective, networked and civically engaged entrepreneurs. While it is difficult for governments to influence culture, creating the correct institutional environment may encourage desired behaviour that becomes reinforced over time within the community culture of localities, with the education system and local role models able to play a key role in fostering entrepreneurship.

In sum, while there is a growing tendency in the literature to advocate the resilience approach, there needs to be an increasing focus on how resilience thinking is applied in practice through different policy approaches. This involves examination of the role of governance institutions in supporting or indeed undermining resilience, and how the private sector, including individual entrepreneurs, businesses and sectors, responds to crisis, whether this is global economic challenges regional changes or localised challenges such as riots. We acknowledge that resilience is an emerging concept and thus will take time to become embedded in social science theory and policy practice. However, its strength lies in its application across a range of different contexts. This volume brings together key research and provides a springboard for further examination and application of this important topic as governments and entrepreneurs around the world seek to minimise and/or respond positively to external shocks. As well as taking forward the theoretical contribution of resilience, it is hoped that the volume provides guidance to policymakers in terms of how to foster more resilient economies and people. With greater understanding of the concept and its application, more resilient futures can be secured.

References

Aas, B., Buvik, A. and Cakic, D. (2008), 'Outsourcing of logistics activities in a complex supply chain: a case study from the Norwegian oil and gas industry'. *International Journal of Procurement Management* 1: 280–296.

ACEA (2015), *The Automobile Industry Pocket Guide 2015/2016*. Brussels: ACEA Communications Department.

Acs, Z.J., Desai, S. and Hessels, J. (2008), 'Entrepreneurship, economic development and institutions'. *Small Business Economics* 31(2/3): 219–234.

Adams, T. (2015), 'Self-driving cars: from 2020 you will become a permanent backseat driver', *Guardian*, 13 September, www.theguardian.com/technology/2015/sep/13/self-driving-cars-bmw-google-2020-driving (accessed 5 May 2016).

AEA (2011), *Local and Regional Carbon Dioxide Emissions Estimates for 2005–2009 for the UK: Technical Report*. Didcot: AEA Technology.

Agder, W.N. (2003), 'Social capital, collective action, and adaptation to climate change'. *Economic Geography* 79(4): 387–404.

Agrawal, A. and Cockburn, I. (2003), 'The anchor tenant hypothesis: exploring the role of large, local, R&D-intensive firms in regional innovation systems'. *International Journal of Industrial Organization* 21(9): 1227–1253.

Aguilera, D.C. (1998), *Crisis Intervention: Theory and Methodology*. Missouri: Mosby.

A'Hearn, B. and Venables, A.J. (2013), 'Regional disparities: internal geography and external trade'. In G. Toniolo (ed.), *The Oxford Handbook of the Italian Economy since Unification*. Oxford: Oxford University Press, 599–630.

Aidis, R., Estrin, S. and Mickiewicz, T. (2008), 'Institutions and entrepreneurship development in Russia: a comparative perspective'. *Journal of Business Venturing* 23(6): 656.

Alesch, D., Holly, J., Mittler, E. and Nagy, R. (2001), *Organizations at Risk: What Happens When Small Business and Not-For-Profits Encounter Natural Disasters?* Technical Report, Public Entity Risk Institute, Fairfax, VA.

Alinsky, S. (1971), *Rules for Radicals*. New York: Vintage.

Amoros, J.E. and Bosma, N. (2013), *Global Entrepreneurship Monitor 2013 Global Report*. Babson Park, MA: Global Entrepreneurship Monitor.

Anderson, A.R. (2000), 'Paradox in the periphery: an entrepreneurial reconstruction?'. *Entrepreneurship and Regional Development* 12(1): 91–109.

Anderson, A.R. and Smith, R. (2007), 'The moral space in entrepreneurship: an exploration of ethical imperatives and the moral legitimacy of being enterprising'. *Entrepreneurship and Regional Development* 19(6): 479–497.

Anderson, M.B. (1995), 'Vulnerability to disaster and sustainable development: a general framework for assessing vulnerability'. In M. Munasinghe and C. Clarke (eds), *Disaster Prevention for Sustainable Development: Economic and Policy Issues*. A paper for the Yokohama World Conference on Natural Disaster Reduction, May; International Decade for Natural Disaster Reduction (IDNDR) and the World Bank, 23–27.

Andres, L. and Round, J. (2015), 'The role of "persistent resilience" within everyday life and polity: households coping with marginality within the "Big Society"'. *Environment and Planning A* 47(3): 676–690.

Aoyama, Y. (2009), 'Entrepreneurship and regional culture: the case of Hamamatsu and Kyoto, Japan'. *Regional Studies* 43(3): 495–512.

Arbia, G. and Baltagi, B.H. (eds) (2008), *Spatial Econometrics: Methods and Applications*. Berlin: Springer Science & Business Media.

Arbia, G. and Basile, R. (2005), 'Spatial dependence and nonlinearities in regional growth behaviour in Italy'. *Statistica* 65(2): 145–167.

Arbia, G. and Paelink, J.H.P. (2003), 'Economic convergence or divergence? Modelling the regional dynamics of EU regions'. *Journal of Geographical Systems* 5: 291–314.

Arbolino, R., Di Caro, P. and Marani, U. (2016), *Regional Resilience During the Great Recession: The Role of the European Union Cohesion Policy*. Mimeo.

Arrow, K.J. (1962), 'The economic implications of learning by doing'. *Review of Economic Studies* 29: 155–173.

Arthur, W.B. (2009), 'Complexity and the economy'. In J.B. Rosser (ed.), *Handbook of Research on Complexity*. Cheltenham, UK and Northampton, USA: Edward Elgar Publishing, 12–21.

Asheim, B.T. and Isaksen, A. (2002), 'Regional innovation systems: the integration of local "sticky" and global "ubiquitous" knowledge'. *Journal of Technology Transfer* 27(1): 77.

Atkinson, R. and Kintrea, K. (2000), 'Owner occupation, social mix and neighbourhood impacts'. *Policy and Politics* 28(1): 93–108.

Audretsch, D.B. and Feldman, M.P. (1996), 'R&D spillovers and the geography of innovation and production'. *The American Economic Review* **86**(3): 630–640.

Auer, P. and Cazes, S. (2000), 'The resilience of the long-term employment relationship: evidence from the industrialized countries'. *International Labour Review* **139**(4): 379–408.

Ayres, S. and Pearce, G. (2013), 'A Whitehall perspective on decentralisation in England's emerging territories'. *Local Economy* **28**: 801–816.

Azzam, T. and Riggio, R.E. (2003), 'Community based civic leadership programs: a descriptive investigation'. *Journal of Leadership & Organizational Studies* **10**(1): 55–67.

Bailey, D. and De Propris, L. (2014), 'Editorial: recession, recovery and resilience?'. *Regional Studies* **48**(11): 1757–1760.

Bailey, D. and de Ruyter, A. (2012), 'Re-examining the BMW-Rover affair: a case study of corporate, strategic and government failure?'. *International Journal of Automotive Technology and Management* **12**(2): 117–136.

Bailey, D. and Kobayashi, S. (2008), 'Life after Longbridge? Crisis and restructuring in the West Midlands auto cluster'. In M. Farschi, O. Janne and P. McCann (eds), *Industrial Regeneration and Regional Policy Options in a Global Economy*. Cheltenham, UK and Northampton, USA: Edward Elgar Publishing, 129–154.

Bailey, D. and Turok, I. (2016), 'Editorial: resilience revisited'. *Regional Studies* **50**(4): 557–560.

Bailey, D., Bellandi, M., Caloffi, A. and De Propris, L. (2010), 'Place-renewing leadership: trajectories of change for mature manufacturing regions in Europe'. *Policy Studies* **31**: 457–474.

Bailey, D., Kobayashi, S. and MacNeill, S. (2008), 'Rover and out? Globalization, the West Midlands auto cluster, and the end of MG Rover'. *Policy Studies* **29**(3): 267–279.

Bailey, N. and Pill, M. (2015), 'Can the state empower communities through localism? An evaluation of recent approaches to neighbourhood governance in England'. *Environment and Planning C: Government and Policy* **33**: 289–304.

Bailey, N., Barker, A. and Macdonald, K. (1996), *Partnership Agencies in British Urban Policy*. London: UCL Press.

Balland, P.A., Rigby, D. and Boschma, R. (2015), 'The technological resilience of US cities'. *Cambridge Journal of Regions, Economy and Society* **8**(2): 167–184.

Bamiatzi, V. and Kirchmaier, T. (2014), 'Strategies for superior performance under adverse conditions: a focus on small and medium-sized high-growth firms'. *International Small Business Journal* **32**(3): 259–284.

Bamiatzi, V., Cavusgil, S.T., Jabbour, L. and Sinkovics, R.R. (2014), 'Does business group affiliation help firms achieve superior performance during industrial downturns? An empirical examination'. *International Business Review* **23**(1): 195–211.

Banahene, K.O., Anvuur, A.M. and Dainty, A.R. (2014), 'Conceptualising organisational resilience: an investigation into project organising'. In A. Raiden and E. Aboagye-Nimo (eds), *Proceedings 30th Annual ARCOM Conference*, 1–3 September 2014, Portsmouth: Association of Researchers in Construction Management, 795–804.

Bank of Italy (2015a), *Economie Regionali – L'economia delle regioni Italiane*. December, Rome.

Bank of Italy (2015b), *Bollettino Economico n.4*, October, Rome.

Barca, F. (2009), *An Agenda for a Reformed Cohesion Policy: A Place-based Approach to Meeting European Union Challenges and Expectations*. Brussels: DG Regio.

Barca, F., McCann, P. and Rodríguez-Pose, A. (2012), 'The case for regional development intervention: place-based versus place-neutral approaches?'. *Journal of Regional Science* **52**(1): 134–152.

Baron, R. (2008), 'The role of affect in the entrepreneurial process'. *Academy of Management Review* **33**(2): 328–340.

Barton, A. (1970), *Communities in Disasters*. New York: Anchor.

Bartz, W. and Winkler, A. (2016), 'Flexible or fragile? The growth performance of small and young businesses during the global financial crisis – evidence from Germany'. *Journal of Business Venturing* **31**(2): 196–215.

Bathelt, H., Malmberg, P. and Maskell, P. (2004), 'Clusters and knowledge: local buzz, global pipelines and the process of knowledge creation'. *Progress in Human Geography* **28**: 31–56.

Bathelt, H., Munro, A.K. and Spigel, B. (2013), 'Challenges of transformation: innovation, re-bundling, and traditional manufacturing in Canada's technology triangle'. *Regional Studies* **47**(7): 1111–1130.

Baumol, W.J. (1990), 'Entrepreneurship: productive, unproductive and destructive'. *Journal of Political Economy* **98**(5): 892–921.

BBC News Online (2006), 'Q&A: Why Peugeot is leaving the UK', 18 April, http://news.bbc.co.uk/1/hi/business/4919922.stm (accessed 5 May 2016).

Beck, N. and Katz, J.N. (1995), 'What to do (and not to do) with time-series cross-section data'. *American Political Science Review* **89**(3): 634–647.

Beine, M., Bos, C.S. and Coulombe, S. (2012), 'Does the Canadian economy suffer from Dutch Disease?'. *Resource and Energy Economics* **34**(4): 468–492.

Beinhocker, E.D. (2007), *The Origin of Wealth: Evolution, Complexity, and the Radical Remaking of Economics*. London: Random House.

Bénabou, R. and Tirole, J. (2006), 'Belief in a just world and redistributive politics'. *Quarterly Journal of Economics* **121**(2): 699–746.

Benneworth, P. and Charles, D. (2005), 'University spin-off policies and economic development in less successful regions: learning from two decades of policy practice'. *European Planning Studies* **13**: 537–557.

Bentley, G. (2000), 'The automotive industry: change and challenge for the RDAs'. In G. Bentley and J. Gibney (eds), *Regional Development Agencies and Business Change*. Aldershot: Ashgate, 125–150.

Bentley, G. (2007), 'Dealing with strategic change: a trio of automotive industry closures in the West Midlands'. *Strategic Change* **16**(8): 361–370.

Bentley, G., Bailey, D. and MacNeill, S. (2013), 'Restructuring in the European auto industry'. In P. McCann, F. Giarratani and G. Hewings (eds), *Handbook of Economic Geography and Industry Studies*. Cheltenham, UK and Northampton, MA, USA: Edward Elgar Publishing, 67–96.

Bentley, G., Pugalis, L. and Shutt, J. (2017), 'Leadership and systems of governance: the constraints on the scope for leadership of place-based development in sub-national territories'. *Regional Studies* **51**(2): 194–209.

Berglund, H. (2007), 'Researching entrepreneurship as lived experience'. In H. Neergaard and J.P. Ulhøi (eds), *Handbook of Qualitative Research Methods in Entrepreneurship*. Cheltenham, UK and Northampton, MA, USA: Edward Elgar Publishing, 75–93.

Berglund, H. and Hellström, T. (2002), 'Enacting risk in independent technological innovation'. *International Journal of Risk Assessment and Management* **3**(2–4): 205–221.

Beugelsdijk, S. (2007), 'Entrepreneurial culture, regional innovativeness and economic growth'. *Journal of Evolutionary Economics* **17**(2): 75–82.

Beugelsdijk, S. and Maseland, R. (2011), *Culture in Economics: History, Methodological Reflections and Contemporary Applications*. Cambridge: Cambridge University Press.

Bhamra, R. and S. Dani (2011), 'Creating resilient SMEs'. *International Journal of Production Research* **49**(18): 5373–5374.

Bhamra, R., Dani, S. and Burnard, K. (2011), 'Resilience: the concept, a literature review and future directions'. *International Journal of Production Research* **49**(18): 5375–5393.

BIS (2010), *Local Growth: Realising Every Place's Potential*. Cm 7961, 28 October 2010.

Bjarnason, S. and Coldstream, P. (eds) (2003), *The Idea of Engagement: Universities in Society*. London: Association of Commonwealth Universities.

Blatt, R. (2009), 'Resilience in entrepreneurial teams: developing the capacity to pull through'. *Frontiers of Entrepreneurship Research* **29**(11).

Bodnar, G.M., Consolandi, C., Gabbi, G. and Jaiswal-Dale, A. (2013), 'Risk management for Italian non-financial firms: currency and interest rate exposure'. *European Financial Management* **19**(5): 887–910.

Bonanno, G. (2004), 'Loss, trauma, and human resilience have we underestimated the human capacity to thrive after extremely aversive events?'. *American Psychologist* **59**(1): 20–28.

Bonanno, G. (2005), 'Resilience in the face of potential trauma'. *Current Directions in Psychological Science* **14**(3): 135–138.

Bonanno, G., Papa, A. and O'Neill, K. (2001), 'Loss and human resilience'. *Applied and Preventative Psychology* **10**(3): 193–206.

Bosch Worldwide (2016), *Bosch in Figures*, www.bosch.com/en/com/bosch_group/bosch_figures/bosch-figures.php (accessed 4 May 2016).

Boschma, R. (2004), 'Competitiveness of regions from an evolutionary perspective'. *Regional Studies* **38**(9): 1001–1014.

Boschma, R. (2015), 'Towards an evolutionary perspective on regional resilience'. *Regional Studies* **49**(5): 733–751.

Boschma, R. and Capone, G. (2015), 'Institutions and diversification: related versus unrelated diversification in a varieties of capitalism framework'. *Research Policy* **44**(10): 1902–1914.

Boschma, R. and Frenken, K. (2006), 'Why is economic geography not an evolutionary science? Towards an evolutionary economic geography'. *Journal of Economic Geography* **6**(3): 273–302.

Boschma, R. and Frenken, K. (2009), 'Some notes on institutions in evolutionary economic geography'. *Economic Geography* **85**(2): 151–158.

Boschma, R. and Frenken, K. (2011), 'The emerging empirics of evolutionary economic geography'. *Journal of Economic Geography* **11**(2): 295–307.

Boschma, R. and Frenken, K. (2015), *Evolutionary Economic Geography*. Papers in Evolutionary Economic Geography #15.18. Utrecht: Utrecht University.

Boschma, R. and Lambooy, J. (1999), 'The prospects of an adjustment policy based on collective learning in old industrial regions'. *Geojournal* **49**: 391–399.

Boschma, R. and Martin, R. (2007), 'Editorial: constructing an evolutionary economic geography'. *Journal of Economic Geography* **7**(5): 537–548.

Boschma, R. and Martin, R. (eds) (2010), *The Handbook of Evolutionary Economic Geography*. Cheltenham, UK and Northampton, USA: Edward Elgar Publishing.

Boschma, R., Balland, P.A. and Kogler, D.F. (2015), 'Relatedness and technological change in cities: the rise and fall of technological knowledge in US metropolitan areas from 1981 to 2010'. *Industrial and Corporate Change* **24**(1): 223–250.

Boschma, R., Minondo, A. and Navarro, M. (2013), 'The emergence of new industries at the regional level in Spain: a proximity approach based on product relatedness'. *Economic Geography* **89**(1): 29–51.

Boyte, H.C. (2005), 'Reframing democracy: governance, civic agency, and politics'. *Public Administration Review* **65**: 536–546.

Brakman, S., Garretsen, H. and van Marrewijk, C. (2015), 'Regional resilience across Europe: on urbanisation and the initial impact of the Great Recession'. *Cambridge Journal of Regions, Economy and Society* **8**(2): 225–240.

Brennan, A., Rhodes, J. and Tyler, P. (2000), 'The nature of local area social exclusion in England and the role of the labour market'. *Oxford Review of Economic Policy* **16**(1): 129–146.

Briguglio, L., Cordina, G., Farrugia, N. and Vella, S. (2009). 'Economic vulnerability and resilience: concepts and measurements'. *Oxford Development Studies* **37**(3): 229–247.

Bristow, G. (2010), 'Resilient regions: re-"place"ing regional competitiveness'. *Cambridge Journal of Regions, Economy and Society* **3**(1): 153–167.

Bristow, G. and Healy, A. (2014), 'Regional resilience: an agency perspective'. *Regional Studies* **48**(5): 923–935.

Bristow, G. and Healy, A. (2015), 'Crisis response, choice and resilience: insights from complexity thinking'. *Cambridge Journal of Regions, Economy and Society* **8**(2): 241–256.

Bristow, G., Porter, J. and Cooke, P. (2012), *Path Interdependence, Firm Innovation and Resilience: A Complex Adaptive Systems Perspective.* Working Paper CASS, Cardiff, Cardiff University.

Brooks, C., Vorley, T. and Williams, N. (2016), 'The role of civic leadership in fostering economic resilience in city regions'. *Policy Studies* **37**(1): 1–16.

Bruton, G., Ahlstrom, D. and Li, H-L. (2010), 'Institutional theory and entrepreneurship: where are we now and where do we need to move in the future'. *Entrepreneurship Theory and Practice* **34**(3): 421–440.

Bruton, G., Ahlstrom, D. and Obloj, K. (2008), 'Entrepreneurship in emerging economies: where are we today and where should the research go in the future'. *Entrepreneurship Theory and Practice* **32**(1): 1–14.

Bryman, A. (2012), *Social Research Methods*, 4th edn. Oxford: Oxford University Press.

Bryson, J.R., Clark, J.J and Vanchan, V. (eds) (2015), *The Handbook of Manufacturing Industries in the World Economy.* Cheltenham, UK and Northampton, MA, USA: Edward Elgar Publishing.

Buchanan, D.A. (2012), 'Case studies in organizational research'. In

G. Symon and C. Cassell (eds), *The Practice of Qualitative Organizational Research: Core Methods and Current Challenges.* London: Sage Publications, 373–392.

Buchanan, D.A. and Denyer, D. (2013), 'Research tomorrow's crisis: methodological innovations and wider implications'. *International Journal of Management Reviews* **15**(2): 205–224.

Buck, N. and While, A. (2015), 'Competitive urbanism and the limits to smart city innovation: the UK Future Cities initiative'. *Urban Studies,* DOI:10.1177/0042098015597162.

Bulkens, M., Minca, C. and Muzaini, H. (2015), 'Storytelling as method in spatial planning'. *European Planning Studies* **23**(11): 2310–2326.

Burnard, K. and Bhamra, R. (2011), 'Organisational resilience: development of a conceptual framework for organisational responses'. *International Journal of Production Research* **49**(18): 5581–5599.

Cable, V. and Pickles, E. (2010), *Local Enterprise Partnerships: Open Letter to Local Authority Leaders and Business Leaders.* London: HM Government.

Cadigan, S.T. (2009), *Newfoundland and Labrador: A History.* Toronto: University of Toronto Press.

Cainelli, G., Montresor, S. and Marzetti, G.V. (2012), 'Production and financial linkages in inter-firm networks: structural variety, risk-sharing and resilience'. *Journal of Evolutionary Economics* **22**(4): 711–734.

Calhoun, C. (2011), 'Civil society and the public sphere'. In M. Edwards (ed.), *The Oxford Handbook of Civil Society.* New York: Oxford University Press, 311–323.

Callahan, R. (2007), 'Governance: the collision of politics and cooperation'. *Public Administration Review* **67**: 290–301.

Camagni, R. and Capello, R. (2015), 'Rationale and design of EU cohesion policies in a period of crisis'. *Regional Science Policy & Practice* **7**(1): 25–47.

Canova, F., Coutinho, L. and Kontolemis, Z. (2012), *Measuring the Macroeconomic Resilience of Industrial Sectors in the EU and Assessing the Role of Product Market Regulations.* European Economy Occasional Papers No. 112. Brussels: European Commission.

Cardona, O.D. (2004), 'The need for rethinking the concepts of vulnerability and risk from a holistic perspective: a necessary review and criticism for effective risk management'. In G. Bankoff, G. Frerks and D. Hilhorst (eds), *Mapping Vulnerability: Disasters, Development and People.* London: Earthscan.

Carr, R. (2015), *The Next LEPs: Unlocking Growth Across Our Localities.* London: Localis.

Carrington, W.J., McCue, K. and Pierce, B. (1996), 'The role of employer/ employee interactions in labor market cycles: evidence from the self-employed'. *Journal of Labor Economics* **14**(4): 571–602.

Cellini, R. and Torrisi, G. (2014), 'Regional resilience in Italy: a very long-run analysis'. *Regional Studies* **48**(11): 1779–1796.

Cellini, R., Di Caro, P. and Torrisi, G. (2016), 'Regional resilience in Italy: do employment and income tell the same story?'. In R. Huggins and P. Thompson (eds), *Handbook of Regions and Competitiveness*. Cheltenham, UK and Northampton, MA, USA: Edward Elgar Publishing.

Cerra, V. and Saxena, S.C. (2008), 'Growth dynamics: the myth of economic recovery'. *American Economic Review* **98**(1): 439–457.

Champion, T. and Townsend, A. (2013), 'Great Britain's second-order city regions in recessions'. *Environment and Planning A* **45**(2): 362–382.

Chapman, K., MacKinnon, D. and Cumbers, A. (2004), 'Adjustment or renewal in regional clusters? A study of diversification amongst SMEs in the Aberdeen oil complex'. *Transactions of the Institute of British Geographers* **29**(3): 382–396.

Chesbrough, H. (2006), *Open Innovation*. Boston: Harvard Business School Press.

Cho, M-R. and Hassink, R. (2009), 'The limits to locking-out through restructuring: the textile industry in Daegu, South Korea'. *Regional Studies* **43**(9): 1183–1198.

Christopherson, S. and Clark, J. (2007), *Remaking Regional Economies: Power, Labor, and Firm Strategies in the Knowledge Economy*. New York: Routledge.

Christopherson, S.J., Michie, J. and Tyler, P. (2010), 'Regional resilience: theoretical and empirical perspectives'. *Cambridge Journal of Regions, Economy and Society* **3**: 3–10.

Cioccio, L. and Michael, E.J. (2007), 'Hazard or disaster: tourism management for the inevitable in Northeast Victoria'. *Tourism Management* **28**(1): 1–11.

Clark, A.E. (2003), 'Unemployment as a social norm: psychological evidence from panel data'. *Journal of Labor Economics* **21**(2): 323–351.

Clark, J. (2013), *Working Regions: Reconnecting Innovation and Production in the Knowledge Economy*. New York: Routledge.

Clark, J. and Christopherson, S. (2009), 'Integrating Investment and Distribution: A Critical Regionalist Approach to Progressive Regionalism'. *Journal of Planning Education and Research (JPER)* **28**(3): 341–54.

Clark, J., Huang, H-I. and Walsh, J.P. (2010), 'A typology of innovation districts: what it means for regional resilience'. *Cambridge Journal of Regions, Economies, and Society* **3**(1): 121–37.

Clarke, N. and Cochrane, A. (2013), 'Geographies and politics of localism: the localism of the United Kingdom's coalition government'. *Political Geography* **34**: 10–23.

Clavel, P. (1994), 'The evolution of advocacy planning'. *American Planning Association. Journal of the American Planning Association* **60**(2): 146.

Coe, N.M. (2011), 'Geographies of production I: an evolutionary revolution?'. *Progress in Human Geography* **35**(1): 81–91.

Cook, J., Pringle, S., Bailey, D., Cammis, S., Wilkinson, C. and Amison, P. (2013), *Economic Shocks Research: A Report to the Department for Business, Innovation and Skills*. Cambridge: SQW.

Cooke, P. (2005), 'Regionally asymmetric knowledge capabilities and open innovation exploring "Globalisation 2" – a new model of industry organisation'. *Research Policy* **34**(8): 1128.

Cooke, P. and Morgan, K. (1991), *The Intelligent Region: Industrial and Institutional Innovation in Emilia-Romagna*. Regional Industrial Research Report 7. Cardiff: University of Wales College of Cardiff.

Cooke, P. and Rehfeld, D. (2011), 'Path dependence and new paths in regional evolution: in search of the role of culture'. *European Planning Studies* **19**(11): 1909–1929.

Cope, J. (2011), 'Entrepreneurial learning from failure: an interpretive phenomenological analysis'. *Journal of Business Venturing* **26**(6): 604–623.

Corden, W.M. (1982), 'Booming sector and Dutch Disease economics: survey and consolidation'. *Oxford Economic Papers* **36**(3): 359–380.

Corey, C.M. and Deitch, E.A. (2011), 'Factors affecting business recovery immediately after Hurricane Katrina'. *Journal of Contingencies and Crisis Management* **19**(3): 169–181.

Courvisanos, J. (2009), 'Political aspects of innovation'. *Research Policy* **38**(7): 1117–1124.

Cowell, M.M. (2013), 'Bounce back or move on: regional resilience and economic development planning'. *Cities* **30**: 212–222.

Cowell, M.M. (2015), *Dealing with Deindustrialization: Adaptive Resilience in American Midwestern Regions*. London: Routledge.

Cowling, M., Liu, W. and Ledger, A. (2012), 'Small business financing in the UK before and during the current financial crisis'. *International Small Business Journal* **30**(7): 778–800.

Cowling, M., Liu, W., Ledger, A. and Zhang, N. (2015), 'What really happens to small and medium-sized enterprises in a global economic recession? UK evidence on sales and job dynamics'. *International Small Business Journal* **33**(5): 488–513.

Cox, E., Broadbridge, A. and Raikes, L. (2014), *Building Economic Resilience? An Analysis of Local Enterprise Partnerships' Plans*. Newcastle: IPPR North.

Crescenzi, R., Luca, D. and Milio, S. (2016), 'The geography of the economic crisis in Europe: national macroeconomic conditions, regional structural factors and short-term economic performance'. *Cambridge Journal of Regions, Economy and Society* **9**(1): 13–32.

Crespo, J., Suire, R. and Vicente, J. (2014), 'Lock-in or lock-out? How structural properties of knowledge networks affect regional resilience'. *Journal of Economic Geography* **14**(1): 199–219.

Cross, R. (1993), 'On the foundations of hysteresis in economic systems'. *Economics and Philosophy* **9**(1): 53–74.

Cross, R. and Allen, A. (1988), 'On the history of hysteresis'. In R. Cross (ed.), *Unemployment, Hysteresis and the Natural Rate Hypothesis*. Oxford: Blackwell, 26–39.

Crouch, C. and Hill, S. (2004), 'Regeneration in Sheffield: from council dominance to partnership'. In C. Crouch, P. Le Galès, C. Trigilia and H. Vorlzkow (eds), *Changing Governance of Local Economies: Responses to European Local Production Systems*. Oxford: Oxford University Press.

Cumbers, A., Mackinnon, D. and Chapman, K. (2003), 'Innovation, collaboration, and learning in regional clusters: a study of SMEs in the Aberdeen oil complex'. *Environment and Planning A* **35**(9): 1689–1706.

Curley, M. (2016), 'Twelve principles for open innovation 2.0'. *Nature* **533**(7603).

Dabinett, G. and Ramsden, P. (1999), 'Urban policy in Sheffield: regeneration, partnerships and people'. In R. Imrie and H. Thomas (eds), *British Urban Policy: An Evaluation of the Urban Development Corporations*. London: Sage Publications, 168–185.

Dahlhamer, J. and Tierney, K. (1998), 'Rebounding from disruptive events: business recovery following the Northridge earthquake'. *Sociological Spectrum* **18**: 121–141.

Daniele, V. and Malanima, P. (2007), 'Il prodotto delle regioni e il divario Nord-Sud in Italia (1861–2004)'. *Rivista di politica economica*, 267–315.

Davidsson, P. (1995), 'Culture, structure and regional levels of entrepreneurship'. *Entrepreneurship and Regional Development* **7**(1): 41–62.

Davidsson, P. and Gordon, S.R. (2016), 'Much ado about nothing? The surprising persistence of nascent entrepreneurs through macroeconomic crisis'. *Entrepreneurship Theory and Practice* **40**(4): 915–941.

Davidsson, P. and Honig, B. (2003), 'The role of social and human capital among nascent entrepreneurs'. *Journal of Business Venturing* **18**(3): 301–331.

Davidsson, P. and Wiklund, J. (2001), 'Levels of analysis in entrepreneurship research: current research practice and suggestions for the future'. *Entrepreneurship: Theory & Practice* **25**(4): 81.

Davies, S. (2011), 'Regional resilience in the 2008–2010 downturn:

comparative evidence from European countries'. *Cambridge Journal of Regions, Economy and Society* **4**(3): 369–382.

Davis, J. (2006), 'And then there were four. . . a thumbnail history of oil industry restructuring, 1971–2005'. In J. Davis (ed.), *The Changing World of Oil: An Analysis of Corporate Change and Adaptation*. Aldershot: Ashgate, 1–12.

Davoudi, S. and Porter, L. (2012), 'Resilience: a bridging concept or a dead end?'. *Planning Theory and Practice* **13**(2): 299–333.

Dawley, S. (2014), 'Creating new paths? Offshore wind, policy activism, and peripheral region development'. *Economic Geography* **90**(1): 91–112.

Dawley, S., MacKinnon, D., Cumbers, A. and Pike, A. (2015), 'Policy activism and regional path creation: the promotion of offshore wind in north east England and Scotland'. *Cambridge Journal of Regions, Economy and Society* **8**(2): 257–272.

Dawley, S., Marshall, N., Pike, A., Pollard, J. and Tomaney, J. (2014), 'Continuity and evolution in an old industrial region: the labour market dynamics of the rise and fall of Northern Rock'. *Regional Studies* **48**: 154–172.

Dawley, S., Pike, A. and Tomaney, J. (2010), 'Towards the resilient region?'. *Local Economy* **25**(8): 650–667.

De la Torre, A., Pería, M.S.M. and Schmukler, S.L. (2010), 'Bank involvement with SMEs: beyond relationship lending'. *Journal of Banking and Finance* **34**(9): 2280–2293.

Deakins, D. and Freel, M. (1998), 'Entrepreneurial learning and the growth process in SMEs'. *The Learning Organization* **5**(3): 144–155.

Deas, I., Hincks, S. and Headlam, N. (2013), 'Explicitly permissive? Understanding actor interrelationships in the governance of economic development: the experience of England's Local Enterprise Partnerships'. *Local Economy* **28**: 718–773.

Demmer, W.A., Vickery, S.K. and Calantone, R. (2011), 'Engendering resilience in small-and medium-sized enterprises (SMEs): a case study of Demmer Corporation'. *International Journal of Production Research* **49**: 5395–5413.

Dewald, J. and Bowen, F. (2010), 'Storm clouds and silver linings: responding to disruptive innovations through cognitive resilience'. *Entrepreneurship Theory and Practice* **34**(1): 197–218.

Dewe, P.J., O'Driscoll, M.P. and Cooper, C.L. (2012), 'Theories of psychological stress at work'. In R.J. Gatchel and I.Z. Schultz (eds), *Handbook of Occupational Health and Wellness*. New York: Springer, 23–38.

Di Caro, P. (2014), 'Shocking aspects of Mezzogiorno: resilience, vulnerability and regional growth'. *Rassegna Economica* **77**(2).

Di Caro, P. (2015a), 'Recessions, recoveries and regional resilience:

evidence on Italy'. *Cambridge Journal of Regions, Economy and Society* **8**(2): 273–291.

Di Caro, P. (2015b), 'Testing and explaining economic resilience with an application to Italian regions'. *Papers in Regional Science*. DOI: 10.1111/pirs.12168.

DiMaggio, P.J. and Powell, W.W. (1983), 'The iron cage revisited: institutional isomorphism and collective rationality in organizational fields'. *American Sociological Review* **48**(1): 147–160.

DiMaggio, P.J. and Powell, W.W. (1991), 'Introduction'. In W.W. Powell and P.J. DiMaggio (eds), *The New Institutionalism in Organizational Analysis*. Chicago: University of Chicago Press, 1–38.

Diodato, D. and Weterings, A.B. (2015), 'The resilience of regional labour markets to economic shocks: exploring the role of interactions among firms and workers'. *Journal of Economic Geography* **15**(4): 723–742.

Djankov, S., La Porta, R., Lopez de Silanes, F. and Shleifer, A. (2002), 'The regulation of entry'. *The Quarterly Journal of Economics* **117**(1): 1–37.

Doern, R. (2016), 'Entrepreneurship and crisis management: the experiences of small businesses during the London 2011 riots'. *International Small Business Journal* **34**(3): 276–302.

Doloreux, D. and Shearmur, R. (2009), 'Maritime clusters in diverse regional contexts: the case of Canada'. *Marine Policy* **33**(3): 520–527.

Doran, J. and Fingleton, B. (2015), 'Resilience from the micro perspective'. *Cambridge Journal of Regions, Economy and Society* **8**(2): 205–223.

Drakopoulou Dodd, S. and Hynes, B.C. (2012), 'The impact of regional entrepreneurial contexts upon enterprise education'. *Entrepreneurship & Regional Development* **24**(3/4): 741–766.

Drakopoulou Dodd, S., Jack, S. and Anderson, A. (2013), 'From admiration to abhorrence: the contentious appeal of entrepreneurship across Europe'. *Entrepreneurship & Regional Development* **25**(1–2): 69–89.

Dubé, J. and Polèse, M. (2015), 'Resilience revisited: assessing the impact of the 2007–09 recession on 83 Canadian regions with accompanying thoughts on an elusive concept'. *Regional Studies* **50**(4): 615–628.

Eisenhardt, K.M. and Graebner, M.E. (2007), 'Theory building from cases: opportunities and challenges'. *Academy of Management Journal* **50**(1): 25–32.

El Harbi, S. and Anderson, A.R. (2011), 'Institutions and the shaping of different forms of entrepreneurship'. *Journal of Socio-Economics* **39**(3): 436–444.

Elster, J. (1976), 'A note on hysteresis in the social sciences'. *Synthese* **33**(2/4): 371–391.

Eraydin, A. (2016) 'Attributes and characteristics of regional resilience:

defining and measuring the resilience of Turkish Regions'. *Regional Studies* **50**(4): 600–614.

Estrin, S. and Mickiewicz, T. (2011), 'Entrepreneurship in transition economies: the role of institutions and generational change'. In M. Minniti (ed.), *The Dynamics of Entrepreneurship*. Oxford: Oxford University Press.

Etherington, D. and Jones, M. (2009), 'City-regions: new geographies of uneven development and inequality'. *Regional Studies* **43**: 247–265.

Etherington, D. and Jones, M. (2016), 'The city-region chimera: the political economy of metagovernance failure in Britain'. *Cambridge Journal of Regions, Economy and Society*, DOI:10.1093/cjres/rsw007.

Etienne, H.F. and Faga, B. (eds) (2014), *Planning Atlanta*. Chicago: American Planning Association, Planners Press.

Ettlinger, N. (2003), 'Cultural economic geography and a relational and microspace approach to trusts, rationalities, networks, and change in collaborative workplaces'. *Journal of Economic Geography* **3**(1): 1–28.

Etzioni, A. (1987), 'Entrepreneurship, adaptation and legitimation: a macro-behavior perspective'. *Journal of Economic Behavior and Organization* **8**(2): 175–189.

Etzkowitz, H. and Leydesdorff, L.A. (1997), *Universities and the Global Knowledge Economy: A Triple Helix of University-Industry-Government Relations*. London and New York: Pinter.

European Commission (2010), *Examining the Links between Organised Crime and Corruption*. Brussels: European Commission.

European Commission (2012), *Flash Barometer 354: Entrepreneurship Country Report Greece*. Brussels: European Commission.

European Commission (2014), *Cohesion Policy and Greece*. Brussels: European Commission.

Evans, D.S. and Leighton, L.S. (1990), 'The determinants of changes in US self-employment 1968–1987'. *Small Business Economics* **1**(2): 111–120.

Evenhuis, E. (2016), The Political Economy of Adaptation and Resilience in Old Industrial Regions: A Comparative Study of South Saarland and Teesside. Unpublished PhD thesis. Centre for Urban and Regional Development Studies; Department of Geography, Sociology, and Politics, Newcastle University, Newcastle-upon-Tyne.

Faggian, A., Gemmiti, R. and Santini, I. (2016), *Farther from Europe? Italian Cities and Metropolitan Areas Responses to the Crisis*. Mimeo.

Falkner, E.M. and Hiebl, M.R. (2015), 'Risk management in SMEs: a systematic review of available evidence'. *The Journal of Risk Finance* **16**(2): 122–144.

Featherstone, K. (2010), 'The Greek sovereign debt crisis and EMU: a failing state in a skewed regime'. *Journal of Common Market Studies* **49**(2): 193–217.

Featherstone, K. and Papadimitriou, D. (2008), *The Limits of Europeaniza-tion: Reform Capacity and Policy Conflict in Greece.* Basingstoke and New York: Palgrave Macmillan.

Feldman, M. (2000), 'Location and innovation: the new economic geog-raphy of innovation, spillovers, and agglomeration'. In G. Clark, M. Feldman and M. Gertler (eds), *The Oxford Handbook of Economic Geography.* New York: Oxford University Press.

Feldman, M. (2003), 'The locational dynamics of the US biotech indus-try: knowledge externalities and the anchor hypothesis'. *Industry and Innovation* **10**(3): 311.

Feldman, M. and Florida, R. (1994), 'The geographic sources of innova-tion: technological infrastructure and product innovation in the United States'. *Annals of the Association of American Geographers* **84**(2): 210.

Felton, E., Gibson, M.N., Flew, T., Graham, P. and Daniel, A. (2010), 'Resilient creative economies? Creative industries on the urban fringe'. *Continuum* **24**(4): 619–630.

Ferrera, M. (2008), *Il fattore D: perché il lavoro delle donne farà crescere l'Italia.* Milan: Mondadori.

Fiaschi, D., Gianmoena, L. and Parenti, A. (2011), 'The dynamics of labour productivity across Italian provinces: convergence and polariza-tion'. *Rivista italiana degli economisti,* **16**(2): 209–240.

Filippov, S. and Kalotay, K. (2011), 'Global crisis and activities of multi-national enterprises in new EU member states'. *International Journal of Emerging Markets* **6**(4): 304–328.

Finegold, D. and Soskice, D. (1988), 'The failure of training in Britain: analysis and prescription'. *Oxford Review of Economic Policy* **4**(3): 21–53.

Fingleton, B., Garretsen, H. and Martin, R. (2012), 'Recessionary shocks and regional employment: evidence of the resilience of UK regions'. *Journal of Regional Science* **52**(1): 109–133.

Fink, S. (1986), *Crisis Management: Planning for the Inevitable.* New York: AMACON.

Flach, F.F. (2003), *Resilience: Discovering a New Strength at Times of Stress.* New York: Hatherleigh Press.

Florida, R. (2002), *The Rise of the Creative Class.* New York: Basic Books.

Florida, R., Mellander, C. and Stolarick, K. (2008), 'Inside the black box of regional development – human capital, the creative class and toler-ance'. *Journal of Economic Geography* **8**(5): 615–659.

Fogli, A., Hill, E. and Perri, F. (2012), 'The geography of the great recession'. In *NBER International Seminar on Macroeconomics.* Chicago: University of Chicago Press.

Forester, J. (1982), 'Planning in the face of power'. *Journal of the American Planning Association* **48**(1): 67.

Foster, K. (2006), *A Case Study Approach to Understanding Regional Resilience*. Macarthur Foundation Research Network on Building Resilient Regions.

Fotopoulos, G. (2014), 'On the spatial stickiness of UK new firm formation rates'. *Journal of Economic Geography* **14**(3): 651–679.

Fotopoulos, G. and Giotopoulos, I. (2010), 'Gibrat's law and persistence of growth in Greek manufacturing'. *Small Business Economics* **35**(1): 191–202.

Fredrickson, B.L., Tugade, M.M., Waugh, C.E. and Larkin, G.R. (2003), 'What good are positive emotions in crises? A prospective study of resilience and emotions following the terrorist attacks on the United States on September 11th, 2001'. *Journal of Personality and Social Psychology* **84**(2): 365–376.

Frenken, K. (ed.) (2007), *Applied Evolutionary Economics and Economic Geography*. Cheltenham, UK and Northampton, MA, USA: Edward Elgar Publishing.

Frenken, K. and Boschma, R.A. (2007), 'A theoretical framework for evolutionary economic geography: industrial dynamics and urban growth as a branching process'. *Journal of Economic Geography* **7**(5): 635–649.

Freytag, A. and Thurik, R. (2007), 'Entrepreneurship and its determinants in a cross-country setting'. *Journal of Evolutionary Economics* **17**(2): 117–131.

Friedman, M. (1993), 'The plucking model of business fluctuations revisited'. *Economic Enquiry* **31**: 171–177.

Fritsch, M. and Mueller, P. (2005), 'How persistent are regional start-up rates? An empirical analysis'. *Research of Technological Innovation, Management and Policy* **9**: 71–82.

Fromhold-Eisebith, M. (2015), 'Sectoral resilience: conceptualizing industry-specific spatial patterns of interactive crisis adjustment'. *European Planning Studies* **23**(9): 1675–1694.

Fusco, L. (2006), *Offshore Oil: An Overview of Development in Newfoundland and Labrador*. St. John's, Newfoundland: Memorial University.

García-Teruel, P.J. and Martinez-Solano, P. (2007), 'Effects of working capital management on SME profitability'. *International Journal of Managerial Finance* **3**(2): 164–177.

Gardiner, B., Martin, R., Sunley, P. and Tyler, P. (2013), 'Spatially unbalanced growth in the British economy'. Presentation at workshop on *Local Economic Growth: Recession, Resilience and Recovery*, 11–12 July, McGrath Centre, St Catharine's College, Cambridge.

Garud, R. and Karnøe, P. (2001), 'Path creation as a process of mindful deviation'. In R. Garud and P. Karnøe (eds), *Path Dependence and Creation*. London: Lawrence Erlbaum, 1–38.

Georgescu-Roegen, N. (1966), *Analytical Economics: Issues and Problems*. Cambridge, MA: Harvard University Press.

Gilly, J.P., Kechidi, M. and Talbot, D. (2014), 'Resilience of organisations and territories: the role of pivot firms'. *European Management Journal* **32**(4): 596–602.

Glaeser, E.L. (2005), 'Reinventing Boston: 1630–2003'. *Journal of Economic Geography* **5**(2): 119–153.

Glasmeier, A. (2000), *Manufacturing Time: Global Competition in the Watch Industry, 1795–2000*. New York: The Guilford Press.

Global Entrepreneurship Monitor (2013), *Entrepreneurship in Greece during 2012–2013: Are There Any Signs of Recovery in Small Entrepreneurship?* Babson Park, MA: Global Entrepreneurship Monitor.

Glover, J. (2012), 'Rural resilience through continued learning and innovation'. *Local Economy* **27**(4): 355–372.

Göcke, M. (2002), 'Various concepts of hysteresis applied in economics'. *Journal of Economic Surveys* **16**(2): 167–188.

Goddard, J.B. and Chatterton, P. (1999), 'Regional Development Agencies and the knowledge economy: harnessing the potential of universities'. *Environment and Planning C: Government and Policy* **17**: 685–699.

Goldfinch, S. and Hart, P.T. (2014), 'Leadership and institutional reform: engineering macroeconomic policy change in Australia'. *Governance* **16**(2): 235–270.

Goodwin, M., Jones, M. and Jones, R. (2012), *Rescaling the State: Devolution and the Geographies of Economic Governance*. Manchester: Manchester University Press.

Grabher, G. (1993), 'The weakness of strong ties: the lock-in of regional development in the Ruhr area'. In G. Grabher (ed.), *The Embedded Firm: On the Socioeconomics of Interfirm Relations*. London and New York: Routledge, 255–277.

Grabher, G. and Stark, D. (1997), 'Organising diversity: evolutionary theory, network analysis and post socialism'. *Regional Studies* **31**: 533–544.

Grandey, A.A. and Cropanzano, R. (1999), 'The conservation of resources model applied to work–family conflict and strain'. *Journal of Vocational Behavior* **54**(2): 350–370.

Grant, R. and Baden-Fuller, C. (2004), 'A knowledge accessing theory of strategic alliances'. *Journal of Management Studies* **41**(1): 61–84.

Greif, A. (1994), 'Cultural beliefs and the organization of society: a historical and theoretical reflection on collectivist and individualist societies'. *Journal of Political Economy* **102**(5): 912–950.

Greif, A. (2006), *Institutions and the Path to the Modern Economy*. New York: Cambridge University Press.

Guglielmetti, C. (2012), 'The consequences of the international crisis for European SMEs: vulnerability and resilience'. In B. Dallago and C. Guglielmetti (eds), *The Consequences of the International Crisis for European SMEs: Vulnerability and Resilience*, Vol. 27. London and New York: Routledge, 1–16.

Guiso, L., Sapienza, P. and Zingales, L. (2004), 'The role of social capital in financial development'. *American Economic Review* **94**(3): 526–556.

Guseva, A. (2007), 'Friends and foes: informal networks in the Soviet Union'. *East European Quarterly* **41**(1): 2–9.

Hall, P. and Preston, P. (1988), *The Carrier Wave: New Information Technology and the Geography of Innovation 1846–2003*. London: Unwin Hyman.

Hambleton, R. (2009), 'Civic leadership for Auckland: an international perspective'. *Auckland Governance Research Papers* **4**: 515–552.

Hambleton, R. and Howard, J. (2013), 'Place-based leadership and public service innovation'. *Local Government Studies* **39**: 47–70.

Hambleton, R. and Sweeting, D. (2004), 'US-style leadership for English local government?'. *Public Administration Review* **64**: 474–488.

Han, Y. and Goetz, S.J. (2015), 'The economic resilience of US counties during the Great Recession'. *The Review of Regional Studies* **45**(2): 131–149.

Hannigan, T.J., Cano-Kollmann, M. and Mudambi, R. (2015), 'Thriving innovation amidst manufacturing decline: the Detroit auto cluster and the resilience of local knowledge production'. *Industrial and Corporate Change* **24**(3): 613–634.

Hansen, K.E.H. (2016), 'Local labour markets and socio-economic change: evidence from Danish towns, 2008–2013'. *European Planning Studies*, 1–22.

Hanson, K.J. (2009), 'The path to regional competitiveness: business-civic leadership and geoeconomics in metropolitan Philadelphia'. *International Journal of Public Sector Management* **22**: 210–220.

Hassink, R. (2007), 'The strengths of weak lock-ins: the renewal of the Westmünsterland textile industry'. *Environment and Planning A* **39**(5): 1147–1165.

Hassink, R. (2010a), 'Locked in decline? On the role of regional lock-ins in old industrial areas'. In R. Boschma and R. Martin (eds), *The Handbook of Evolutionary Economic Geography*. Cheltenham, UK and Northampton, MA, USA: Edward Elgar Publishing, 450–468.

Hassink, R. (2010b), 'Regional resilience: a promising concept to explain differences in regional economic adaptability?'. *Cambridge Journal of Regions, Economy and Society* **3**: 521–535.

Hassink, R. and Shin, D.-H. (2005), 'The restructuring of old industrial areas in Europe and Asia'. *Environment and Planning A* **37**(4): 571–580.

Hassink, R., Klaerding, C. and Marques, P. (2014), 'Advancing evolutionary economic geography by engaged pluralism'. *Regional Studies* **48**(7): 1295–1307.

Haughton, G. and Allmendinger, P. (2008), 'The soft spaces of local economic development'. *Local Economy* **23**(2): 138–148.

Hauser, C., Tappeiner, G. and Walde, J. (2007), 'The learning region: the impact of social capital and weak ties on innovation'. *Regional Studies* **41**(1): 75–88.

Hayton, J.C., George, G. and Zahra, S.A. (2002), 'National culture and entrepreneurship: a review of behavioural research'. *Entrepreneurship Theory and Practice* **26**(4): 33–55.

Hayward, M.L.A., Forster, W.R., Sarasvathy, S.D. and Fredrickson, B.L. (2010), 'Beyond hubris: how highly confident entrepreneurs rebound to venture again'. *Journal of Business Venturing* **25**(6): 569–578.

Hellier, D. (2015), 'Vorsprung durch technik: US tech giants v Germany in the driverless car race'. *Guardian*, 4 August, www.theguardian.com/business/2015/aug/04/vorsprung-durch-technic-us-tech-germany-driverless-car (accessed 5 May 2016).

Henning, M., Stam, E. and Wenting, R. (2013), 'Path dependence research in regional economic development: cacophony or knowledge accumulation?'. *Regional Studies* **47**(8): 1348–1362.

Henrekson, M. (2007), 'Entrepreneurship and institutions'. *Comparative Labour Law and Policy Journal* **28**(3): 717–742.

Henrekson, M. and Stenkula, M. (2010), 'Entrepreneurship and public policy'. In Z. Acs and D.B. Audretsch (eds), *Handbook of Entrepreneurship Research*. London: Springer, 595–637.

Herbane, B. (2010), 'Small business research: time for a crisis-based view'. *International Small Business Journal* **28**(1): 43–64.

Herbane, B., Elliot, D. and Swartz, E.M. (2004), 'Business continuity management: time for a strategic role?'. *Long Range Planning* **37**: 435–457.

Herd, M. and Mutiga, M. (2016), '100 resilient cities announces hundredth member, but "work is only just beginning"'. *Guardian*, www.theguardian.com/cities/2016/may/25/rockefeller-100-resilient-cities-washington-lagos-manchester-belfast (accessed 2 February 2017).

Hervas-Oliver, J.L., Jackson, I. and Tomlinson, P.R. (2011), '"May the ovens never grow cold": regional resilience and industrial policy in the north Staffordshire ceramics industrial district – with lessons from Sassoulo and Castellon'. *Policy Studies* **32**(4): 377–395.

Hill, E.W., Wial, H. and Wolman, H. (2008), *Exploring Regional Economic*

Resilience. Working Paper 2008–04, Institute of Urban and Regional Development, University of California, Berkeley.

Hilpert, U. (1992), *Archipelago Europe – Islands of Innovation: Synthesis Report*, Vol. 18, Prospective Dossier No. 1, *Science, Technology and Economic Cohesion in the Community*. Brussels: FAS, EC, Science, Research and Development, DG/XII/411/92.

Hindle, K. (2004), 'Choosing qualitative methods for entrepreneurial cognition research: a canonical development approach'. *Entrepreneurship Theory and Practice* **28**(6): 575–607.

Hjemdal, O., Friborg, O., Stiles, T.C., Rosenvinge, J.H. and Martinussen, M. (2006), 'Resilience predicting psychiatric symptoms: a prospective study of protective factors and their role in adjustment to stressful life events'. *Clinical Psychology & Psychotherapy* **13**(3): 194–201.

HM Government (2013), *Growth Deals: Initial Guidance for Local Enterprise Partnerships*. London: Stationery Office.

HM Treasury and Business Innovation and Skills (2013), *Government's Response to the Heseltine Review*. London: Stationery Office.

Hobfoll, S.E. (1988), *The Ecology of Stress*. New York: Hemisphere Publishing Corporation.

Hobfoll, S.E. (1989), 'Conservation of resources: a new attempt at conceptualizing stress'. *American Psychologist* **44**: 513–524.

Hobfoll, S.E. (2001), 'The influence of culture, community, and the nested-self in the stress process: advancing conservation of resources theory'. *Applied Psychology: An International Review* **50**(3): 337–421.

Hobfoll, S.E. (2002), 'Social and psychological resources and adaptation'. *Review of General Psychology* **6**(4): 307–324.

Hobfoll, S.E. and Lilly, R.S. (1993), 'Resource conservation as a strategy for community psychology'. *Journal of Community Psychology* **21**(2): 128–148.

Hobfoll, S.E. and Shirom, A. (2001), 'Conservation of resources theory: applications to stress and management in the workplace'. In R.T. Golembiewski (ed.), *Handbook of Organizational Behavior*, 2nd edn. New York: Marcel Dekker, 57–80.

Hobfoll, S.E., Tracy, M. and Galea, S. (2006), 'The impact of resource loss and traumatic growth on probable PTSD and depression following terrorist attacks'. *Journal of Traumatic Stress* **19**(6): 867–878.

Hodgson, G.M. and Knudsen, T. (2010), *Darwin's Conjecture: The Search for General Principles of Social and Economic Evolution*. Chicago: University of Chicago Press.

Hofstede, G. (1980), *Culture's Consequences: Internal Differences in Work Related Values*. Beverly Hills, CA: Sage Publications.

Hofstede, G., Noorderhaven, N.G., Thurik, A.R., Uhlaner, L.M.,

Wennekers, A.R.M. and Wilderman, R.E. (2004), 'Culture's role in entrepreneurship: self-employment out of dissatisfaction'. In T.E. Brown and J. Ulijn (eds), *Innovation, Entrepreneurship and Culture: The Interaction between Technology, Progress and Economic Growth*. Cheltenham, UK and Northampton, MA, USA: Edward Elgar Publishing, 162–203.

Holstein, J.A. and Gubrium, J.F. (1994), 'Phenomenology, ethnomethodology, and interpretive practice'. In N.K. Denzin and Y.S. Lincoln (eds), *Handbook of Qualitative Research*. London: Sage Publications.

Holweg, M., Davies, P. and Podpolny, D. (2009), *The Competitive Status of the UK Automotive Industry*. Buckingham: PICSIE Books.

Hoover, M. and Fisher, L. (1949), *Research in Regional Economic Growth: Problems in the study of Economic Growth*, Vol. I. Cambridge, MA: National Bureau of Economic Research.

Hope, K. (2015), *Annual Report on European SMEs 2014/2015*. Brussels: European Commission.

House, J.D. (1999), *Against the Tide: Battling for Economic Renewal in Newfoundland and Labrador*. Toronto: University of Toronto Press.

House, J.D. (2003), 'Myths and realities about petroleum-related development: lessons for British Columbia from Atlantic Canada and the North Sea'. *Journal of Canadian Studies* 37: 9–34.

Howell, A. (2015), 'Resilience as enhancement: governmentality and political economy beyond "responsibilisation"'. *Politics* 35, 67–71.

Hu, X. and Hassink, R. (2015), *Overcoming the Dualism between Adaptation and Adaptability in Regional Economic Resilience*. Papers in Evolutionary Economic Geography (PEEG) # 15.33, Utrecht University.

Hu, X. and Hassink, R. (2016), 'Explaining differences in the adaptability of old industrial areas'. In U. Hilpert (ed.), *Routledge Handbook of Politics & Technology*. London and New York: Routledge, 162–172.

Hudson, R. (2005), 'Rethinking change in old industrial regions: reflecting on the experiences of north east England'. *Environment and Planning A* 37(4): 581–596.

Hudson, R. (2010), 'Resilient regions in an uncertain world: wishful thinking or a practical reality?'. *Cambridge Journal of Regions, Economy and Society* 3(1): 11–25.

Huggins, R. and Izushi, H. (2007), *Competing for Knowledge: Creating, Connecting, and Growing*. London and New York: Routledge.

Huggins, R. and Thompson, P. (2012), 'Entrepreneurship and community culture: a place-based study of their interdependency'. *Entrepreneurship Research Journal* 2(1).

Huggins, R. and Thompson, P. (2013), 'Competitiveness and the post-regional political economy'. *Local Economy* 28: 884–893.

Huggins, R. and Thompson, P. (2015a), 'Culture and place-based development: a socio-economic analysis'. *Regional Studies* **49**(1): 130–159.

Huggins, R. and Thompson, P. (2015b), 'Local entrepreneurial resilience and culture: the role of social values in fostering economic recovery'. *Cambridge Journal of Regions, Economy and Society* **8**(2): 313–330.

Huggins, R. and Thompson, P. (2016), 'Socio-spatial culture and entrepreneurship: some theoretical and empirical observations'. *Economic Geography* **92**(3): 269–300.

Huggins, R. and Williams, N. (2009), 'Enterprise and public policy: a review of Labour government intervention in the United Kingdom'. *Environment and Planning C: Government and Policy* **27**(1): 19–41.

Huggins, R. and Williams, N. (2011), 'Entrepreneurship and regional competitiveness: the role and progression of policy'. *Entrepreneurship and Regional Development* **23**: 907–932.

Huggins, R., Izushi, H. and Thompson, P. (2013), 'Regional competitiveness: theories and methodologies for empirical analysis'. *Journal of CENTRUM Cathedra: The Business and Economics Research Journal* **6**(2): 155–172.

Hycner, R.H. (1985), 'Some guidelines for the phenomenological analysis of interview data'. *Human Studies* **8**: 279–303.

Ibert, O. and Schmidt, S. (2014), 'Once you are in you might need to get out: adaptation and adaptability in volatile labor markets – the case of musical actors'. *Social Sciences* **3**(1): 1–23.

Industry Canada (2016), 'Imports and domestic exports, customs-based, by North American Industry Classification System (NAICS), Canada, provinces and territories, monthly (dollars)'. *Trade Data Online* (accessed 7 June 2016).

Ingirige, B., Wedawatta, G. and Amaratunga, D. (2010), 'Building up resilience of construction sector SMEs and their supply chains to extreme weather events'. *International Journal of Strategic Property Management* **14**(4): 362–375.

Innis, A. (1933), *Problems of Staples Production in Canada*. Toronto: Ryerson Press.

Ironson, G., Wynings, C., Schneiderman, N., Baum, A., Rodriguez, M. and Greenwood, D. (1997), 'Posttraumatic stress symptoms, intrusive thoughts, loss, and immune function after Hurricane Andrew'. *Psychosomatic Medicine* **59**: 128–141.

Irvine, W. and Anderson, A. (2004), 'Small tourist firms in rural areas: agility, vulnerability and survival in the face of crisis'. *International Journal of Entrepreneurial Behavior & Research* **10**(4): 229–246.

Jack, S.L. and Anderson, A.R. (1999), 'Entrepreneurship education within the enterprise culture: producing reflective practitioners'. *International Journal of Entrepreneurial Behaviour and Research* **5**(3): 110–125.

Jacobs, J. (1969), *The Economy of Cities*. New York: Vintage Books.

Jensen, M.B., Johnson, B., Lorenz, E. and Lundvall, B.A. (2007), 'Forms of knowledge and modes of innovation'. *Research Policy* **36**(5): 680–693.

Jessop, B. (2004), 'Multi-level governance and multi-level meta-governance'. In I. Bache and M. Flinders (eds), *Multi-Level Governance*. Oxford: Oxford University Press, 49–74.

Johnson, P. and Robinson, P. (2014), 'Civic hackathons: innovation, procurement, or civic engagement?'. *Review of Policy Research* **31**(4): 349–357.

Johnstone, H. and Lionais, D. (2004), 'Depleted communities and community business entrepreneurship: revaluing space through place'. *Entrepreneurship and Regional Development* **16**(3): 217–233.

Jonas, A.E.G. (2011), 'Region and place: regionalism in question'. *Progress in Human Geography* **36**: 263–272.

Jüttner, U., Peck, H. and Christopher, M. (2003), 'Supply chain risk management: outlining an agenda for future research'. *International Journal of Logistics: Research and Applications* **6**(4): 197–210.

Kaplan, H.B. (1999), 'Toward an understanding of resilience: a critical review of definitions and models'. In M.D. Glantz and J.R. Johnson (eds), *Resilience and Development: Positive Life Adaptations*. New York: Plenum, 17–83.

Kaplanoglou, G. and Rapanos, V.T. (2013), 'Tax and trust: the fiscal crisis in Greece'. *South European Society and Politics* **18**(3): 283–304.

Kapsali, M. and Butler, J. (2011), 'Politics'. In R. Prouska and M. Kapsali (eds), *Business and Management Practices in Greece: A Comparative Context*. Basingstoke: Palgrave.

Katsimi, M. and Moutos, T. (2010), 'EMU and the Greek crisis: the political-economy perspective'. *European Journal of Political Economy* **26**: 568–576.

Katz, B. and Warner, J. (2014), *The Rise of Innovation Districts: A New Geography of Innovation in America*. Washington, DC: Brookings Institution.

Kearns, A. and Forrest, R. (2000), 'Social cohesion and multilevel urban governance'. *Urban Studies* **37**(5/6): 995–1017.

Keeble, D. (1989), 'High technology and regional development in Britain: the case of the Cambridge phenomenon'. *Environment and Planning C* **7**(2): 152–172.

Keogh, W. (1998), 'Small, technology-based firms in the UK oil and gas industry: innovation and internationalisation strategies'. *International Small Business Journal* **17**: 57–72.

Kim, C.-J. and Nelson, C.R. (1999), 'Friedman's plucking model of business fluctuations: tests and estimates of permanent and transitory components'. *Journal of Money, Credit, and Banking* **33**: 317–334.

Kim, G. (2007), 'The analysis of self-employment levels over the life-cycle'. *Quarterly Review of Economics and Finance* **47**(3): 397–410.

King, N. (2004), 'Using templates in the thematic analysis of text'. In C. Cassell and G. Symon (eds), *Essential Guide to Qualitative Methods in Organizational Research*. London: Sage Publications, 256–270.

King, N., Carroll, C., Newton, P. and Dornan, T. (2002), 'You can't cure it so you have to endure it: the experience of adaptation to diabetic renal disease'. *Qualitative Health Research* **12**(3): 329–346.

Kitchin, R. (2014), 'The real-time city? Big data and smart urbanism'. *GeoJournal* **79**(1): 1–14.

Kitchin, R. (2015), 'Making sense of smart cities: addressing present shortcomings'. *Cambridge Journal of Regions, Economy and Society* **8**(1): 131–136.

Kitching, J., Smallbone, D., Xheneti, M. and Kašperová, E. (2011), *Adapting to a Fragile Recovery: SME Responses to Recession and Post-Recession Performance*. Paper presented at the 34th Institute for Small Business and Entrepreneurship conference, Sheffield, 9–10 November.

Knack, S. and Keefer, P. (1997), 'Does social capital have an economic payoff? A cross-country investigation'. *Quarterly Journal of Economics* **112**(4): 1251–1288.

Koellinger, P. (2008), 'Why are some entrepreneurs more innovative than others?'. *Small Business Economics* **31**(1): 21–37.

Komninos, N. and Tsarchopoulos, P. (2013), 'Toward intelligent Thessaloniki: from an agglomeration of apps to smart districts'. *Journal of the Knowledge Economy* **4**: 149.

Koufopoulos, D.N. and Morgan, N.A. (1994), 'Competitive pressures force Greek entrepreneurs to plan'. *Long Range Planning* **27**(4): 435–448.

Krueger, N.F. and Carsrud, A.L. (1993), 'Entrepreneurial intentions: applying the theory of planned behaviour'. *Entrepreneurship & Regional Development* **5**: 315–330.

Lagendijk, A. (1997), 'Towards an integrated automotive industry in Europe: "A merging filière" perspective'. *European Urban and Regional Studies* **4**(1): 5–18.

Lagravinese, R. (2015), 'Economic crisis and rising gaps North–South: evidence from the Italian regions'. *Cambridge Journal of Regions, Economy and Society* **8**(2): 331–342.

Lai, Y., Saridakis, G., Blackburn, R. and Johnstone, S. (2016), 'Are the HR responses of small firms different from large firms in times of recession?'. *Journal of Business Venturing* **31**(1): 113–131.

Lang, T. (2012), 'How do cities and regions adapt to socio-economic crisis?

Towards an institutionalist approach to urban and regional resilience'. *Raumforschung und Raumordnung* **70**(4): 285–291.

Le Feuvre, M., Medway, D., Warnaby, G., Ward, K. and Goatman, A. (2016), 'Understanding stakeholder interactions in urban partnerships'. *Cities* **52**: 55–65.

Lee, N. (2014), 'Grim down south? The determinants of unemployment increases in British cities in the 2008–2009 recession'. *Regional Studies* **48**(11): 1761–1778.

Lee, N., Sameen, H. and Cowling, M. (2015), 'Access to finance for innovative SMEs since the financial crisis'. *Research Policy* **44**(2): 370–380.

Levie, J. (2007), 'Immigration, in-migration, ethnicity and entrepreneurship in the United Kingdom'. *Small Business Economics* **28**(2/3): 143–169.

Liddle, J. (2012), 'Sustaining collaborative leadership in city-regions: an examination of local enterprise partnerships in England'. In M. Sotarauta, L. Horlings and J. Liddle (eds), *Leadership and Change in Sustainable Regional Development*. Abingdon: Routledge, 37–59.

Lindqvist, G. (2009), *Disentangling Clusters: Agglomeration and Proximity Effects*. Stockholm: Economic Research Institute, Stockholm School of Economics.

Lumpkin, G.T. and Dess, G.G. (1996), 'Clarifying the entrepreneurial orientation construct and linking it to performance'. *Academy of Management Review* **21**(1): 135–172.

Luthans, F. (2002), 'The need for and meaning of positive organizational behavior'. *Journal of Organizational Behavior* **23**(6): 695–706.

Luthar, S. and Becker, B. (2000), 'The construct of resilience: a critical evaluation and guidelines for future work'. *Child Development* **7**: 543–562.

Luthar, S.S., Cicchetti, D. and Becker, B. (2000), 'The construct of resilience: a critical evaluation and guidelines for future work'. *Child Development* **71**(3): 543–562.

MacKinnon, D. and Derickson, K.D. (2013), 'From resilience to resourcefulness: a critique of resilience policy and activism'. *Progress in Human Geography* **37**(2): 253–270.

MacKinnon, D., Cumbers, A., Pike, A., Birch, K. and McMaster, R. (2009), 'Evolution in economic geography: institutions, political economy, and adaptation'. *Economic Geography* **85**(2): 129–150.

Macko, A. and Tyszka, T. (2009), 'Entrepreneurship and risk taking'. *Applied Psychology* **58**(3): 469–487.

Macpherson, A. and Holt, R. (2007), 'Knowledge, learning and small firm growth: a systematic review of the evidence'. *Research Policy* **36**(2): 172–192.

Malecki, E.J. (2004), 'Jockeying for position: what it means and why it matters to regional development policy when places compete'. *Regional Studies* **38**(9): 1101–1120.

Malerba, F. (2002), 'Sectoral systems of innovation and production'. *Research Policy* **31**(6): 247–264.

Malerba, F. and Nelson, R. (2011), 'Learning and catching up in different sectoral systems: evidence from six industries'. *Industrial and Corporate Change* **20**(6): 1645–1675.

Mallak, L. (1998), 'Putting organizational resilience to work'. *Industrial Management* **40**(6): 8–13.

Malmberg, A. and Maskell, P. (1997), 'Towards an explanation of industry agglomeration and regional specialization'. *European Planning Studies* **5**(1): 25–41.

Manolova, T.S. and Yan, A. (2002), 'Institutional constraints and strategic responses of new and small firms in a transforming economy: the case of Bulgaria'. *International Small Business Journal* **20**(2): 163–184.

Manolova, T.S., Eunni, R.V. and Gyoshev, B.S. (2008), 'Institutional environments for entrepreneurship: evidence from emerging economies in Eastern Europe'. *Entrepreneurship Theory and Practice* **32**(1): 203–218.

March, J.G. (1991), 'Exploration and exploitation in organizational learning'. *Organization Science* **2**(1): 71–87.

Markusen, A. (2003), 'Fuzzy concepts, scanty evidence, policy distance: the case for rigour and policy relevance in critical regional studies'. *Regional Studies* **37**(6–7): 701–717.

Marshall, A. (1930), *Principles of Economics*. London: Macmillan.

Martin, R. (2010), 'Roepke lecture in economic geography. Rethinking regional path dependence: beyond lock-in to evolution'. *Economic Geography* **86**(1): 1–27.

Martin, R. (2011), 'The local geographies of the financial crisis: from the housing bubble to economic recession and beyond'. *Journal of Economic Geography* **11**(4): 587–618.

Martin, R. (2012), 'Regional economic resilience, hysteresis and recessionary shocks'. *Journal of Economic Geography* **12**: 1–32.

Martin, R. (2016), 'Shocking aspects of regional development: towards an economic geography of resilience'. In G.C. Clark, M.A. Feldman and M. Gertler (eds), *New Handbook of Economic Geography*. Oxford: Oxford University Press.

Martin, R. and Simmie, J. (2008), 'Path dependence and local innovation systems in city-regions'. *Innovation: Management, Policy & Practice* **10**: 183–196.

Martin, R. and Sunley, P. (1998), 'Slow convergence? The new endogenous growth theory and regional development'. *Economic Geography* **74**(3): 201–227.

Martin, R. and Sunley, P. (2003), 'Deconstructing clusters: chaotic concept or policy panacea?'. *Journal of Economic Geography* **3**(1): 5–35.

Martin, R. and Sunley, P. (2006), 'Path dependence and regional economic evolution'. *Journal of Economic Geography* **6**(4): 395–437.

Martin, R. and Sunley, P. (2007), 'Complexity thinking and evolutionary economic geography'. *Journal of Economic Geography* **7**(5): 16–45.

Martin, R. and Sunley, P. (2010), 'The place of path dependence in an evolutionary perspective on the economic landscape'. In R. Boschma and R. Martin (eds), *Handbook of Evolutionary Economic Geography*. Cheltenham, UK and Northampton, MA, USA: Edward Elgar Publishing, 62–92.

Martin, R. and Sunley, P. (2011a), 'Conceptualising cluster evolution: beyond the life-cycle model?'. *Regional Studies* **45**(10): 1299–1318.

Martin, R. and Sunley, P. (2011b), 'Regional competitiveness: clusters or dynamic competitive advantage?'. In R. Huggins and H. Izushi (eds), *Competition, Competitive Advantage, and Clusters: The Ideas of Michael Porter*. Oxford: Oxford University Press, 211–238.

Martin, R. and Sunley, P. (2015), 'On the notion of regional economic resilience: conceptualization and explanation'. *Journal of Economic Geography* **15**(1): 1–42.

Martin, R., Sunley, P. and Tyler, P. (2015), 'Local growth evolutions: recession, resilience and recovery'. *Cambridge Journal of Regions, Economy and Society* **8**(2): 141–148.

Martin, R., Sunley, P.J., Gardiner, B. and Tyler, P. (2013), *Resilience and Local Economic Growth Paths*. Presentation at workshop on Local Economic Growth: Recession, Resilience and Recovery 11–12 July, McGrath Centre, St Catharine's College, Cambridge.

Martin, R., Sunley, P., Gardiner, B. and Tyler, P. (2016), 'How regions react to recessions: resilience and the role of economic structure'. *Regional Studies* **50**(4): 561–585.

Maskell, P. and Malmberg, A. (2007), 'Myopia, knowledge development and cluster evolution'. *Journal of Economic Geography* **7**(5): 604–618.

Masten, A.S. (1994), 'Resilience in individual development: successful adaptation despite risk and adversity'. In M. Wang and E. Gordon (eds), *Risk and Resilience in Inner City America: Challenges and Prospects*. Hillsdale, NJ: Erlbaum, 3–25.

Masten, A.S. (2001), 'Ordinary magic: resilience processes in development'. *American Psychologist* **56**(3): 227–238.

Masten, A.S., Best, K. and Garmezy, N. (1990), 'Resilience and development: contributions from the study of children who overcame adversity'. *Development and Psychopathology* **2**(4): 425–444.

Masten, A.S., Burt, K.B., Roisman, G.I., Obradovic, J., Don, J.D. and

Tellegen, A. (2004), 'Resources and resilience in the transition to adulthood: continuity and change'. *Development and Psychopathology* **16**: 1071–1094.

Matsaganis, M. and Leventi, C. (2013), 'The distributional impact of the Greek crisis in 2010'. *Fiscal Studies* **24**(1): 83–108.

Mattes, J. (2012), 'Dimensions of proximity and knowledge bases: innovation between spatial and non-spatial factors'. *Regional Studies* **46**(8): 1085–1099.

Mayr, S., Mitter, C. and Aichmayr, A. (2017), 'Corporate crisis and sustainable reorganization: evidence from bankrupt Austrian SMEs'. *Journal of Small Business Management* **55**(1): 108–127.

McMullen, J.S. (2011), 'Delineating the domain of development entrepreneurship: a market-based approach to facilitating inclusive economic growth'. *Entrepreneurship Theory and Practice* **35**(1): 185–215.

McNeill, D. (2015), 'Global firms and smart technologies: IBM and the reduction of cities'. *Transactions of the Institute of British Geographers* **40**(4): 562–574.

Meegan, R., Kennett, P., Jones, G. and Croft, J. (2014), 'Global economic crisis, austerity and neoliberal urban governance in England'. *Cambridge Journal of Regions, Economy and Society* **7**: 137–153.

Michener, K.J. and McLean, I.W. (1999), 'US regional growth and convergence'. *Journal of Economic History* **59**: 1016–1042.

Miller, B. (1992), 'Collective action and rational choice: place, community, and the limits to individual self-interest'. *Economic Geography* **68**(1): 22–42.

Minniti, M. (2005), 'Entrepreneurship and network externalities'. *Journal of Economic Behavior and Organization* **57**(1): 1–27.

Moavenzadeh, J. (2006), *Offshoring Automotive Engineering: Globalization and Footprint Strategy in the Motor Vehicle Industry*. Washington: National Academy of Engineering.

Modica, M. and Reggiani, A. (2014), 'Spatial economic resilience: overview and perspectives'. *Networks and Spatial Economics* **15**(2): 1–23.

Morgan, K. (2007), 'The learning region: institutions, innovation and regional renewal'. *Regional Studies* **41**: 147–159.

Morgan, K. (2013), 'Path dependence and the state: the politics of novelty in old industrial regions'. In P. Cooke (ed.), *Re-framing Regional Development: Evolution, Innovation and Transition*. London: Routledge, 318–340.

Mouawad, D.C. (2009), 'A governance blueprint for the 'federalist' Manchester city region'. *International Journal of Public Sector Management* **22**: 203–209.

Moussiopoulos, N., Achillas, C., Vlachokostas, C., Spyridi, D. and

Nikolaou, N. (2010), 'Environmental, social and economic information management for the evaluation of sustainability in urban areas: a system of indicators for Thessaloniki, Greece'. *Cities* **27**(5): 377–384.

Mueller, P. (2006), 'Entrepreneurship in the region: breeding ground for nascent entrepreneurs?'. *Small Business Economics* **27**(1): 41–58.

Nadin, S. and Cassell, C. (2004), 'Using data matrices'. In C. Cassell and G. Symon (eds), *Essential Guide to Qualitative Methods in Organizational Research*, London: Sage Publications, 271–287.

Nathan, M., Rosso, A., Gatten, T., Majmudar, P. and Mitchell, A. (2013), *Measuring the UK's Digital Economy with Big Data*. London: Growth Intelligence and National Institute of Economic and Social Research.

Neffke, F., Hartog, M., Boschma, R. and Henning, M. (2014), *Agents of Structural Change: The role of Firms and Entrepreneurs in Regional Diversification*. Working paper, University of Utrecht.

Neffke, F., Henning, M. and Boschma, R. (2011), 'How do regions diversify over time? Industry relatedness and the development of new growth paths in regions'. *Economic Geography* **87**(3): 237–265.

Nelson, R.R. (1994), 'The co-evolution of technology, industrial structure, and supporting institutions'. *Industrial and Corporate Change* **3**(1): 47–63.

Nelson, R.R. and Winter, S.G. (1982), *An Evolutionary Theory of Economic Change*. Cambridge, MA: Belknap Press of Harvard University Press.

Neven, D. and Gouymte, C. (2008), 'Regional convergence in the European Community'. *Journal of Common Market Studies* **33**: 47–65.

Nifo, A. and Vecchione, G. (2015), 'Measuring institutional quality in Italy'. *Rivista economica del Mezzogiorno* **29**(1–2): 157–182.

Noorderhaven, N., Thurik, R., Wennekers, S. and van Stel, A. (2004), 'The role of dissatisfaction and per capita income in explaining self-employment across 15 European countries'. *Entrepreneurship Theory and Practice* **28**(5): 447–466.

North, D.C. (1956), 'Exports and regional economic growth: a reply'. *Journal of Political Economy* **64**(2): 165–168.

North, D.C. (1990), *Institutions, Institutional Change, and Economic Performance*. Cambridge: Cambridge University Press.

North, D.C. (1994), 'Economic performance through time'. *American Economic Review* **84**(3): 359–367.

O'Dougherty-Wright, M., Masten, A.S. and Narayan, A.J. (2013), 'Resilience processes in development: four waves of research on positive adaptation in the context of adversity'. In S. Goldstein and R.B. Brooks (eds), *Handbook of Resilience in Children*. Berlin: Springer, 15–37.

OECD (2013), *Regions at a Glance 2013*. Paris: Organisation for Economic Co-operation and Development.

OECD (2015), *Local Economic Resilience and Adaptability to Long-Term Challenges*. LEED Webinar Series. Paris: Organisation for Economic Co-operation and Development.

Offer, J. (1998), 'Pessimist's charter'. *Accountancy* **121**(4): 50–51.

Office for National Statistics (2016), 'Time series: gross domestic product (GDP) – CVM', www.ons.gov.uk/economy/grossdomesticproductgdp/timeseries/abmi (accessed 10 January 2016).

Olson, M. (1982), *The Rise and Decline of Nations; Economic Growth, Stagflation, and Social Rigidities*. New Haven: Yale University Press.

Orens, R. and Reheul, A.M. (2013), 'Do CEO demographics explain cash holdings in SMEs?'. *European Management Journal* **31**(6): 549–563.

Ormerod, P. (2010), 'Risk, recessions and the resilience of capitalist economies'. *Risk Management* **12**: 83–99.

Page, S. (2010), 'Integrative leadership for collaborative governance: civic engagement in Seattle'. *The Leadership Quarterly* **21**: 246–263.

Pal, R., Torstensson, H. and Mattila, H. (2014), 'Antecedents of organizational resilience in economic crises: an empirical study of Swedish textile and clothing SMEs'. *International Journal of Production Economics* **147**(B): 410–428.

Papyrakis, E. and Gerlagh, R. (2007), 'Resource abundance and economic growth in the United States'. *European Economic Review* **51**(4): 1011–1039.

Parker, S.C., Congregado, E. and Golpe, A.A. (2012), 'Is entrepreneurship a leading or lagging indicator of the business cycle? Evidence from UK self-employment data'. *International Small Business Journal* **30**(7): 736–753.

Paroutis, S., Bennett, M. and Heracleous, L. (2014), 'A strategic view on smart city technology: the case of IBM smarter cities during a recession'. *Technological Forecasting and Social Change* **89**: 262–272.

Parrilli, M.D., Curbelo, J.L. and Cooke, P. (2012), 'Introduction'. In P. Cooke, M.D. Parrilli and J.L. Curbelo (eds), *Innovation, Global Change and Territorial Resilience*. Cheltenham, UK and Northampton, MA, USA: Edward Elgar Publishing, 1–22.

Paunov, C. (2012), 'The global crisis and firms' investments in innovation'. *Research Policy* **41**(1): 24–35.

Pearson, C. and Clair, J. (1998), 'Reframing crisis management'. *Academy of Management Review* **23**: 59–76.

Peck, F., Connelly, S., Durnin, J. and Jackson, K. (2013), 'Prospects for "place-based" industrial policy in England: the role of Local Enterprise Partnerships'. *Local Economy* **28**: 828–41.

Peck, J. (2002), 'Political economies of scale: fast policy, interscalar relations, and neoliberal workfare'. *Economic Geography* **78**(3): 331.

Peck, J. and Theodore, N. (2015), *Fast Policy: Experimental Statecraft at the Thresholds of Neoliberalism*. Minneapolis: University of Minnesota Press.

Pedone, R. (1997), 'Disaster recovery – are you prepared for business disruption?'. *Long Island Business News*, November 3: 23–24.

Pendall, R., Foster, K.A. and Cowell, M. (2010), 'Resilience and regions: building understanding of the metaphor'. *Cambridge Journal of Regions, Economy and Society* **3**: 71–84.

Pennings, J.M. and Garcia, P. (2004), 'Hedging behavior in small and medium-sized enterprises: the role of unobserved heterogeneity'. *Journal of Banking and Finance* **28**(5): 951–978.

Perloff, H.S., Dunn, E.S., Lampard, E.E. and Muth, R.F. (1960), *Regions, Resources, and Economic Growth*. Baltimore: Johns Hopkins Press for Resources for the Future.

Perrings, C. (2006), 'Political ecology and ecological resilience: an integration of human and ecological dynamics'. *Ecological Economics* **35**(3): 323–336.

Pike, A., Dawley, S. and Tomaney, J. (2010), 'Resilience, adaptation and adaptability'. *Cambridge Journal of Regions, Economy and Society* **3**: 59–70.

Piperopoulos, M. (2009), 'Economics, business and society in Greece: towards a national innovation system'. *International Journal of Economics and Business Research* **1**(3): 277–290.

Polèse, M. (2009), *The Wealth and Poverty of Regions: Why Cities Matter*. Chicago: University of Chicago Press.

Ponomarov, S.Y. and Holcomb, M.C. (2009), 'Understanding the concept of supply chain resilience'. *The International Journal of Logistics Management* **20**: 124–143.

Ponzio, S. and Di Gennaro, L. (2004), *Growth and Markov Chains: An Application to Italian Provinces*. II PhD Conference in Economics, Research in Economics: Aims and Methodologies.

Popp, A. and Wilson, J. (2007), 'Life cycles, contingency, and agency: growth, development, and change in English industrial districts and clusters'. *Environment and Planning A* **39**(12): 2975–2992.

Porteous, P. (2013), 'Localism: from adaptive to social leadership'. *Policy Studies* **34**: 523–540.

Power, A., Plöger, J. and Winkler, A. (2010), *Phoenix Cities: The Fall and Rise of Great Industrial Cities*. Bristol: Policy Press.

Prisk, M. (2011), 'LEPs: fast solutions'. *Local Government Chronicle*, 19 May.

Puffer, S.M., McCarthy, D.J. and Boisot, M. (2010), 'Entrepreneurship in Russia and China: the impact of formal institutional voids'. *Entrepreneurship Theory and Practice* **34**(3): 441–467.

Pugalis, L. (2012), 'The governance of economic regeneration in England: emerging practice and issues'. *Journal of Urban Regeneration and Renewal* **5**(3): 235–252.

Pugalis, L. (2016), 'Austere state strategies: regenerating for recovery and the resignification of regeneration'. *Local Government Studies* **42**(1): 52–74.

Pugalis, L. and Bentley, G. (2013), 'Storming or performing? Local Enterprise Partnerships two years on'. *Local Economy* **28**(7–8): 863–874.

Pugalis, L. and Bentley, G. (2014), 'State strategies and entrepreneurial governance'. In L. Pugalis and J. Liddle (eds), *Enterprising Places: Leadership and Governance Networks*. Bingley: Emerald, 123–148.

Pugalis, L. and Townsend A.R. (2013), 'Trends in place-based economic strategies: England's fixation with "fleet-of-foot" partnerships'. *Local Economy* **28**: 696–717.

Pugalis, L. and Townsend, A.R. (2014), *Planning for Growth: The Role of Local Enterprise Partnerships in England*. Interim report. London: Royal Town Planning Institute.

Pugalis, L., Townsend, A.R. and Johnston, L. (2014), 'Pushing it! Austerity urbanism and dispersed leadership through "fleet-of-foot" mechanisms in times of crisis'. In J. Diamond and J. Liddle (eds), *European Public Leadership in Crisis?* Bingley: Emerald, 1–25.

Pugalis, L., Townsend, A.R., Gray, N. and Ankowska, A. (2015), *Planning for Growth: The Role of Local Enterprise Partnerships in England*. Final report. London: Royal Town Planning Institute.

Pugalis, L., Townsend, A.R., Gray, N. and Ankowska, A. (2016), 'New approaches to growth planning at larger-than-local scales'. *Journal of Urban Regeneration & Renewal* **10**(1): 73–88.

Putnam, R. (1993), *Making Democracy Work: Civic Traditions in Modern Italy*. Princeton, NJ: Princeton University Press.

Putnam, R. (2000), *Bowling Alone: The Collapse and Revival of American Community*. New York: Simon and Schuster.

Quinn, M. (2013), 'New Labour's regional experiment: lessons from the East Midlands'. *Local Economy* **28**: 738–751.

Raco, M. (1999), 'Competition, collaboration and the new industrial districts: examining the institutional turn in local economic development'. *Urban Studies* **36**(5/6): 951–968.

Raco, M. and Street, E. (2012), 'Resilience planning, economic change and the politics of post-recession development in London and Hong Kong'. *Urban Studies* **49**(5): 1065–1087.

Rantisi, N.M. (2002), 'The local innovation system as a source of "variety": openness and adaptability in New York City's Garment District'. *Regional Studies* **36**(6): 587.

Reading the Riots (2012), *Reading the Riots: Investigating England's Summer of Disorder*. *The Guardian* and the London School of Economics and Political Science, http://eprints.lse.ac.uk/46297/1/Reading%20the%20riots(published).pdf (accessed 14 February 2017).

Reid, S. (2007), 'Identifying social consequences of rural events'. *Event Management* 11(1–2): 89–98.

Rey, S.J. and Janikas, M.V. (2005), 'Regional convergence, inequality and space'. *Journal of Economic Geography* 5: 155–176.

Robinson, D. (2007), 'The search for community cohesion: key themes and dominant concepts of the public policy agenda'. *Urban Studies* 42(8): 1411–1427.

Robson, B. (2014), 'Does England no longer have an urban policy?'. *Town Planning Review* 85: 1–5.

Rodríguez-Pose, A. (2001), 'Local production systems and economic performance in Britain, France, Germany and Italy'. In C. Crouch, P. Le Galès, C. Trigilia and H. Voelzkow (eds), *Local Production Systems in Europe. Rise or Demise?* Oxford: Oxford University Press, 25–45.

Rodríguez-Pose, A. and Storper, M. (2006), 'Better rules or stronger communities? On the social foundations of institutional change and its economic effects'. *Economic Geography* 82(1): 1–25.

Romer, P.M. (1986), 'Increasing returns and long-run growth'. *Journal of Political Economy* 94(5): 1002–1037.

Romer, R. (2001), *Advanced Macroeconomics*. Boston: McGraw-Hill.

Rosenberg, M. (1979), *Conceiving the Self*. New York: Basic Books.

Rosenstein-Rodan, P.N. (1943), 'Problems of industrialisation of Eastern and South-Eastern Europe'. *The Economic Journal* 53(210): 202–211.

Rosenstein-Rodan, P.N. (1961), 'Notes on the Theory of the "Big Push"'. In H.S. Ellis (ed.), *Economic Development for Latin America*. London: Palgrave Macmillan.

Rossi, U. (2015), 'The variegated economics and the potential politics of the smart city'. *Territory, Politics, Governance* 4(3): 337–353.

Rossiter, W. and Price, L. (2013), 'Local economic strategy development under Regional Development Agencies and Local Enterprise Partnerships: applying the lens of the multiple streams framework'. *Local Economy* 28: 852–862.

Rouse, J. and Jayawarna, D. (2006), 'The financing of disadvantaged entrepreneurs'. *International Journal of Entrepreneurial Behaviour and Research* 12(6): 388–400.

Runyan, R.C. (2006), 'Small business in the face of crisis: Identifying barriers to recovery from a natural disaster'. *Journal of Contingencies and Crisis Management* 14: 12–26.

Sæther, B., Isaksen, A. and Karlsen, A. (2011), 'Innovation by co-evolution in natural resource industries: the Norwegian experience'. *Geoforum* **42**(3): 373–381.

Safford, S. (2009), *Why the Garden Club Couldn't Save Youngstown: The Transformation of the Rust Belt*. Cambridge, MA: Harvard University Press.

Saridakis, G. (2012), 'Introduction to the special issue on enterprise activity, performance and policy during times of crisis'. *International Small Business Journal* **30**(7): 733–735.

Sassen, S. (2001), *The Global City: New York, London, Tokyo*. Princeton, NJ: Princeton University Press.

Schamp, E.W. (2005), 'Decline of the district, renewal of firms: an evolutionary approach to footwear production in the Pirmasens area Germany'. *Environment and Planning A* **37**(4): 617–634.

Schamp, E.W. (2010), 'On the notion of co-evolution in economic geography'. In R. Boschma and R. Martin (eds), *The Handbook of Evolutionary Economic Geography*. Cheltenham, UK and Northampton, USA: Edward Elgar Publishing, 432–449.

Schmidt, V.A. (2010), 'Taking ideas and discourse seriously: explaining change through discursive institutionalism as the fourth "new institutionalism"'. *European Political Science Review* **2**(1): 1–25.

Schumpeter, J.A. (1939), *Business Cycles: A Theoretical, Historical and Statistical Analysis of the Capitalist Process*. New York: McGraw-Hill.

Schumpeter, J.A. (1942), *Capitalism, Socialism and Democracy*. New York: Harper.

Schwartz, S.H. (1994), 'Are there universal aspects in the structure and contents of human values?'. *Journal of Social Issues* **50**(4): 19–45.

Scott, M. and Bruce, R. (1987), 'Five stages of growth in small business'. *Long Range Planning* **20**(3): 45–52.

Scott, W.R. (2007), *Institutions and Organizations: Ideas and Interests*. Thousand Oaks, CA: Sage Publications.

Sensier, M., Bristow, G. and Healy, A. (2016), 'Measuring regional economic resilience across Europe: operationalizing a complex concept'. *Spatial Economic Analysis* **11**(2): 1–24.

Sepulveda, L. and Syrett, S. (2007), 'Out of the shadows? Formalisation approaches to informal economic activity'. *Policy & Politics* **35**(1): 87–104.

Setterfield, M. (2010), *Hysteresis*. Working paper 10–04, Department of Economics, Trinity College.

Shaw, K. (2012), 'Interface: applying the resilience perspective to planning: critical thoughts from theory and practice – "reframing" resilience: challenges for planning theory and practice'. *Planning Theory & Practice* **13**(2): 308–331.

Sheffi, Y. (2002), 'Supply chain management under the threat of international terrorism'. *International Journal of Logistics Management* **12**(2): 1–12.

Sheffi, Y. (2005), *The Resilient Enterprise*. Cambridge, MA: MIT Press.

Sheffield City Region (2006), 'Sheffield City Region Development Programme', www.sheffieldcityregion.org.uk/general-documents (accessed 1 April 2014).

Sheffield City Region (2010), 'Shaping the Future of the Sheffield City Region Economy', www.sheffieldcityregion.org.uk/general-documents (accessed 1 April 2014).

Sheffield City Region (2013), 'Independent Economic Review', www.sheffieldcityregion.org.uk/wp-content/uploads/2013/10/Independent-Economic-Review.pdf (accessed 1 May 2015).

Sheffield City Region (2014), *Growth Plan*. Sheffield: Sheffield City Region LEP.

Sheffield First (2013), *State of Sheffield 2013*. Sheffield: Sheffield First.

Shelton, T. and Clark, J.J. (2016), 'Technocratic values and uneven development in the "smart city"'. *Metropolitics/Metropolitiques*, May, www.metropolitiques.eu/Technocratic-Values-and-Uneven.html (accessed 14 February 2017).

Shelton, T., Zook, M. and Wiig, A. (2015), 'The "actually existing smart city"'. *Cambridge Journal of Regions, Economy and Society* **8**(1): 13–25.

Shutt, J., Pugalis, L. and Bentley, G. (2012), 'LEPs – living up to the hype? The changing frame work for regional economic development and localism in the UK'. In M. Ward and S. Hardy (eds), *Changing Gear: Is Localism the New Regionalism*. London: Smith Institute, 12–24.

Simmie, J. (2003), 'Innovation and urban regions as national and international nodes for the transfer and sharing of knowledge'. *Regional Studies* **37**(6–7): 607–620.

Simmie, J. (2014a), 'Regional economic resilience: a Schumpeterian perspective'. *Raumforschung und Raumordnung* **72**(2): 103–116.

Simmie, J. (2014b), *Evolutionary Growth Theory and Resilience in UK Cities*. Working paper. Oxford: Oxford Brookes University, Department of Planning.

Simmie, J. and Carpenter, J. (2008), 'Towards an evolutionary and endogenous growth theory explanation of why regional and urban economies in England are diverging'. *Planning Practice & Research* **23**(1): 101–124.

Simmie, J. and Martin, R. (2010), 'The economic resilience of regions: towards an evolutionary approach'. *Cambridge Journal of Regions, Economy and Society* **3**(1): 27–43.

Smallbone, D. and Welter, F. (2001), 'The distinctiveness of entrepreneurship in transition economies'. *Small Business Economics* **16**(4): 249–262.

Smallbone, D. and Welter, F. (2010), 'Entrepreneurship and government policy in former Soviet republics: Belarus and Estonia compared'. *Environment and Planning C: Government and Policy* **28**(2): 195–210.

Smallbone, D., Deakins, D., Battisti, M. and Kitching, J. (2012a), 'Small business responses to a major economic downturn: empirical perspectives from New Zealand and the United Kingdom'. *International Small Business Journal* **30**(7): 754–777.

Smallbone, D., Kitching, J. and Xheneti, M. (2012b), 'Vulnerable or resilient? SMEs and the economic crisis in the UK'. In B. Dallago and C. Guglielmetti (eds), *The Consequences of the International Crisis for European SMEs: Vulnerability and Resilience*, Vol. 27. Abingdon: Routledge, 109–134.

Smallbone, D., Leig, R. and North, D. (1995), 'The characteristics and strategies of high growth SMEs'. *International Journal of Entrepreneurial Behavior & Research* **1**(3): 44–62.

Smith, J.A. (1996), 'Beyond the divide between cognition and discourse: using interpretative phenomenological analysis in health psychology'. *Psychology & Health* **11**(2): 261–271.

SMMT (2015), 'Motor industry facts 2015', www.smmt.co.uk/2015/05/motor-industry-facts-2015 (accessed 10 February 2016).

Soja, E. (2015), 'Accentuate the regional'. *International Journal of Urban and Regional Research* **39**: 372–381.

Souitaris, V. (2001), 'Strategic influences of technological innovation in Greece'. *British Journal of Management* **12**(2): 131–147.

Souitaris, V. (2002), 'Firm-specific competencies determining technological innovation: a survey in Greece'. *R&D Management* **32**(1): 61–77.

Sparrow, J. (1999), 'Using qualitative research to establish SME support needs'. *Qualitative Market Research: An International Journal* **2**(2): 121–134.

Spencer, W.J. and Gomez, C. (2004), 'The relationship among national institutional structures, economic factors, and domestic entrepreneurial activity: a multicountry study'. *Journal of Business Research* **57**(10): 1098–1107.

SQW (2010) 'Local Enterprise Partnerships', www.lgcplus.com/Journals/3/Files/2010/9/24/SQW-LEPs%20report.pdf (accessed March 2014).

Staber, U. (2005), 'Entrepreneurship as a source of path dependency'. In G. Fuchs and P. Shapira (eds), *Rethinking Regional Innovation and Change*, Vol. 30. New York: Springer, 107–126.

Stam, E. (2010), 'Entrepreneurship, evolution and geography'. In R. Boschma and R. Martin (eds), *The Handbook of Evolutionary Economic Geography*. Cheltenham, UK and Northampton, USA: Edward Elgar Publishing, 139–161.

Statistics Canada (2016a), Table 384-0038 – gross domestic product, expenditure-based, provincial and territorial, annual (dollars unless otherwise noted). CANSIM (database).

Statistics Canada (2016b), Table 228-0060 – merchandise imports and domestic exports, customs-based, by North American Product Classification System (NAPCS), Canada, provinces and territories, monthly (dollars). CANSIM (database).

Statistics Canada (2016c), Table 282-0008 – labour force survey estimates (LFS), by North American Industry Classification System (NAICS), sex and age group, annual (persons unless otherwise noted). CANSIM (database).

Staw, B.M. (1976), 'Knee-deep in the big muddy: a study of escalating commitment to a chosen course of action'. *Organizational Behavior and Human Performance* **16**(1): 27–44.

Steen, M. and Hansen, G.H. (2013), 'Same sea, different ponds: cross-sectorial knowledge spillovers in the North Sea'. *European Planning Studies* **22**(10): 2030–2049.

Steen, M. and Karlsen, A. (2014), 'Path creation in a single-industry town: the case of Verdal and Windcluster Mid-Norway'. *Norsk Geografisk Tidsskrift – Norwegian Journal of Geography* **68**(2): 133–143.

Storey, D.J. and Johnson, S. (1987), 'Regional variations in entrepreneurship in the UK'. *Scottish Journal of Political Economy* **34**(2): 161–173.

Storper, M. (1997), *The Regional World: Territorial Development in a Global Economy*. London: Guilford Press.

Storper, M. (2008), 'Community and economics'. In A. Amin and J. Roberts (eds), *Community, Economic Creativity and Organization*. Oxford: Oxford University Press, 37–68.

Strambach, S. (2010), 'Path dependence and path plasticity: the co-evolution of institutions and innovation – the German customized business software industry'. In R. Boschma and R. Martin (eds), *Handbook of Evolutionary Economic Geography*. Cheltenham, UK and Northampton, USA: Edward Elgar Publishing, 406–431.

Strambach, S. and Halkier, H. (2013), 'Reconceptualising change: path dependency, path plasticity and knowledge combination'. *Zeitschrift für Wirtschaftsgeographie* **57**(1–2): 1–14.

Strambach, S. and Klement, B. (2016), 'Resilienz aus wirtschaftsgeographischer Perspektive: Impulse eines 'neuen' Konzepts'. In R. Wink (ed.), *Resilienz aus interdisziplinärer Perspektive*. Heidelberg: Spektrum-Verlag, 263–294.

Streeck, W. and Thelen, K. (2005), 'Institutional changes in advanced political economies'. In W. Streeck and K. Thelen (eds), *Beyond Continuity:*

Institutional Change in Advanced Political Economies. Oxford: Oxford University Press, 1–39.

Sullivan-Taylor, B. and Branicki, L. (2011), 'Creating resilient SMEs: why one size might not fit all'. *International Journal of Production Research* **49**: 5565–5579.

Svimez (2012), *La condizione e il ruolo delle donne per lo sviluppo del Sud*, Rome.

Swanstrom, T. (2008), *Regional Resilience: A Critical Examination of the Ecological Framework*. Institute of Urban and Regional Development (IURD) working paper 2008-07. Berkeley: University of California.

Swinney, P. and Thomas, E. (2015), *A Century of Cities: Urban Economic Change since 1911*. London: Centre for Cities.

Tabellini, G. (2010), 'Culture and institutions: economic development in the regions of Europe'. *Journal of the European Economic Association* **8**(4): 677–716.

Thomas, B.C., Williams, R., Thompson, P. and Packham, G. (2013), 'Use of the Internet and SME characteristics to expand scale and geographical scope of sales: the case of the United Kingdom'. *International Journal of Technology Diffusion* **4**(3): 1–37.

Thompson, P., Jones-Evans, D. and Kwong, C. (2009), 'Women and home-based entrepreneurship: evidence from the United Kingdom'. *International Small Business Journal* **27**(2): 227–239.

Thompson, P., Jones-Evans, D. and Kwong, C. (2012), 'Entrepreneurship in deprived urban communities: the case of Wales'. *Entrepreneurship Research Journal* **2**(1).

Thornton, P.H., Ribeiro-Soriano, D. and Urbano, D. (2011), 'Sociocultural factors and entrepreneurial activity: an overview'. *International Small Business Journal* **29**(2): 105–118.

Tiebout, C.M. (1956a), 'A pure theory of local expenditures'. *Journal of Political Economy* **64**(5): 416–424.

Tiebout, C.M. (1956b), 'Exports and regional economic growth'. *Journal of Political Economy* **64**(2): 160–164.

Tierney, K., Nigg, M. and Dahlhamer, J. (1996), 'The impact of the 1993 Midwest Floods: Business vulnerability and disruption in Des Moines'. In R. Sylves and W. Waugh (eds), *Disaster Management in the US and Canada*, 2nd edn. Springfield, MA: Charles C. Thomas, 214–233.

Tiessen, J.H. (1997), 'Individualism, collectivism, and entrepreneurship: a framework for international comparative research'. *Journal of Business Venturing* **12**(5): 367–384.

Todo, Y., Nakajima, K. and Matous, P. (2015), 'How do supply chain networks affect the resilience of firms to natural disasters? Evidence from the Great East Japan Earthquake'. *Journal of Regional Science* **55**(2): 209–229.

Tonoyan, V., Strohmeyer, R., Habib, M. and Perlitz, M. (2010), 'Corruption and entrepreneurship: how formal and informal institutions shape small firm behavior in transition and mature market economies'. *Entrepreneurship: Theory and Practice* **34**(5): 803–832.

Tovey, A. (2015), 'The fall and rise of Britain's car industry'. *The Telegraph*, 11 April, www.telegraph.co.uk/finance/newsbysector/industry/engineer ing/11529330/The-fall-and-rise-of-Britains-car-industry.html (accessed 10 March 2016).

Townsend, A.M. (2013), *Smart Cities: Big Data, Civic Hackers, and the Quest for a New Utopia*. New York: W.W. Norton & Company.

Townsend, A. and Champion, T. (2014), 'The impact of recession on city regions: the British experience, 2008–13'. *Local Economy* **29**(1–2): 38–51.

Treado, C.D. (2010), 'Pittsburgh's evolving steel legacy and the steel technology cluster'. *Cambridge Journal of Regions, Economy and Society* **3**(1): 105–120.

Trickett, L. and Lee, P. (2010), 'Leadership of "subregional" places in the context of growth'. *Policy Studies* **31**: 429–440.

Tuchman, B.W. (1984), *The March of Folly: From Troy to Vietnam*. New York: Random House.

Uhlaner, L. and Thurik, R. (2007), 'Postmaterialism influencing total entrepreneurial activity rates across nations'. *Journal of Evolutionary Economics* **17**(2): 161–185.

Van de Vrande, V., De Jong J.P., Vanhaverbeke, W. and De Rochemont, M. (2009), 'Open innovation in SMEs: trends, motives and management challenges'. *Technovation* **29**(6): 423–437.

Van Winden, W. and de Carvalho, L. (2011), *Model Knowcities*. Nieuwerkerk: Urban IQ.

Verbano, C. and Venturini, K. (2013), 'Managing risks in SMEs: a literature review and research agenda'. *Journal of Technology Management and Innovation* **8**(3): 186–197.

Ville, S. and Wicken, O. (2013), 'The dynamics of resource-based economic development: evidence from Australia and Norway'. *Industrial and Corporate Change* **22**(5): 1341–1371.

Wade, R. (1987), 'The management of common property resources: finding a cooperative solution'. *World Bank Research Observer* **2**(2): 219–234.

Walker, E. and Brown, A. (2004), 'What success factors are important to small business owners?'. *International Small Business Journal* **22**(6): 577–594.

Walker, J. and Cooper, M. (2011), 'Genealogies of resilience: from systems ecology to the political economy of crisis adaptation'. *Security Dialogue* **42**(2): 143–160.

Walker, E., Wang, C. and Redmond, J. (2008), 'Women and work–life balance: is home-based business ownership the solution?'. *Equal Opportunities International* **27**(3): 258–275.

Weick, K.E. and Sutcliffe, K.M. (2007), *Managing the Unexpected*, 2nd edn. San Francisco: Jossey-Bass.

Weick, K.E., Sutcliffe, K.M. and Ostfeld, D. (2005), 'Organizing and the process of sensemaking'. *Organization Science* **16**(4): 409–421.

Welsh, M. (2014), 'Resilience and responsibility: governing uncertainty in a complex world'. *The Geographical Journal* **180**: 15–26.

Welter, F. (2011), 'Contextualising entrepreneurship: conceptual challenges and ways forward'. *Entrepreneurship Theory and Practice* **35**(1): 165–184.

Welter, F. and Smallbone, D. (2011), 'Institutional perspectives on entrepreneurial behaviour in challenging environments'. *Journal of Small Business Management* **49**(1): 107–125.

Wennekers, S. and Thurik, R. (1999), 'Linking entrepreneurship and economic growth'. *Small Business Economics* **13**(1): 27–55.

Wennekers, S., Thurik, R., van Stel, A. and Noorderhaven, N. (2007), 'Uncertainty avoidance and the rate of business ownership across 21 OECD countries, 1976–2004'. *Journal of Evolutionary Economics* **17**(2): 133–160.

Wennekers, S., van Stel, A., Thurik, R. and Reynolds, P. (2005), 'Nascent entrepreneurship and the level of economic development'. *Small Business Economics* **24**(3): 293–309.

Westlund, H. and Bolton, R. (2003), 'Local social capital and entrepreneurship'. *Small Business Economics* **21**(1): 77–113.

Westman, M. and Eden, D. (1997), 'Effects of a respite from work on burnout: vacation relief and fade-out'. *Journal of Applied Psychology* **82**(4): 516–527.

White, I. and O'Hare, P. (2014), 'From rhetoric to reality: which resilience, why resilience, and whose resilience in spatial planning?'. *Environment and Planning C: Government and Policy* **32**(5): 934–950.

Williams, N. and Vorley, T. (2014), 'Economic resilience and entrepreneurship: lessons from the Sheffield City Region'. *Entrepreneurship & Regional Development* **26**(3–4): 257–281.

Williams, N. and Vorley, T. (2015a), 'The impact of institutional change on entrepreneurship in a crisis-hit economy: the case of Greece'. *Entrepreneurship and Regional Development* **27**(1–2): 28–49.

Williams, N. and Vorley, T. (2015b), 'Institutional asymmetry: how formal and informal institutions affect entrepreneurship in Bulgaria'. *International Small Business Journal* **33**(8): 840–861.

Williams, N., Vorley, T. and Ketikidis, P. (2013), 'Economic resilience and entrepreneurship: a case study of the Thessaloniki City Region'. *Local Economy* **28**(4): 399–415.

Wink, R. (2014), 'Regional economic resilience: European experiences and policy issues'. *Raumforschung und Raumordnung* **72**(2): 85–91.

Wolfe, D. (2010), 'The strategic management of core cities: path dependence and economic adjustment in resilient regions'. *Cambridge Journal of Regions, Economy and Society* **3**: 139–152.

Wolfe, D. and Gertler, M. (2006), 'Local antecedents and trigger events: policy implications of path dependence for cluster formation'. In P. Braunerhjelm and M. Feldman (eds), *Cluster Genesis: Technology-Based Industrial Development*. Oxford: Oxford University Press.

Wong, P.K., Ho, Y.P. and Autio, E. (2005), 'Entrepreneurship, innovation and economic growth: evidence from GEM data'. *Small Business Economics* **24**(3): 335–350.

World Bank (2016), *Doing Business 2016*. Washington, DC: World Bank.

World Economic Forum (2015), *The Global Competitiveness Report 2015–2016*. Geneva: World Economic Forum.

Wößmann, L. (2001), 'Der Aufstieg und Niedergang von Regionen: Die dynamische Markttheorie von Heuß in räumlicher Sicht'. *Jahrbuch für Regionalwissenschaft* **21**(1): 65–89.

Xavier, S.R., Kelley, D., Kew, J., Herrington, M. and Vorderwülbecke, A. (2012), *GEM 2011 Global Report*. Babson Park, MA: Global Entrepreneurship Monitor.

Xu, Y. and Warner, M.E. (2015), 'Understanding employment growth in the recession: the geographic diversity of state rescaling'. *Cambridge Journal of Regions, Economy and Society* **8**(2): 359–377.

Yamamoto, D. (2011), 'Regional resilience: prospects for regional development research'. *Geography Compass* **5**: 723–736.

Index